Praise for *Race, Religion, and the Pulpit*

"The book provides an interesting and thoughtful analysis of the challenges and responses of a black church and its pastor in the urban Midwest at a moment of dramatic economic, social, and cultural transition."

—*Middle West Review*

"Robert L. Bradby has long been regarded as a revered religious leader, a strategic political thinker, and a stubbornly enigmatic figure. In this biographical study, Julia Marie Robinson conveys a set of fresh insights on Bradby's life and times, particularly in her exploration of his Canadian origins and interracial identity as well as the flows of black peoples across the fluid U.S.–Canadian border. Robinson's volume makes a distinctive contribution to the ongoing debates about Bradby, to the history of Second Baptist, and to our understanding of the intellectual and political histories of religion in black urban life in places like Detroit."

—Angela D. Dillard, professor of Afroamerican and African studies
and in the Residential College at the University of Michigan

"The influence of Rev. Bradby and Detroit's Second Baptist Church is clearly outlined in *Race, Religion, and the Pulpit*, and Robinson brings a new perspective to the issues of twentieth-century race relations in urban Detroit. It is a historical narrative to be considered for any scholar interested in race relations and the history of urban Detroit and brings considerable attention to Detroit's Baptist influence while elucidating the life of a positive influence in the making of urban Detroit."

—*Michigan Historical Review*

"*Race, Religion, and the Pulpit* is first and foremost a biography not just of one rather extraordinary man, the Reverend Bradby, but also of the city of Detroit at a time of great change and growth. Through the personal narrative of Bradby, we are able to appreciate the international and fluid character of vital cities like Detroit in the early twentieth century. We see that there was much movement between the U.S. and Canada for both black Americans and white Americans and that this ability to move and to seek new communities of support shaped self-identity and broader race relations alike. For any scholar who assumes that American racial categories were already determined by the turn of the century, Julia Marie Robinson offers a very different view."

—Heather Ann Thompson, author of *Blood in the Water:
The Attica Prison Uprising of 1971 and Its Legacy*,
winner of the Pulitzer Prize and the Bancroft Prize

"Robinson's study of the Rev. Robert L. Bradby unearths valuable material useful to a range of scholarly interests."

T0273886

RACE,
RELIGION,
and the
PULPIT

GREAT LAKES BOOKS

A complete listing of the books in this series can
be found online at wsupress.wayne.edu

EDITOR

Thomas Klug

Sterling Heights, Michigan

RACE,

RELIGION,

and the

PULPIT

REV. ROBERT L. BRADBY AND THE MAKING OF URBAN DETROIT

JULIA MARIE ROBINSON

Wayne State University Press
Detroit

Library of Congress Control Number: 2014952941

ISBN 978-0-8143-5143-7 (paperback)
ISBN 978-0-8143-3291-7 (jacketed cloth)
ISBN 978-0-8143-4037-0 (ebook)

Bradby family photos are reproduced courtesy of Angela Bradby-
Greene, Family Historical Collection. Historic photos of Second Baptist
Church in Detroit are reproduced courtesy of the Archives Research
Center at Second Baptist Church of Detroit.

Cover design by Tracy Cox.

Wayne State University Press rests on Waawiyaataanong, also referred to
as Detroit, the ancestral and contemporary homeland of the Three Fires
Confederacy. These sovereign lands were granted by the Ojibwe, Odawa,
Potawatomi, and Wyandot Nations, in 1807, through the Treaty of Detroit.
Wayne State University Press affirms Indigenous sovereignty and honors
all tribes with a connection to Detroit. With our Native neighbors, the press
works to advance educational equity and promote a better future for the
earth and all people.

Wayne State University Press
Leonard N. Simons Building
4809 Woodward Avenue
Detroit, Michigan 48201-1309

Visit us online at wsupress.wayne.edu.

To my parents,
Edisel H. Robinson and Annetta M. Robinson
&
The Members of Second Baptist Church in Detroit, Michigan

CONTENTS

ACKNOWLEDGMENTS

As the minister of Second Baptist Church of Detroit, . . . would it be right without any reason at all to break from these who have struggled so hard . . . to make me what I am?

Rev. Robert L. Bradby

Second Baptist, the first church established for free blacks in the territory of Michigan in 1836, has long stood as a monument of faith and sociopolitical empowerment for black Detroiters. Reverend Robert L. Bradby, Second Baptist's nineteenth pastor, was a seminal figure in the church's illustrious history, especially between 1910 and 1930, when the church held the reputation as the "home of strangers." During the first wave of the Great Migration at the turn of the twentieth century, African Americans were seeking a way to escape the inequalities of the South. Making their way northward, many were drawn to Detroit's most influential pastor, said to be dedicated to establishing the Kingdom of God among Detroit's newcomers. As a modus operandi in the culture of Second Baptist, the Kingdom of God represented a theological understanding of Christian praxis and racial uplift. The theological orientation of the Kingdom blended the promises inherent in the Gospel messages of salvation and the sociopolitical strategies of black uplift. In Detroit, Reverend Bradby proclaimed this Kingdom theology from the pulpit of Second Baptist, which became a transformative ideology that empowered and shaped the city's black urban community.

The intertwined history of Second Baptist, Rev. Robert L. Bradby, and the urbanization of Detroit lies in the familiar settings of church offices, pews, and Sunday school rooms. Old church bulletins, letters, and anniversary booklets tell stories of struggle, faith, and progress. One is always astonished at what materials lie right under one's nose, or—in my case—right above my head. I grew up attending services at Second Baptist. The church had three floors, and on the second floor stood the former office of Reverend Bradby. Second Baptist's late church historian, Dr. Nathaniel Leach, kept his study in that space. Today, the office door of the late Dr. Leach still holds the name R. L. Bradby, written in faded gold letters.

During the numerous times I sat as a child up in the balcony of Second Baptist, only a few yards from Leach's study, I never realized how much that office and the clutter of papers therein would shape my life and career. It took a graduate assignment at Michigan State University to take me back to the second floor of the church. And it was then that I remembered a story told by my grandfather, William Lensey Robinson. Often, absentmindedly, rotating a disfigured gold ring around what was left of his right index finger, my grandfather would tell the story of how his finger became a nub at the Ford Motor Company stamping plant. Rev. Robert L. Bradby's written recommendation had secured my grandfather a job at Ford Motor Company, an act that marked my grandfather's good standing as a member of Second Baptist. Incidentally, my grandfather named his son, my father, Edisel Henry Robinson. My father's name echoed the first name of Ford Motor Company's illustrious founder, Henry Ford, and his first son, Edsel Ford. The naming of my father after Henry Ford and his son may have possibly been in tribute to the automotive magnate, or it just might have been the name that appealed best to my grandfather. Whatever the reason, the interwoven stories of my grandfather's experience at Ford Motor Company, my father's name, Second Baptist, and Reverend Bradby became the basis of my doctoral dissertation and now the narrative you have before you.

I owe much gratitude to Second Baptist's most celebrated historian. Baptized by Reverend Bradby in 1924, Dr. Leach became a devout member of Second Baptist Church. Among his many services to the church was the tremendous task of collecting and preserving the church's phenomenal history. Collecting photos, bulletins, and church minutes, Leach was able to publish the first dissertation on the church, titled *The Second Baptist Connection: Reaching Out to Freedom, History of Second Baptist Church of Detroit*. By 1977, Leach had enough historical data to establish the church as a historical landmark, highlighting the church's impressive history as one of the last stages in the Underground Railroad. That same year, Leach organized the Second Baptist Historical Committee, which was charged with preserving the church's rich history. Leach remained the presiding chair of the committee until his health failed in 2004. The Bentley Historical Library at the University of Michigan, Ann Arbor, has also recognized Dr. Nathaniel Leach's contribution to Second Baptist and Detroit's dynamic history by copying much of his work on microfilm. I am incredibly indebted to Dr. Leach and the Second Baptist Historical Committee for taking such care of the church's historical documents. Despite Leach's untimely death in 2005, his legacy continues to live on in the church's vibrant history. I am extremely honored to be able to share the story of Second Baptist, or "Second," as congregants refer to their historic black church. I am also grateful to the church members of Second Baptist, many of whom provided deeper insight into the personhood of Reverend Bradby.

I owe a great deal of thanks to a number of archivists at the University of Michigan's Bentley Historical Library, the Burton Historical Library, and the Benson Ford Research Center, who tirelessly supported this project over the years. I must also thank Gwen S. Robinson, a superb researcher at the W.I.S.H. Centre in Chatham, Ontario, and an officer in the Chatham-Kent Black Historical Society. She placed in my hands some of the most crucial data concerning Robert L. Bradby's Canadian background and members of the black Baptist communities who lived along Ontario's southern borders. Her expertise in the field of African Canadian history and her willingness to help were overwhelming.

In my research for this project, I also had the unique opportunity to interview one of the descendants of Robert L. Bradby, his granddaughter, Gabrielle Bradby-Green. Gabby, as I call her, was a breath of fresh air and revitalization in the project. Her skill in preserving her family's history was remarkable. She provided one of the most inspiring interviews and offered insightful analysis on her family's background and movements in Detroit. The Angela Bradby and Gabrielle Bradby-Green Family Historical Collection has been preserved in her care, and the papers in the collection filled crucial gaps in Bradby's early life and education.

Gabby put me in contact with two other archivists, the late Edgar Hastings Allard of Tucson, Arizona, and Judith Ledbetter of Charles City County, Virginia. Allard was a self-made historian and researcher. His research on the Bradby family tree was extensive and organized along the lines of a first-rate archivist. In 2002, Allard wrote an unpublished report on Bradby's descendants, tracing the Baptist minister's ancestry through its paternal lines. Although Ed died in 2005, his work and life shall always be remembered. I am truly thankful to have shared the passion of the Bradby family line with such a remarkable person and archivist.

Judith F. Ledbetter is a well-trained archivist and the director of the Charles City County Center for Local History in Charles City County, Virginia. A personable researcher and genealogist, Judith generously shared information on families from Charles City County who had fled to Canada just prior to the Civil War. Her resources enhanced the Canadian connections in Bradby's paternal ancestry and also pointed to solid ties to Native American ancestry in his family line. I am truly thankful to Judith for all her help and assistance during my time in Virginia.

In many ways, a scholar is the product of the friends and colleagues who take precious time to review and comment on a manuscript. I am very grateful to my friend and college roommate, Melissa Weber, for her careful reading and initial editing of the project. Once the manuscript was accepted by Wayne State University Press, my acquisition editor, Kathryn Wildfong, was extremely patient, forthright, and nurturing as I weathered the stages of editing.

The expert guidance of Pero Dagbovie and Angela Dillard will forever be remembered. Prominent scholars, each provided tremendous guidance and constructive criticism throughout the revision process. I am especially grateful to Dr. Dagbovie, who first reviewed my manuscript back in 2002 and then the revised version in 2013. His intuitive comments have continually guided the evolution of my research project. Sincere appreciation also goes to Cheryl D. Hicks, Heather Ann Thompson, Sonya Ramsey, and Rogina Scott-Franklin for their counsel, encouragement, support, and friendship during my academic career. Finally, I must thank my friend, Shirley A. Bess; my parents, Edisel H. Robinson and Annetta M. Robinson; and my son, Kenneth C. Robinson, who added balance, strength, laughter, and faith throughout this journey.

NOTE ON
USAGE AND TERMINOLOGY

In this book I use various terms to refer to peoples of African descent in North America and southern Ontario. The designations *black* and *African American* are used interchangeably throughout this work. I refer to people of African descent living or born in Canada as African Canadians. Recognizing that each of these terms has continually been a socially constructed category, made more complex in the United States with the influx of immigrants from African Diaspora communities, this work employs *black*, *African American*, and *African Canadian* to refer to people once identified as *colored* and *Negro*. In direct quotes I have followed the example of my sources. The words *Negro*, *colored*, and *mulatto* appear in primary documents from the nineteenth and twentieth centuries, and I have chosen to maintain the continuity and usage of the aforementioned terms within this work.

The following narrative also uses the terms *race man* and *race woman*. Again, recognizing that racial designations operate as a metalanguage, often constructed through aspects of gender and class, the words *race man* and *race woman* are used to reflect the terminology and connotations of reformers, activists, and community leaders who use these words to denote a person, highly motivated and committed to the social, political, and economic advancement of African Americans. Also, the word *elite* in this work refers to wealthy whites and upper-middle-class African Americans, many of whom were educated, held prominent positions in Detroit's political spheres, and operated successful businesses.

While recognizing the multifaceted nature of what has historically been referred to as the *black church*, this study acknowledges that the black church is not a monolith, and that all predominantly African American church congregations are not all the same. However, because each church within the African American community has emerged and experienced a shared racial past in America, this work understands that local black churches have a common ground as each has sought to overcome the vicissitudes of racism, antiblack terrorism, and black disenfranchisement in North America. Therefore, this book uses the term *local black church* to speak to the individualistic as well as the communal nature of predominantly African American Protestant churches, especially in the Baptist denomination.

RACE,
RELIGION,
and the
PULPIT

INTRODUCTION

We are now dedicating ourselves to a larger and more extensive promotion of the program of the Kingdom of God, and we accept the challenge very humbly and dedicate ourselves to complete surrender to His will and to follow him whithersoever He may lead.

Rev. Robert L. Bradby

The proverbial stepchild of historically white Protestant and Catholic institutions, the African American church has been varied in its form and function in African American communities. It has created mimetic spaces of empowerment and positive identity constructions that have often transcended geographical and denominational boundaries. From the earliest days of what some scholars called the "invisible institution" that existed in the slave quarters of farms and plantations[1] to the brick and mortar of local black churches, Christianity, as it was interpreted through a black hermeneutical lens, operated as one of the most fertile seedbeds of institutionalized black activism. Indeed, during the antebellum period, enslaved African peoples created their own forms of Christianity in response to a religion that sanctioned their enslavement from New Testament texts like I Timothy 6:1, Colossians 3:22, and I Peter 2:18. Born out of the stories of deliverance from the book of Exodus, the salvific messages of the synoptic gospels, and the variations of African traditional religion from West and Central Africa carried over during the African Diaspora, African slaves crafted a Christianity that theologically affirmed the humanity of their black bodies and their divinely ordained position as children of God. These sacred affirmations filtered through the horrors of slavery and rose like a river after emancipation, flooding local African American communities with an institutional form of Christianity that had been converted to the African American experience of enslavement and their continued struggle for liberation, hence, the local black church. And though scholars argue that African American churches are among the most idiosyncratic of all social organizations, and thereby incapable of being understood as monoliths, the "black church" as an institution still exists as a prominent space for social, political, and theological empowerment within many African American communities.[2]

With the doctrines of Christianity constituting the "organizing principle"[3] around which life was structured for many African Americans at the turn of the twentieth century, black believers created a gospel that identified God as the "God of the oppressed,"[4] a savior who called black men and women to fight the good fight of social equality in the face of racial discrimination. With the infamous "separate but equal" codes running rampant in the Jim Crow South after 1896, the "spiritual strivings"[5] for equality and a better experience of freedom were often made manifest through the prophetic voices of African American pastors. Functioning as a living symbol of empowerment, respectability, and even resistance, the black pastor wielded considerable influence on behalf of African American Christians, with many pastors operating as powerful intermediaries between the black community and the larger white world.

The pulpit of the local black church was the heart of the black pastor's dynamic and pervasive influence in the African American community. As a sacralized space that functioned as a prophetic critique of American culture and a priestly conduit of divine intervention, the pulpit in the black church exposed the latent power of the divine to intersect the oppressive realities of racist sentiment and white supremacy. Aphorisms of faith and hope that emanated from the black pulpit established theological justification for black equality, protest, and agitation against white power structures. As such, the pulpit and the ministers who stood therein were emblematic of the continuous overlapping of sacred imperatives within secular agendas. This blending of the sacred and profane in African American Christianity continually challenges traditional interpretations that hold imaginaries of the sacred and profane in opposition to each other in religious life. Complicating the arguments of scholars like Mircea Eliade and Émile Durkheim, the sacred construct in African American Christian imagination has "historically defied this polarity."[6] Here the pulpit in African American culture, with its convoluted blending of sacred and profane realities, produced prophetic critiques of American society and created an ideological apparatus of power in African American Christian communities by which to transform the social, political, and economic landscapes of urban America. By virtue of their centrality in American culture, churches were community builders. They were spaces of communal gatherings that brought people from diverse backgrounds into networks of exchange, not just for worship, but also for economic, political, and social transactions.

During the early years of the Great Migration, between 1910 and 1930, African Americans from the South headed toward northern cities in the Northeast, Midwest, and West. As this first wave of black migrants filtered into these areas, local black churches became one of the most crucial conduits in the making and reshaping of black urban communities. Among northern cities that appealed to southern black migrants, Detroit was a highly sought location, considered one of America's northern "promised lands" because of the city's need for cheap labor to accommodate the demands of it's thriving industries during the interwar years. Black churches in the city began to swell with new congregants from the South. Encouraged by the call from the pulpit to meet the needs of their displaced brothers and sisters, urban black churches in Detroit set about mobilizing their congregants to help their southern counterparts start a new life. In doing so, neighborhoods were expanded, political lines were redrawn, and the industrial working force of Detroit would be forever changed. A black presence would be felt throughout Detroit's cultural milieu, and it was in part due to the transformative interactions between racial uplift and a religious imperative that was heralded from the *pulpit* of local black churches. Ideas of racial uplift intersected with African American Christian paradigms that were filtered through black pulpits proclaiming the good news of Jesus Christ. Although this phenomenon took place in many black churches in Detroit, there was one church, and one minister in particular, that demonstrated the fullness of this black Christian ethos—Second Baptist Church of Detroit. "Second," as many of its members called it, and it's nineteenth pastor, the Reverend Robert Lewis Bradby, exposed the potent power of the pulpit in the making of urban Detroit. Thus, religion, as it functioned through black Christian paradigms, became the catalyst for economic empowerment and the formation of an urban African American working class.

Using biography as a critical lens by which to understand the historical intersections of race and religion in America, *Race, Religion, and the Pulpit* seeks to give light to an important figure in African American history, one who's life has been peripherally acknowledged in historical scholarship. These marginal treatments of Second Baptist's most distinguished minister depict Rev. Robert L. Bradby as "a conflicted character, fraught with ambivalence,"[7] while treatises viewed him as an "enormously powerful pastor of Second Baptist Church,"[8] one who viewed "meeting the Exodusters as part of his calling [in taking] the social gospel to the streets."[9] Though portrayed as a minor figure in Detroit's history, historians could not ignore the minister's powerful influence in Detroit during the interwar years, with many historians claiming Bradby as a "self-made man and prominent religious leader,"[10] one who walked a "fine line . . . between providing sermons and services that appealed to southern migrants and maintaining the respect of secular leaders."[11] In most accounts of Reverend Bradby, no matter how small, historians highlight the minister's dynamic relationship with Henry Ford and the Ford Motor Company. Indeed, scholars identify Bradby as a black leader who "greatly valued . . . ties to the Ford family which enabled [him] to dictate the nature of community building."[12]

Despite a number of thoughtful monographs on Second Baptist's nineteenth minister, Bradby still remains an opaque figure in the history of Detroit and in African American history.[13] *Race, Religion, and the Pulpit* expands upon earlier arguments surrounding Reverend Bradby by offering a more detailed account of the minister's life, his theological strivings toward racial uplift, and the nature of his political connections among Detroit's white elites. This study lends depth to earlier histories on Detroit during the interwar years, bringing to the fore the role of religion and how ideas of the sacred functioned in the sociopolitical and economic landscapes of twentieth-century Detroit.

The first two chapters of this study address the early years of Bradby's life and the sociohistorical context in which the minister came to prominence. Titled "American-Canadian Beginnings," chapter 1 notes Bradby's birth during the latter period of the Reconstruction era and his rise to adulthood among African Canadian Baptists in southern Ontario. Here, mid-nineteenth-century migratory patterns and kinship networks between African Americans and Native Americans are examined in light of Bradby's ancestry. Key in this section is an analysis of African Canadian Baptist communities and the ways in which formations of black Canadian Baptist societies often transcended nation-state borders between Canada and the United States because of the injustices of racial discrimination in both nations. This was especially true during the antebellum era when, as early as the 1840s, black Baptist churches in Canada were fighting against the institution of slavery. By the 1850s, when the Fugitive Slave Act was in effect, African Canadian Baptist communities were actively encouraging fugitive slaves to take refuge in their communities.[14] And as hundreds of fugitive slaves entered Canada from Detroit, Second Baptist became one of the last stops before crossing the Canadian border to freedom. As part of the Underground Railroad, fugitive slaves were clandestinely ushered through the doors of Second Baptist, given food and rest in the church's basement, and then shipped during the night across the Detroit River to Canada at places like Windsor and Fort Malden near Amherstburg.[15]

Indeed, the founding members of Second Baptist had been helping fugitive slaves since as early as 1833. Thornton and Ruth Blackburn, for example, had escaped to Detroit from a plantation in Louisville, Kentucky, in 1831. When the Blackburns' master sent an agent to Detroit to retrieve his property two years later, the wives of two founding members of Second Baptist helped one of the Blackburns escape to Canada. Although Second Baptist would not be established until 1836, the black worshipping community within the predominantly white First Baptist Church of Detroit, Michigan, organized in 1827, were recorded in the church's minutes as a small black membership that "expected complete integration, complete freedom."[16] Mrs. Madison J. Lightfoot and Mrs. George French, free women of color who upheld the sentiments of their community, went to pay a visit to Mrs. Blackburn, who had been arrested along with her husband. The visitation was fortuitous, as Ruth Blackburn walked out of jail after exchanging clothes with Mrs. French and escaped to Canada.[17] Her husband, Thornton Blackburn, also eventually escaped, on June 16, 1833, when a "mob of Negroes took him by force and helped him to escape to Sandwich in Canada" as he was being escorted to the steamboat headed back to Kentucky. Although Thornton Blackburn was arrested again in Windsor, he was later released, and he traveled to Toronto, Ontario, where he became a property owner. He later traveled back to Louisville, Kentucky, to help his mother escape from slavery in 1843, possibly with the help of Second Baptist, which by that time was founded as the first black Baptist church in state of Michigan and was a prominent conduit of the Underground Railroad.[18] The Blackburn affair in the early history of Second Baptist was a foreshadowing of other transnational connections between

African American and African Canadian communities in the Baptist faith along the borders of Canada and the United States. Reverend Bradby's early life in particular was indicative of these multifaceted connections as people of color sought to enhance their experience of freedom after slavery.

Chapter 2, "Home of Strangers," places the minister and Second Baptist in the first wave of the Great Migration and the expansion of Detroit's automotive industry. Focusing on Bradby's tremendous influence as a pastor and race leader in early twentieth-century Detroit, this chapter highlights the various ministries Second Baptist created to meet the needs of migrant newcomers, which created a reputation of the church among migrants as being the "home of strangers" in the city. Here, the multivaried functions of the local black Baptist church in the urbanization and industrialization of northern cities are explored through the history of Second Baptist Church during this period.

Chapters 3 and 4 investigate the nature of relationships between Second Baptist, its members, and prominent white elites in Detroit. Chapter 3, "The Power in the Pew," offers a gendered analysis of Second Baptist and the informal power structures backing Reverend Bradby's grassroots leadership in Detroit. It is clear in this section that the foundation of Bradby's leadership and the effectiveness of Second Baptist in providing financial, educational, and social resources that helped migrants find a sense of home in Detroit's promised land rested upon the dynamic activities of Second Baptist's black churchwomen. Titled "The Black Preacher and the Automotive Mogul," chapter 4 describes Bradby's relationship with Ford Motor Company and Henry Ford and the ways in which that relationship created and shaped Detroit's rising black middle class.

Chapter 5 and the conclusion of this work address Bradby's role as a race leader and model of black uplift in Detroit. Titled "The Black Pulpit, Politics, and Establishing the Kingdom of God," chapter 5 examines Bradby's role in the organizing years of Detroit's NAACP chapter, the Sweet trials of the mid-1920s, and the Scottsboro Boys trials in the 1930s. A prominent presence during the controversial rise of the United Auto Workers union in Detroit in the 1940s, Reverend Bradby demonstrated the power black ministers wielded in transcending the sacred sphere of the church in order to evoke civil rights reform in the secular arenas of urban spaces. The conclusion of this history provides a final synopsis of Reverend Bradby's life and addresses the nature of the minister's activism in light of the religious imperatives of his time.

BRADBY AS A COMPLEX LEADER AND SPOKESPERSON

Born in Middlemiss, Ontario, in 1877 to a white mother and Native American father, Bradby's early life provides a window of analysis into the ways in which people of color constructed their sense of identity and belonging within white hegemonic contexts. Indeed, with his extremely light skin and straight hair, Bradby could have racially passed for white. Yet his decision and self-declaration of "I am Negro,"[19] reveals the myriad ways in which racial identity was created at the turn of the twentieth century and is indicative of scholar Baz Dreisinger's argruments around "proximity." For Dreisinger, proximity is crucial "in the processes of racial passing because passing occurs within carefully constructed, clearly demarcated spaces."[20]

The fact that Bradby embraced a black identity demands further attention to the ways in which he situated himself culturally and in proximity to the nonwhite cultures of his time. Indeed, "proximity" may have been a way in which many mixed-raced peoples constructed and often reconstructed their identity in light of the racial culture of their day. For Bradby, attempting to balance the lines between socially constructed categories of white, black, Native American, and colored in his life made for a complex process of self-identification, one in which he crafted in proximity to the black race a decision that would have lasting effects as the minister began his tenure at the first African American church established in the state of Michigan—Second Baptist Church of Detroit.

Bradby's life and ultimate rise as one of Detroit's most influential ministers tell the larger story of how race and religion collided to shape Detroit's urban landscape in the early twentieth century. His life demonstrates the interplay between the complexities of racial identity construction, the didactic tropes of black advancement, and contested terrains of African American uplift ideology. His brand of activism constituted a hybridity of black middle-class discourse and Social Gospel imperatives inherent in the concept of the Kingdom of God. Bradby was a leader who moved beyond a "simplistic messianic or dichotomous, construction of black leadership (e.g., accommodation vs. resistance),"[21] to a figure much more complicated by his liminal position as a mediator between southern migrants and the metropolis's black elites, between the city's black urban population and Detroit's white power structures, and between Second Baptist's faith community and black political groups like the Detroit Urban League and the city's local chapter of the National Association for the Advancement for Colored People (NAACP). Underlining these *in-between* spaces in Bradby's life were the minister's own social constructions of his mixed-race heritage, a social construction that would ultimately reflect the minister's identification with the African American race.

As a minister Bradby was triangularly situated between the ideological appropriations of Christian faith, complex notions of black uplift, and the tenets of progressivism. Such *in-between* spaces and triangular conscious-ness caused Second Baptist's nineteenth minister to reconstruct traditional notions of black uplift ideology beyond that of merely seeking to "rehabilitate the race's image by embodying [a] respectability [that] was enacted through an ethos of service to the masses."[22] Uplift for Bradby was infused with sacred paradigms heavily embedded within Christian theology. Here, "uplift," Bradby style, was an ideology solidly tied to theological imperatives of what Reverend Bradby understood as the divine call to establish the Kingdom of God in the lives of black folks. While this was indeed an "ethos of services to the masses," it was also a salvific cry to the black community to usher in concrete evidence of God's reality and presence in the lives of black people—the Kingdom of God. Here, the Kingdom of God was the presence of the divine reality and movement of God manifested in the ordinary experiences of supplying every need of the black community, especially the migrant. In this respect, issues of respectability and prescribed bourgeois agendas came secondary to the "in-breaking" of God's divine presence through a Christian praxis to those African Americans in need in Detroit's secular spheres. His-torians note that "racial uplift ideology cannot be regarded as an indepen-dent black perspective,"[23] so one must allow that Reverend Bradby reflected a unique brand of uplift ideology. Uplift for Reverend Bradby was rooted in the theological imperatives of what he understood as the Kingdom of God. This theologically based modus operandi enabled Bradby to unite religious principles with socioeconomic and political agendas, ultimately reflecting the competing philosophies inherent in the Social Gospel and contesting traditional understandings of black uplift ideology.

Establishing "a larger and more extensive program of the 'Kingdom of God'" was for Reverend Bradby the Christian expression of black uplift. This divine initiative of establishing the Kingdom of God was understood as God's will and the destiny of Second Baptist Church in Detroit. All members of Second Baptist were "called" to this task and were demanded to "surrender" to do God's will, following His divine mandate "whithersoever He may lead."[24] From 1910 to 1940, this divine mandate drove Reverend Bradby and the members of Second Baptist to engage in a number of activities that strongly reflected the influence of the Social Gospel and its call to establish God's *kingdom*. As a result, Second Baptist became one of the most renowned places of refuge for southern migrants during the interwar years. Among migrants and old-time Detroiters, Second Baptist held the reputation as the "home of strangers." Reverend Bradby's guidance of this "home of strangers" reflected his understanding of the Kingdom of God and demonstrated a theological perspective grounded in the rhetoric of the Social Gospel, progressive reformers, and the multifaceted and contested manifestations of black uplift efforts.

THEOLOGICAL UNDERPINNINGS: THE "KINGDOM OF GOD"

In order to understand the depths of Reverend Bradby's motivations for black uplift and the ways in which he structured the numerous ministries of Second Baptist, it is important to understand the nature of his theological orientation. Formed from the rivers of progressivism and Social Reform during the interwar years, the concept of the Kingdom of God shaped, guided, and directed the pulpit of Second Baptist and ordered the daily agendas of Reverend Bradby throughout his thirty-six-year ministry in Detroit. The Kingdom of God operated as an ideological apparatus in the sociopolitical consciousness of the Progressive Era and was the psychological birth child of the Social Gospel movement. It was a theology and a philosophy that permeated the minds of many reformers and ministers living in North America's urban industrial landscape. The phrase *Kingdom of God* initially made its mark in the consciousness of Christian America through the proclamation and writings of such figures as Washington Gladden and Walter Rauschenbusch in the late nineteenth century. The latter was one of the most prominent theologians of the movement. Rauschenbusch demanded a Christianity that confronted poverty, crime, and unemployment. Facing the horrors of New York City's Hell's Kitchen district, the theologian wrote of a Christian imperative that sought to eradicate evil proclivities inherent in urban industrial cities.[25]

During his tenure at Rochester Theological Seminary, Rauschenbusch built upon his visions from Hell's Kitchen and produced "some of the most influential statements of the new social Christianity."[26] In *Christianity and the Social Crisis* (1907) he argued, "There are two great entities in human life—the human soul and the human race—and religion is to save both. The soul is to seek righteousness and eternal life; the race is to seek righteousness and the *Kingdom of God*."[27] Thus Rauschenbusch and other proponents of social Christianity placed the concept of the Kingdom of God at the center of progressive reform. The Kingdom of God was not just an ephemeral reality that could only be glimpsed in the afterlife. For adherents of the Social Gospel, the Kingdom of God was literally a sphere in reality that was brought about by Christian charity toward those whom society had spurned—the orphan, the widow, the poor, and the sick. This concept of the Kingdom of God also carried a "double consciousness" of sorts, one that recognized heaven as an invisible reality, while at the same time seeking and struggling for its earthly physicality and presence in the lives of the downtrodden. In short, the Kingdom of God spoke to the immanent presence of God in the everyday realities of life. Here, "all areas of life might be sanctified and must be related to Christ's kingly rule. . . . Christ was the prophetic Lord who called men and women into the common life to struggle with every form of social evil rather than being simply the comforting Savior of an individualistic religion."[28]

While men like "Gladden and other proponents of the Social Gospel engaged in racial reform [through] missionary societies [that] foster[ed] black education,"[29] it was local black ministers like Reverdy C. Ransom, for example, who set the stage for concepts like the Kingdom of God to really impact black urban communities in the North. Accepting a new pastorate in Allegheny City, Pennsylvania, upon his graduation from the prestigious Wilberforce University, Ransom carried his education in social Christianity to the black urban areas of the city. As the black minister walked the "alleys and climbed the dark stairways of the wretched tenements, or walked out on the shanty boats where [his] people lived on the river,"[30] the messages of the Social Gospel were shaped to fit the African American experience of suffering in a racialized world. These experiences kindled in Ransom a "vision of the need for social service" among African American communities. This vision, in turn, caused Ransom and many other black ministers to embrace a Social Gospel that spoke to the needs of African Americans everywhere. As historian Ronald White points out, "Ransom and many black pastors in post–Civil War America took responsibility for the whole life of their people."[31]

These attitudes Ransom and other black ministers held reflected key conceptualizations of the Kingdom of God and echoed the voice of Rauschenbusch himself. The role of the minister of the Gospel, Rauschenbusch asserted, "can soften the increasing class hatred of the working class. He can infuse the spirit of moral enthusiasm into the economic struggle of the dispossessed and lift it to something more than a 'stomach question.'"[32]

The Kingdom of God for Social Gospel adherents implied the reality of God's rule that transcended and even destroyed class distinctions and pushed for social justice among the disenfranchised. Yet for black preachers like Ransom, Rauschenbusch's concept of the Kingdom and the role of preachers held tremendous implications beyond ordinary class distinctions. The Kingdom of God spoke to the dilemma of racial inequality and gave divine sanction to the black struggle for social justice. As Rauschenbusch notes, "We have been cursed for a generation with the legacy of sectional hatred, and the question of the status of the black race has not been solved even at such cost. If Pharaoh again hardens his heart, he will again have to weep for his first born and be whelmed in the Red Sea."[33] Black proponents of the Social Gospel recognized this fact, and many embraced the concept of the Kingdom of God as the leading force behind their reform practices.

Writing one year prior to Bradby's tenure at Second Baptist, Social Gospel leader Washington Gladden, considered the "father of the Social Gospel," and Frank Mason North proclaimed the basic concepts of the Social Gospel movement, particularly as it related to urban ministry. Frank Mason North's address, titled "The City and the Kingdom," was presented at Chautauqua, New York, on July 9, 1909.[34] North's address posited "the centrality of the kingdom of God in the teaching of Jesus and how that message related to the church's mission in the city."[35] For North, "the way to the Kingdom is not over the ruins of the city, but through its streets . . . the Kingdom is coming! We dream of it, we work for it. The city is here, the very heart of the divine strategy, the key of the mighty campaign." In October of that same year, Washington Gladden's sermon to the American Board of Commissioners for Foreign Missions carried North's theology of the Kingdom further, stating "the nation is to be an important agency in the kingdom."[36]

The writings of Gladden, North, and Rauschenbusch, and their emphasis on a theological praxis of establishing the Kingdom of God through Christian social activism and racial reform, caught the ears of progressive reformers across racial lines. Yet for black preachers, especially those serving in the African Methodist Episcopal and black Baptist churches, the message of the Social Gospel and its emphasis on the Kingdom of God transformed the traditional "otherworldly" role of the black church and ushered in a "this-worldly" consciousness among black church culture. Here, the Kingdom of God constituted a blending of the secular needs of African Americans with the sacred imperatives of black Christian faith. African American preachers who embraced the Social Gospel and its message of the Kingdom of God created sacred institutions that were prophetic in their critique of American racism and progressive in their reform efforts toward the socioeconomic and political realities of African Americans.

While scholars note that "in social-gospel thought, the nation, city, and church were all instruments to be utilized to achieve the larger kingdom of God,"[37] one of the most transformative mechanisms for change among blacks living in early twentieth-century America was the church. Although "ill equipped to operate as a national uniform entity in programmatic or political approaches," local black churches continued to thrive because of their ability to operate as "political and cultural short-hand and all-purpose stand-in for the dearth of other black institutions, especially in the twentieth century when large institutional responses to racial inequality were required."[38] Jim Crow segregation and prevailing attitudes of black inferiority kept black Social Gospel activists from accessing the nation and the city to effect change in their world. So it was the church—for black preachers committed to the tenets of the Social Gospel and the advancement of African Americans as rightful citizens entitled to all the protections under the Constitution—that became the primary vehicle for establishing the Kingdom of God. Thus Reverend Bradby's leadership of Second Baptist Church gives telling evidence of how African American Christian leaders used the Gospel message to usher in a transformative ideology and a divine impetus for black people of faith to exact change in the social, economic, and political structures of their communities. The sacred space that emanated such calls for change and provided Second Baptist church members with a transcendent sense of empowerment beyond the classist and discriminatory pressures of white hegemony was the black pulpit. Weaving together the ever-conscious reality of racial struggle in the sacred tropes of Judeo-Christian messages of hope and deliverance, the pulpit stood as a transformative sphere within Second Baptist under the proclamations of its most noted minister, Rev. Robert L. Bradby. It was a space that transcended the sacred domains of the church in order to redefine and reshape the black urban experience during the early twentieth century.[39]

1

AMERICAN-CANADIAN BEGINNINGS

I do not need to recite the injuries and injustices heaped upon our group by that organization [the Ku Klux Klan], un-American as it is and un-Christian . . . seeking to promote its religious hate and its racial differences . . . and then compels me because I am Negro to go in the back gate.

Rev. Robert L. Bradby to C. E. Sorensen
(Papers of Henry Ford, Henry Ford Museum and
Greenfield Village Research Center, Dearborn, Michigan)

They insistently refuse to serve colored people sitting at the counter. Their excuse always is that the seats are reserved, which of course is not true. I have just come from there, asking them to be courteous and considerate. The assistant manager's exact words to me were: "I will be dead a thousand years before a nigger will ever sit down at my counter."

Rev. Robert L. Bradby to Prosecutor Harry S. Toy
(Second Baptist Papers, Reel 3)

In some circles of Detroit's Second Baptist congregation, it is still whispered that Bradby was really a white man. Indeed, with his finely textured hair and extremely light skin, he almost countered the black identity he openly claimed from the church's pulpit. Born to a white mother and Native American father, one hundred miles from the US-Canada border in southern Ontario, Bradby was continually confronted with racialized America's bigoted demands "to go in the back gate" during his life, because in his words, "I am Negro."[1] How was it that a person who may have had the capacity to pass for white deliberately chose to pass for black? In answer to such a question, the following narrative explores how Bradby's early life defied rigid racial classifications, thereby revealing the fluidity of racial constructions by individuals born *in-between the lines of racial categories.*

Central to the fluidity of racial categories is understanding what W.E.B. Du Bois related as "the problem of the twentieth century . . . the problem of the colorline."[2] The color line for Du Bois spoke to the innumerable ways in which race and racism have historically shaped American society. Addressing the intersections of race and class within forms of societal domination and resistance, Du Bois recognized the transcendent "problem of the color-line" as it crossed over nations and states in defining the status of people of color and whites.

Born during the last days of the Reconstruction era in America when southern legislators vigorously established the notorious black codes, which restricted the gains African Americans received under the Civil Rights Act of 1866, Bradby began his childhood in Canada under the shadow of America's color line. His mixed-raced ancestry placed him squarely between racial constructions of whiteness and blackness and mirrored the cultural realities of interracial sexual practices in the nineteenth century.

RACIAL MIXING IN THE NINETEENTH CENTURY

Sex between people of different races in the nineteenth century was a common practice. In fact, interracial sex between whites, blacks, and Native Americans was so prevalent that state legislatures moved to create a number of miscegenation laws as early as the colonial period. Maryland, for example, passed the first miscegenation statute in 1661, criminalizing marriage between a black man and a white woman. By 1662, state legislatures in places like Virginia began to designate mixed-race individuals as "mulatto," "Negro," or "Indian" under the legal notion of hypodescent, which meant "anyone with a known black ancestor is considered black."[3] Under this statute the Virginia legislature ruled that "children got by an Englishman upon a Negro woman . . . shall be held bond or free only according to the condition of the mother." Recognizing the fact that white men sired numerous offspring with black women, the law allowed that "children born of a black mother and a white father would follow the common law applicable to farm animals." This law was in direct opposition to traditional English common law that established that the children follow the status of the father.[4]

The creation of miscegenation laws and racial categories for children produced by these multiracial unions in the colonies spoke to British colonial fears that were based on moral and economic grounds. Morally, the idea that "blacks descended from Ham of Genesis and that their blackness was a punishment for sexual excess" fed British colonials' terror of immoral "mongrel" children running rampant in society. Economically, relations between white women and black male slaves would produce "legally free children, thereby depriving the slave owner of potential slaves."[5]

While miscegenation fears rested primarily with black and white sexual interactions, white sexual relations with Native Americans were also included in white supremacist fears of mongrelization. In Virginia, where the first ban on interracial marriage was passed in 1705, a mulatto was defined as the "the child of an Indian, or the child, grandchild, or great grandchild of a Negro."[6] And any individual with "one Indian parent and one white parent was mulatto"; while another person with one Indian grandparent and three white grandparents was, by implication, legally white.[7] These classifications of interracial children were designed to keep those identified as "'mulattoes' on the black side of the colorline."[8] In fact, by 1723, Virginia legislatures "den[ied] equal citizenship [to] free mulattoes in a wide range of categories," including the right to possess firearms and the right to vote. In 1785, however, Virginia's laws had changed slightly toward mixed-raced people, as the legal definition of a mulatto was redefined as "one-fourth part or more [of] Negro blood."[9] This change in definition allowed those with one-eighth black ancestry (one great-grandparent of African descent) to legally pass for white; whereas previously, these individuals would have been branded as mulattoes. This subtle change in the law basically allowed "white into a mixed category." Yet toward the close of the century, Virginia laws had become more stringent when in 1793, the Virginia General Assembly passed a law demanding all free blacks and mulattoes to register with the clerk of the court where they resided.[10] Native Americans and free people of color were required to obtain court certificates as proof of their freeborn status by local county officials based on the word of a white person who could vouch for their free status.[11]

Thus, by the eighteenth century, Virginian laws were ever more focused on ways by which to legally define racial blackness within its borders. And because many Native American lands were often situated next to slave territories, which in turn produced levels of intermingling and collaboration between blacks and Indians, Virginia had to grapple with trying to control and define an essentially multiracial group that engaged in "intermarriage . . . [and] forged ties based on the extension of clan affiliations to Indian mothers and . . . the children of such unions." As scholar Melinda Micco asserts, "'from the first law banning intermarriage to the final Virginia antimiscegenation statute overturned in 1967,' the central imperative of the United States and state governments has been to prevent intermixture between peoples of diverse origins so that morphological differences that code as race might be more neatly maintained."[12]

By the turn of the nineteen century, Virginia law was still trying to code multiracial groups and their offspring when the state defined all people of mixed blood as black. This meant that anyone who had a trace of Native American and black—or Native American and white—ancestry was broadly cast under the definition of "Negro." Thus "mix blood[ed] [people were] in the white mind . . . firmly classed as Negroes and in effect lumped on that side of the race bar . . . with a disparate collage of people of Indian and black ancestry, known as mustees, and offspring of Indian and white parents."[13] Thus identities constructed by the state, that is, "mulatto," "Native American," and "Negro," were "rationalized, codified, and judicially affirmed . . . [the] exclusion of black [and mulattoes] from any basic concept of human rights under the law."[14]

Bradby, who was born to a white mother and a Native American and white father, had the tremendous task of negotiating these disparate racial categories that were placed upon him and his parents. The processes by which these social constructions were made lay in the history of his ancestors. Understanding the racial history of Bradby's ancestors offers a fascinating window by which to understand the negotiations of race and self-identity among free people of color at the turn of the nineteenth century.

MYTHS, LEGENDS, AND THE MAKING OF AN IDENTITY

A legend told by E. P. Bradby, chief of the eastern division of the Chickahominy, holds that fifty years prior to the American revolution, a man by the name of Bradby came to Virginia around 1720. He traveled by ship from England to escape religious persecution. Although Virginia in the 1720s was ripe with religious prejudice, just as much as England, the newly arrived Bradby started a family; he sired one child, James Bradby. James Bradby would eventually inherit "all his father's deep desire for freedom in the worship of God" and face the same religious prejudice over his Baptist faith.[15] Although James

Bradby would not abandon the shores of America like his father did Europe, he would "foreswear . . . the habitations of white men [and] choose to make his home with the Chickahominy Indians," living along the rivers of what is now Charles City County, Virginia. The Chickahominy would eventually adopt James Bradby into their community, and Bradby would take one of the Chickahominy women as his wife. The descendants of this union filter through the remnants of the Chickahominy nation today, many still carrying the name Bradby and affirming their Chickahominy lineage, while still other Bradbys mark their lineage from the Pamunkeys. The late chief William Terrill Bradby of the Pamunkey nation noted that "all his namesakes in the two bands stem from a white man, his great-grandfather, who lived about the time of the revolution."[16]

One of James Bradby's descendants was a man by the name of Bolling Bradby. Notwithstanding the brevity of historical information on all of Bolling Bradby's children, it is clear that Bolling Bradby had at least two sons, Henry T. Bradby and James Eldridge Bradby. Both sons were born free in Charles City County, Virginia, and were racially defined as mulatto. The eldest of the two sons was Henry T. Bradby. Born in 1809, Henry Bradby was described as "a bright mulatto man 31 years old the 22 of this month, 5 feet 9 1/2 inches high, no visible mark or scar, was born free in this county."[17] As America adjusted to the end of the African slave trade in 1808 and the South's internal slave economy became rooted in its infrastructure, Henry Bradby grew up as a freeborn resident of Charles City County, Virginia. By the time Henry Bradby had established a family and acquired a small portion of land, the Fugitive Slave Law was in full effect.[18] Congress instituted the Fugitive Slave Act on September 18, 1850, which required the return of runaway slaves to their owner, no matter where they were located in the union. The act made life decidedly harder for both slaves and free people of color, as dishonest slave catchers were known to purposely force free people and runaway slaves into servitude.

By 1854 Henry Bradby and his family's free status was on the verge of being threatened by the country's hardening racial codes. This meant that James Bradby's descendants, the Chickahominys and Pamunkeys as well as the offspring of Native American and white relations connected with these groups, were targeted by Virginia law officials and made to carry "free papers" on the basis on their nonwhite heritage. Such rulings made racial passing almost impossible, especially when a family's racial record was documented and recorded with the words, "mulatto," "colored," or "Negro."

Here, it is important to note the dilemma that racial categorizations forced upon people of color in terms of self-identity, especially at the turn of the nineteenth century. In Virginia, race, that is, black or mulatto, was "assumed to define and determine" a nonwhite person's identity as well as his or her "understanding . . . of [their] self."[19] As this projected racialized identity was forcibly thrown upon people of color by white power structures, this experience often created an internalization of that identity to the point that many "people of color's own self-understandings became oriented toward those specified racial definitions, which in turn created common experiences of racism [and] prejudice."[20]

These hardening racial lines in Virginia, as well as across states north and south of the Mason-Dixon line, were extremely exacerbated by the Fugitive Slave Act. By the mid-1850s, Henry Bradby and his family began to see how tenuous freedom was for free people designated as "mulatto," "Indian," or "Negro." Despite the rise in abolitionism in southern states like Virginia in the 1840s, white society grew increasingly hostile toward these groups, especially after 1854 when parts of the Nebraska-Kansas territories became known as "bleeding Kansas" over the issue of the slavery. Freeborn or established mulattos, Native Americans, and African Americans were under the constant threat of losing their free status and being forced back into slavery. They could neither hold public offices, serve on juries, testify against whites, bequeath property to their children nor vote in some cases.

Adding insult to injury, Native Americans were being forcibly removed from their lands, due to America's drive for westward expansion, the ideas of Manifest Destiny,[21] and racist perceptions of Native Americans as savages. Native Americans as well as individuals produced by white and Native American sexual relations were considered "physically inferior, morally debased, and mentally defective"—mongrels.[22] In the early nineteenth century, interracial sexuality and the children produced by it "was the only thing the great majority of white Americans genuinely agreed on—that mixture was wrong." Most notable in this stream of white supremacist consciousness were fears about the "'blackness' of Indians" based on their mixed blood ancestry as well as their opposition to whites on the subject of Indian removal. The latter attribute made whites consider Native Americans as mixed-blood people who were "not only 'black,' but also 'black-hearted' in their anti-removal attitudes towards whites, and they threatened to pollute whites' bloodstream by intermixture."[23] These ideas justified the brutalization and displacement of thousands of Native peoples between 1830 and 1858 from their homeland.

Amid this cultural consciousness about mixed-raced people in America during the nineteenth century, Henry T. Bradby began to feel uneasy about Virginian views of mixed-race people and sought to distance himself and his family from such prejudicial communities. Choosing Canada as his family's new Canaan Land, Henry Bradby prepared to leave the shores of Virginia. From 1850 to 1860 over twenty thousand people of color were also making the long trek to Canada, adding to the twenty thousand who had settled in the province thirty years earlier. Many of these newcomers settled in the southern part of Ontario, in the counties of Essex and Kent, which border the Detroit River and Lake St. Clair.[24]

Along with the many fugitive slaves entering Canada were Native Americans seeking a better way of life. Blacks, Native Americans, and people of many other races intermingled and settled in such places as Windsor, Sandwich, Amherstburg, Chatham, Buxton, Dawn, and Colchester.[25] By the 1850s in Canada, Native American blood was considered almost equal, if not equal, to black blood. These classifications of "blackness" would harden some seventy-four years later under Virginia's 1924 Racial Integrity Act. This law made it illegal for whites and nonwhites to marry. Walter Plecker, registrar of Virginia's Bureau of Vital Statistics, sought to enforce this law by "launching an aggressive campaign to prevent the 'mongrelization' of the white 'master race' by what he called 'pseudo-Indians.'" In 1924, Plecker demanded that the Indians of Virginia (which included the Chickahominy and Pamunkey tribes) "be classified as 'colored' on birth and marriage certificates and threatened doctors and midwives with jail for noncompliance."[26] Indeed, what had already been a white supremacist ideology in the minds of white Virginians during the 1850s would become a legal and enforceable definition by 1924. Here, Native Americans were constrained within legally defined categories of "blackness" in the same way that African Americans were demarcated.[27]

The roots of this consciousness began to sprout with the implementation of the Fugitive Slave Act and rising tensions of the American Civil War. During this period, Canadian newspapers recorded daily numbers of emigrants flooding the borders of Canada. Emigrants numbered as few as three people in some areas to as many as fifteen people a day in towns all over southern Ontario between 1850 and 1860. Many came to Canada from the slave states of Delaware, Kentucky, Maryland, Missouri, and Virginia. They traveled in groups, some leaving valuable property and family to escape the strong arm of the Fugitive Slave Act.[28] Among the numbers of emigrants seeking Canadian lands were Henry Bradby and his family, but before they could leave Virginia, each member had to register with the county clerk to obtain "free papers." Henry Bradby needed the assistance of a white man by the name of Allen Bradley to certify to the Charles City County, Virginia, courts that he and his children, Sarah, John, and Miles, "were born free in this County."[29] On January 16, 1857, James Eldridge Bradby and his mother Betsy Bradbury (Bradbury a common misspelling of the name Bradby) were also required to obtain "free papers." Described as a "bright mulatto boy eighteen years old in March last," James Eldridge and his mother Betsy would need the same Allen Bradley to confirm their freeborn status. Although the Charles City County minute book recorded James Eldridge under the name Bradbury, the 1861 census of Canada confirms that James Eldridge Bradby is listed alongside Henry T. Bradby's wife and children, as well as his sister, Nancy B. Bradby, and his other brother, Robert W. Bradby, all of whom were located in the township of Chatham in the county of Kent in Ontario. Given that James Eldridge was the son of Betsy Bradbury, it stands to reason that James Eldridge Bradby and Henry T. Bradby may have possibly been half brothers. This connection is confirmed by a marriage certificate between James Eldridge Bradby and Mary C. Rivers on May 16, 1870, in which he names Bolling Bradby as his father.[30] Interestingly, the 1861 census does not record the presence of Betsy Bradbury among Henry Bradby's relatives in Canada. What the 1861 census does record is that Henry T. Bradby, James Eldridge Bradby, and his relatives were of the Baptist faith and all racially identified as "Indian" or "mulatto," with both Henry T. and James Eldridge noted as farmers. Noteworthy here is that this same James Eldridge Bradby (J. Eldridge Bradby) would eventually become the father of Rev. Robert L. Bradby of Detroit in 1877.[31]

THE EARLY YEARS OF ROBERT L. BRADBY

While Henry T. Bradby returned to Virginia after having married an Ojibwa woman sometime after 1865, James Eldridge Bradby remained in Canada and started a new life for himself among bands of colored people in Canada. And though historical records fail to reveal the name of Henry Bradby's Ojibwa wife, he settled among the Ojibwa Indians in what is now known as the Munsee-Delaware Indian Reservation bordering Middlemiss, Ontario. James Eldridge Bradby followed suit and married "first an Indian girl and later a white woman. A son by the latter union is said to have become a . . . preacher." The white woman James Eldridge Bradby married was named Mary Catherine Rivers. Born in Elgin County, Ontario, in 1855 to William and Mary Rivers, Mary Catherine Rivers married James Eldridge Bradby in Southwold, Ontario, on May 16, 1870, at the age of fifteen.[32] James Eldridge Bradby was thirty-two years old at the time. Although historical sources are unclear concerning the ancestry of Mary Catherine Rivers's parents, if one were to trace the lineage from the information provided from James Eldridge and Mary Catherine's 1870 marriage certificate, along with Canadian census records, then Mary Catherine's mother, Mary Ann Rivers, would have been born in West Oxford, Ontario, in 1835.[33] Again, sources are sketchy at best and there is also an assertion within members of the Bradby-Rivers family that argue that a Mary Ann Avery Nevels was the mother of Mary Catherine. Some family members even claim a Mary Ann Avery Rivers Nevels as the mother of Mary Catherine Rivers.[34]

Despite the uncertainty within the maternal line of James Eldridge Bradby's wife, the marriage between James Eldridge and Mary Catherine brought about the birth of Robert L. Bradby, future pastor of Second Baptist Church. Born on September 17, 1877, Bradby was reared in a 12 x 10 log cabin with an "elm bark" roof. The cabin was in the small village of Middlemiss, about 110 miles from Windsor, Ontario. Surviving the death of his mother when he was five years old, Bradby grew up under the tutelage of his father, grandmother, two uncles, and one aunt.[35] Growing up knowing his mother was white and that his father was of mixed white and Native American ancestry must have caused the young Bradby to contemplate his ethnicity.[36] Although his mother Mary Catherine Rivers was white, many of her relatives, known by the name Rivers Adkins, had intermarried with African Americans, African Canadians, and Native Americans. Bradby's aunts and uncles, as well as his father, probably taught him early in life that the white world would see him as either "Negro," "Indian," or something in between—a "mulatto"—despite having a white mother, especially since his father had to obtain "free papers" just to move to Canada. If Bradby's closest relations self-identified under a "mixed-race" status that placed them closer to designations of blackness than any other racial group, then Bradby must have incorporated these perspectives as well.[37]

The experience of free people of color in Canada at the turn of the century would certainly have enforced Bradby's notion that mixed-race people were often treated with the same disdain as African Americans. By the end of the nineteenth century, white communities were notorious for confusing "the descendants of slaves, Loyalists, Maroons, and Refugees with each other,"[38] thereby conflating all free people of color under the term "black." As a result, "all [people of African descent], within a narrowing range of expression, became one; for they remained poor, they remained badly educated, and above all they remained that which they could not alter, black." James Eldridge Bradby's experience in Canada clearly reflects this racial reality. Although there is no mention of James Eldridge Bradby's level of education, it is uncertain whether he could even read. What is known about James Eldridge Bradby is that he appeared to be locked into low-paying labor positions for the remainder of his life. His son, Robert L. Bradby, grew up in Canada under this same oppression. He followed in his father's footsteps through a variety of odd jobs, all of which demanded extremely hard labor.[39] As a child living in Middlemiss, farm work was the daily activity for the young Bradby. Working with his father from Middlemiss to Delaware, Ontario, Bradby labored on local farms "during the summer holidays, driving [a] hay rake and [a] hay fork and team on [a] wagon for loading hay and . . . grains harvested." From age seven to fourteen, he worked for twenty-five cents a day; his other jobs included minding cows and driving them up [during the] night for a pound of butter a week as well as gathering eggs for the farmers." Other times he "herded cattle on horseback with an old horse by the name of Tom, after school hours." At fourteen, Bradby journeyed to Inwood, Ontario, and joined his father at a logging camp. This was a trip that stood out in Bradby's mind. Traveling alone, he remembered "arriving at eight o'clock at night at a shanty located far back in a dense forest." Overcoming the darkness and denseness of the Inwood forest, Bradby partnered with his father in "cutting wood and logs." This was the first of many jobs that Bradby would obtain during this time in Canada.[40]

At the turn of the century, moderate earnings for laborers were gained through the most intensive, backbreaking work, especially in the logging industry. James Eldridge Bradby and his son earned only fifty cents "a cord for wood," which typically took between twelve and fourteen hours to cut.[41] They averaged about six cords a week, earning a total of three dollars that was disbursed in the form of a due bill, which allowed loggers to purchase provisions from "the store owned by the man from whom the wood was cut." In most cases, wages earned were "short changed" by the storeowner as loggers attempted to purchase daily provisions. Working the woods of Inwood for roughly three years, James Eldridge Bradby then took up a job as chief cook at another sawmill in Inwood, where Bradby was made second cook under the nickname Bob. Moving from Inwood to the small Canadian town of Dresden, the younger Bradby then worked for man named C. P. Watson while laboring part time in a stave mill. Between these two jobs, Bradby did other odd jobs around the community of Dresden and then moved on to Sarnia, Ontario, with his father, working a farm for $135 a year. Hard labor continued to be the rule of the day for both father and son as both men ran the entire farm, "doing all the things that went then with the drudgery of farm life [from] hauling cord wood and saw logs [to] being on the road many a time . . . at four o'clock in the morning with the thermometer registering any where from ten to twenty below zero." Finally settling in Chatham, Ontario, the two worked as butchers, bricklayers, and in local sawmills. During his time in Chatham, Bradby also attempted to finally get an education. At the age of twenty, Bradby attended Woodstock Industrial Institute and Chatham Collegiate Institute, where he finished high school.[42]

In spite of the opportunities in Chatham, Bradby and his father were still forced to live in an impoverished situation. Their poverty and status as laborers may haven been reinforced by local prejudice against their mixed-blood heritage. For many people of color, "prejudice against blacks [and mulattoes] was powerful enough that although jobs and business opportunities were plentiful, they tended to be of the lowest-paying kind."[43] Farming, sawmills, and lumberyards were definitely some of the lowest-wage-paying operations in Canada at the turn of the twentieth century. Bradby and his father's experience as laborers in Canada may have reinforced the notion that despite their mulatto ancestry, they experienced the same plight as blacks in Canada. Undoubtedly, for James Eldridge Bradby, the one-drop mentality that made him acquire free papers in Virginia was still a salient fact as he and his son lived inside the borders of Canada.

THE QUESTION OF IDENTITY

Despite these challenges, the question of passing still remains. For both James Eldridge and his son Robert, based on their "bright mulatto" features, could have possibly passed for white in some areas of Canada. The young Robert Bradby could have certainly attempted to pass for white once he moved away from his childhood home, especially given the fairness of his skin and the texture of his hair. Yet he chose not to racially pass for white, which speaks to the convoluted ways in which racial self-constructions can function within a given culture and time period. Part of this complexity rests in studying the phenomena of racial passing. Baz Dreisinger, in her work on whites who chose to pass for black, notes that in some instances, "race is defined in terms of cultural heritage" and not always by phenotype. Observing that proximity was "central to the enterprise of white passing in American culture from the 1830s to the present day. . . . Blackness [was] imagined [to be] transmittable [and] proximity to blackness [was considered to be] invested with the power to turn whites black."[44]

Proximity and cultural heritage figure very strongly in Bradby's sense of identity. Bradby chose to situate himself within the culture of African Canadian Baptists and live within their communities. This proximity had a tremendous impact on Bradby's sense of self and structured the very foundations of his claim as a "Negro."[45] While it is unclear whether Bradby chose to pass for white or black in the beginning of his childhood, his early adult life reveals that he eventually decided to self-identify as black due to his proximity to African Canadians Baptist communities in southern Ontario. His decision to choose blackness over his white and Native American heritage exposes the powerful influence that cultural heritage and social transformation can wield over that of skin color and ancestry. In this respect, Bradby operated in a type of "invisible blackness" that reflected the idea that "white is black," in which "occasionally people who are visibly white declare themselves black, and millions of Americans who are more European than African in their heritage insist, sometimes defiantly, upon their blackness."[46]

Living at the turn of the century, where the one-drop ideology had now transcended national and international borders, Bradby and his father may have been driven to include themselves in the black race and operate in this type of "invisible blackness." The legacies of the Emancipation Proclamation in 1863 sparked continued anxieties in the hearts of white Canadians, with many fearing a "general irruption" of African Americans into Canada. Such fears drove many Canadian whites to "exclude black children from common schools, [while others] refused to work [with] those few new refugees who did arrive, and encouraged those already present to return to the dis-United States." Added to these pressures were the prejudicial images of racist stereotypes of African Americans and Native Americans that filtered into Canada from Europe and America, which often tainted the perspectives of traditionally liberal white Canadians. Indeed, racial discrimination was so pervasive in Canada during this period that "the Negro sank to his nadir in Canada." Bradby and his father lived through this "Canadian nadir" where the one-drop ideology classified mulattos as a "mongrelized race." Such opposition "drove [many] mulattoes to identify themselves with black Americans."[47]

Regardless of the various ideological machinations coursing through Bradby's negotiation of his mixed-race status, the young man's sense of self was surely influenced by what he recorded as his first direct experience with the divine. He writes that one day, while walking down the road in Chatham, Ontario, he was arrested by the Spirit of God, who put him in remembrance of the hymns his father used to sing while working as a logger and cook. During the encounter, Bradby felt driven by the Spirit of God to leave the cattle he was driving and turn his footsteps toward a local African Canadian church. At twenty-two years old, he affirmed his faith in Jesus Christ and chose to be baptized on Easter Sunday in 1899 by submerging his body in the creek that ran behind the First Baptist Church of Chatham. From that time on, Bradby worked under the guidance of Rev. J. H. Penick and was eventually elected as a deacon and the superintendent of the Sunday school.[48] Standing in leadership positions in Chatham's local black faith community may have given the young Bradby a sense of status, belonging, and community after his many years of roaming with his father through various Canadian towns.[49]

Many of the black Baptist communities in what was then known as Upper Canada emerged from small congregations started by fugitive slaves and free blacks entering Canada from Detroit via the Underground Railroad.[50] Black churches in Chatham arose because of the increasing number of African Americans migrating to that area in the 1840s. Founded in 1843, First Baptist "rendered great service, as a soul saving and life-saving station"[51] in Chatham's black community. First Baptist was the first black church established in Chatham, and it became a bastion of black empowerment and resistance to white oppression under the efforts of nine members and their pastor, Elder S. White. The church was known for its active Sunday school, organized in 1857, and its Women's Missionary Society, established in 1883.[52]

BRADBY'S EARLY MINISTRY

As part of this prestigious congregation, Bradby found a home and a "calling," working among a growing church body of over one hundred congregants. Having established himself as a strong, upstanding member of the black worshipping community in Chatham, Bradby soon felt the "call" to preach the Gospel, and the church speedily granted his preaching license. The young minister attracted the attention of and courted one of the female members of First Baptist, a Miss Maud Snell. The two were married on May 14, 1900.[53] Two years later, First Baptist had become so smitten with the young preacher that it elected him as its pastor. Robert L. Bradby became the eighteenth minister to serve as senior pastor.[54]

By the turn of the twentieth century, Bradby had clearly distinguished himself as part of the black race. His acceptance in the African Canadian Baptist community in Chatham solidified a black identity that was reinforced by a black Christian faith. This sacred construction of an African Canadian identity shaped the young Bradby's sense of self and existential purpose as a minister of the Gospel. And as pastor of a vibrant black Canadian society, Reverend Bradby was inducted into a black Christian consciousness that emphasized black freedom and education. The stance of First Baptist of Chatham toward issues of racism and discrimination in Canada reflected that of other black Baptist churches in the area.

IDENTITY POLITICS AMONG BLACK BAPTISTS IN CANADA AND BRADBY

African Canadian Baptists in Canada had traditionally held reciprocal relationships with African American Baptists in the United States. As early as the 1840s, African Americans were crossing the Canadian border in hopes of obtaining freedom. By 1850, the ratification of the Fugitive Slave Act catalyzed blacks on both sides of the US-Canada border to work together to maintain passageways for the Underground Railroad. Thus African Canadian and African American Baptist communities openly transgressed and transcended territorial borders, physically and ideologically, in order to develop a collective identity that coalesced around the shared struggle for black freedom and equality rather than state and country. For many black people migrating back and forth across the border between America and Canada, a double consciousness ensued, one that took on a multilayered meaning of belonging that was fluid in its construction. Whether Canadian born or American born, black people had to contend with the derogatory racial connotations of black skin and African ancestry that brought strong associations to chattel slavery. These associations negatively impacted their socioeconomic and political standing in cultures that existed under the rule of white hegemony.

Reverend Bradby, like other blacks affiliated with local Baptist churches in towns near the US-Canada border, used the Baptist theology of repentance and redemption to create a valorized black identity. Black Baptist churches in Canada and the United States were mirror reflections of each other in terms of theology and black Christian identity at the turn of the twentieth century. For example, the Amherstburg Regular Baptist Association constituted a dynamic manifestation of black collective identity that was not bound by nation-state affiliations. It was, in essence, a sacred sphere that offered fluid spaces of agency and empowerment that affected the social political realities of black believers. Founded in the home of John Liberty, a free Negro, the founders of the Amherstburg Regular Baptist Association (ARBA) held their first meeting in Amherstburg, Ontario, on October 8, 1841. Those who were gathered celebrated their Baptist faith and their commitment to black freedom by naming themselves the Baptist Association for Colored People. Among those at the meeting were representatives from African Canadian Baptist communities in southern Ontario, towns bordering the Detroit River such as Windsor, Chatham, Dresden, Wilberforce, and Dawn. Along with Canadian communities, the association also included five American Baptist churches located in Michigan. These African American Baptist communities included the Second Baptist Church of Detroit, as well as congregations from Marshall, Battle Creek, Ann Arbor, Toledo, and Ypsilanti.[55] This transnational group of black Baptists asserted the following statement as the basis of their organization:

> Believing that the time is now come that we should form ourselves into an Association because we cannot enjoy the privileges we wish as Christians with the white churches in Canada; centuries having rolled along since our fathers were organized as a church; and believing that many of our fathers have gone down to the grave not enjoying their just privileges and rights in the Christian churches among the whites, we invite all the Christian churches of the same faith and order to unite with us in the great Celestial Cause.

> Union is strength, United, we stand; divided, we fall.

> Come up, brethren, from all parts of the provinces and let us see what we can do for ourselves and our children.

> By order and in behalf of the church.[56]

The boundaries of the ARBA were "racial rather than geographical," so the association operated as an international organization, which included three founding members from America: William C. Monroe, George French, and Madison J. Lightfoot. All three black men from America were free people of color and charter members of Second Baptist Church in Detroit in 1836. William C. Monroe was Second Baptist's first pastor and was elected as the organization's second moderator. George French, a deacon at Second Baptist, was the association's first moderator, while Madison J. Lightfoot acted as clerk of the ARBA for more than two years. This national and international interaction between black Baptists within ARBA continued throughout the next seventy-five years, reflecting that black Baptist churches in Canada and in the United States were similar in worship life, doctrine, theology, and racial experience.[57]

BLACK BAPTISTS IN CANADA

During the nineteenth century many black Baptist communities moved to Canada as groups that had been founded in America. These congregations moved to quieter corners of the Canadian border region in an effort to escape threats of enslavement, discriminatory practices, and black codes that sought to limit black people's right to jobs, education, housing, and political engagement. Thus migration to Canada was, for African Americans, a way to gain their civil and political rights and escape the growing threat of civil war in America. Migrating in groups as few as forty to as large as eighty, African American church groups pushed their way past American borders in hopes of a Canadian promised land. Black Baptist communities were sometimes the first Baptist churches established in Canadian areas. The First Baptist Church of Chatham, for example, was founded in 1843 by Elder Stephen White, who was a free person of color. Soon thereafter, three more "Coloured Baptist Churches [emerged] in Chatham under the jurisdiction of either the ARBA, the Anti-slavery Association or independently, like that of Union Baptist Church of Chatham."[58]

Black Baptist communities in Canada were formed quite differently from how their counterparts in the United States were established. Many black congregations resulted from ecclesiastical racism in predominantly white churches. Disgruntled black congregants would form another church, sometimes with the financial blessings of the white church that rejected their membership. For example, in 1836, thirteen free blacks left the First Baptist Church of Detroit in response to discrimination and prejudice. These men and women became the charter members of Second Baptist Church in Detroit. Many black Baptist communities in Canada held the title of "First" in their names. This was a rarity among African American Baptist congregations, which usually held the designation "Second" or "Third" in their names.

REVEREND BRADBY AND THE AMHERSTBURG REGULAR BAPTIST ASSOCIATION

Bradby's participation in the ARBA not only reflected the interconnectedness of black Baptist churches of Canada and America, but it also demonstrated how African American Baptists were migrating to urban centers on both sides of the US-Canada border. Growing cities like Windsor, Ontario, and

Detroit, Michigan, for example, were places where people of African descent could find better employment opportunities and gain the most autonomy and sense of freedom. These two realities would later shape the style of Reverend Bradby's leadership among both African Canadian and African American Baptists at the turn of the twentieth century. As the pastor and leader of First Baptist of Chatham, Bradby was a staunch supporter and energetic member of the ARBA, rising through the ranks of the organization to serve two years as its moderator. Years later, in 1920, Bradby, along with other African American Baptist ministers, would establish a sister organization to the ARBA called the Wolverine Convention of Michigan that consisted of a number of local black churches on the US border. Impressed with the leadership of the young minister, the members of the ARBA wrote, "Whereas our beloved Moderator Rev. R. L. Bradby has closed his second term as presiding officer of the Amherstburg Regular Baptist Association over which he has presided with fairness and impartiality that has merited for him the highest esteem of the constituents of this body." The association also presented Bradby a five-dollar religious book allowance as "tangible evidence of the high esteem in which he is held by this body."[59]

Throughout Bradby's term of service, the ARBA supported the young minister's educational training. Providing ministers with a solid education had long been one of the goals of the ARBA. In 1855 the association had declared, "That we admire education in the highest degree, and recommend our ministers to seek to become educated." Local church bodies in the association were asked to contribute one penny per week to home missionaries when they came to preach. While the goals of the association were progressive, "money was not [always] raised, [and] begging increased [with] some members accus[ing] the church of being a 'nickel-starter and penny-finisher.'" Despite these difficulties, Reverend Bradby received financial assistance from the association for more than two years. The black churchwomen of the ARBA, the Women's Home and Foreign Mission Society, were especially supportive of Bradby's education, giving as much as $300 in one year, a phenomenal amount in the early 1900s. His parishioners, who allowed him a leave of absence during college semesters, also supported him.[60]

BRADBY'S MINISTERIAL EDUCATION

Reverend Bradby enrolled at McMaster University, founded in 1887, which was located on Bloor Street in Toronto, Ontario. He was one of ten African Americans to attend the prestigious university through 1907. The

Amherstburg Regular Baptist Association sent $10 to Bradby, who was majoring in theology, for books and tuition. In 1905, college tuition for a bachelor's degree in theology was $10 annually. For approximately two years, Reverend Bradby studied such subjects as civil polity, moral science, and education. Between ministering as a pastor and being the moderator of the Amherstburg Regular Baptist Association, Bradby attended courses at the university for seven-and-a-half months of the year.[61]

During his tenure at McMaster University, the untimely death of his father occurred on January 4, 1906.[62] The records of enrollment at McMaster do not register Bradby as a student after 1907. Reverend Bradby and his father were extremely close, and James Eldridge Bradby's death may have caused the young minister to suspend his educational goals in order to grieve the loss of his beloved father. The two had been inseparable since Bradby's birth. Even when Bradby married and settled into the life of a minister, James Eldridge Bradby lived with his son and his wife in the same household until his death.[63] Although Bradby never completed his studies at McMaster, his leadership in the black communities of Canada and America later earned him an honorary doctor of divinity degree from Virginia (Lynchburg) Theological Seminary and a law degree from Wilberforce.[64]

EARLY MINISTRY IN CANADA

During his time at McMaster, Reverend Bradby continued to participate in the numerous ministries of the Amherstburg Regular Baptist Association and First Baptist of Chatham. Word of a bright and dynamic minister spread throughout the African Canadian community and even as far as the American city of Detroit. Two years after Bradby had accepted the pastorate of First Baptist of Chatham, he received two separate calls, one from the First Baptist Church of Windsor, Ontario, and another from Second Baptist Church in Detroit, Michigan. Both churches eagerly sought the attractive minister. Bradby accepted the former offer and made his home on the banks of the Detroit River in Canada. In Windsor, Bradby found another vibrant black community devoted to spreading the Gospel of Jesus Christ and uplifting the black race. First Baptist of Windsor relished the leadership of its new minister, and the relationship between Reverend Bradby and First Baptist lasted for more than six years. As the church's pastor, Bradby solidified his role as race leader in the African Canadian Christian communities of Canada. Reflecting on his years at First Baptist, Bradby wrote, "From an ill-supported parish it became self-sustaining. Contact was formed with the larger work of the denomination and the community felt a deeper regard for human uplift." While pastoring First Baptist of Windsor, Reverend Bradby transformed the very structure of the small church. A banister was built, and the church received a new coat of paint and a rebuilt schoolroom, at the cost of $1,200. A new Bible was purchased for the pulpit, and the pews received new hymnbooks. Once the church was refurbished, Bradby turned to the task of rejuvenating stagnant church auxiliaries and also started new ones. He is noted for establishing a Sinking Fund Treasury for the needy and a Literary Society. He reestablished the Baptist Young Peoples Union (BYPU) and the Ladies Aid and Women's Home Missionary Society.

Reverend Bradby's ministry skills impacted S. L. McDowell, who was converted, licensed to preach, and later ordained to the ministry under Bradby's charismatic leadership. In 1910, McDowell became the pastor of University Avenue Baptist Church in Toronto, Ontario. Another man, C. L. Wells, was also converted under Bradby's pastorate. Wells was licensed and ordained to the ministry under Bradby and then became Reverend Bradby's successor at First Baptist. Reverend Bradby's mentorship of Reverend Wells was so successful that Wells was able to build a new house of worship after raising about $14,000, a phenomenal figure for a black community in 1915.[65]

Reverend Bradby's time at First Baptist of Windsor also solidified his calling to the ministry. During his seven-year tenure at the church, Bradby received his formal ordination as a minister of the Gospel. Rev. Dr. Holland Powell, then pastor of Second Baptist Church of Detroit, was part of the ordination council. Powell, who was from Richmond, Virginia, began serving as Second Baptist's seventeenth pastor in December 1901. Powell recorded that when he was first called to Second Baptist, he arrived one month late because he "previously preached at the ordination services of an energetic young man—Robert L. Bradby—in the First Baptist Church in Windsor."[66] Ironically, this "energetic young man" would eventually take Powell's place at Second Baptist nine years later.

By 1909, J. F. Dixon, corresponding secretary of the ARBA, wrote, "Windsor Baptist church still continues to be the flagship of the Association, through the unflagging zeal of Rev. R. L. Bradby. Souls have been added to the church. Windsor church externally and internally, is not only a credit to the Amherstburg Association, but to all Canada."[67] That year Bradby also received another call, to pastor the Third Baptist Church of Toledo, Ohio, which he later accepted. Ministering only eleven months, from December 1, 1909, to November 1, 1910, Bradby made plans for the erection of a new church building and the establishment of another African American church in Canada. Along with another minister named Rev. Edward Burton, Bradby helped organize the Appin Church in Ontario. Appin Church was established with fourteen charter members and was accepted into the ARBA during this period.[68]

By 1910, Second Baptist of Detroit had courted Reverend Bradby to its pastorate a second time. The church's persistence impressed Bradby, and he accepted a position there on November 1, 1910. Although Bradby left his position in Canada, he still continued to hold connections with the ARBA. In 1916 he was one of the keynote speakers of the Amherstburg Association BYPU, where he encouraged young African Americans in the work of the church and Baptist doctrine. As the "Fraternal Delegate" of the Wolverine Convention of Michigan, Reverend Bradby sought to maintain and strengthen his Canadian ties by "extending an invitation to the Association to join the Wolverine Convention of Michigan." The ARBA accepted his invitation and "for the next four years the two Associations worked together, being called the 'Michigan and Ontario Convention.'" While the initial relationship between the ARBA and the Wolverine Convention was amicable, the partnership was later dissolved due to the influx of ministers leaving Ontario to serve in the United States. The members of the ARBA related that "this connection with the Wolverine Convention proved rather costly . . . some of our ablest young ministers attended sessions, made new contacts, [and] were offered more attractive positions . . . thus many of our pulpits were left empty." Although the Michigan and Ontario Convention split around 1925, Reverend Bradby was still very active in the ARBA. By 1924, Bradby was made a lifetime member of the association, further solidifying his ties to his black Canadian Baptist heritage in Canada.[69]

CONCLUSION

Today, the members of Second Baptist still testify to Reverend Bradby's sense of identity and shared struggle with the black race. Indeed, no one could deny that he lived his life as one of the most powerful black ministers to ever walk the streets of Detroit.

The reality of living out his triple consciousness of white, black, and Native American ancestry in a twentieth-century world that narrowed racial categories to a black-white paradigm may have pushed Bradby to ultimately accept blackness as an identity over his Native American and white roots. The early years of his life were central to Reverend Bradby's sense of ministerial calling and the ways in which he constructed his racial identity. His father's mixed ancestry of white and Native American, as it was contextualized through African Canadian Baptist culture, created in the young adult Bradby a hybridity of racial consciousness, one that was embedded in the identification with the poor and those who struggled for equality in the eyes of their white counterparts. Further, the theological paradigms of the black Baptist faith as well as the sociopolitical activism that Bradby was privy to in the ARBA equipped the young minister with the skills of black Christian leadership as he entered his adult years. Thus by the time Reverend Bradby entered the pulpit of Second Baptist, he had fully embraced his identity as a person of "African" descent and had honed his skills as a strong preacher and leader among black people transnationally.

This blended self-construction points to our first glimpse of Reverend Bradby as an *in-between* figure. He is *in between* African Canadians and Native Americans, he is *in between* African Canadians and Canadian Caucasians, and he is *in between* blacks and whites. Geographically, Bradby lives out this fluid racial construction *in between* the nation-state borders of America and Canada. These spatial existences of being *in between* in racial, social, and geographical contexts created a fluidity in Bradby's identity constructions that allowed the young minister to privilege race over nationality. It is this experience of *in between(ness)* that shapes his later life and ministry in America. Thus if Bradby's life represents the varied spaces of racial and social identity mixed-race people experience, his life is also reflective of the ways in which agency was appropriated through sacred paradigms of Christian imperatives steeped in race-conscious agendas. Agency, self-empowerment, and a valorized social identity for those labeled nonwhite in the early twentieth century were often created through Judeo-Christian narratives preached from local pulpits. Second Baptist Church of Detroit was no different, and in the early years of the Great Migration, the church became center stage in the lives of those seeking the new Promised Land of the North. As the church's nineteenth pastor, Bradby stood poised to respond to the masses of black migrants walking the streets of Detroit. His sermons from the pulpit were a mixture of the Gospel message, racial uplift, and the Social Gospel's call to establish the Kingdom of God. The pulpit, for

Bradby, became the means of mobilizing his congregants to meet the needs of their southern companions. His sense of blackness and his faith ordered his actions, which in turn helped to reorder the urban landscape of Detroit during the interwar years. These realities are explored in the subsequent chapter titled "The Home of Strangers."

2

THE HOME OF STRANGERS

Second Baptist Church of Detroit
and the Great Migration

I arrived in Detroit on the third of July, 1923, as a youngster, with my mother and dad and my brother. During that time, it was difficult to find a place to stay, so we ended up on the east side where my dad had rented a room for us. That was 4529 Hastings Street. It was new to me, because I lived in a small town in the South. I liked Second Baptist. I liked Reverend Bradby. He seemed to be warm, not like some of the ministers. And I finally asked my mother and dad if I could join. And they said yes, so I joined in March of 1924.

Katherine E. Reid, member of Second Baptist Church of Detroit

My family joined Second Baptist back before 1920. As more family members came, everyone in our family was more or less required to join Second Baptist Church. My great-grandmother brought her granddaughter, my mother, to Detroit in 1925 when she was a child of nine, from Memphis, Tennessee. My father, a native of Milledgeville, Georgia, became a member upon his marriage to mother in 1939. The story goes that Reverend Bradby could pick up the phone and call Henry Ford and was able to secure jobs for his members. That word, of course, got into the community and certainly beyond the boundaries of the city of Detroit.

Arthur Michael Carter III, member of Second Baptist Church of Detroit

In the spring of 1918, World War I took center stage in the American consciousness. While German U-boats were seen off the shores of North Carolina, large cities like New York were faced with thousands of immigrant newcomers overwhelming their riverfronts. With more than 23.5 million immigrants arriving on North American soil between 1880 and 1920, the United States was faced with the greatest wave of immigration in its history. As travel-weary strangers from southern and eastern Europe, Asia, and South America sought to make a home in the "land of the free," far from the terrors of discrimination and economic oppression in their homelands, another kind of movement made its way to the northern and western portions of the United States. Leaving the Deep South, black migrants joined the waves of other travelers seeking a better way of life. Like their immigrant counterparts, African Americans were "leaving sexual abuse, poverty, and multifaceted disabilities that plagued them [in] their bad 'Old Country'—the rural South."[1] Confronted with the legacies of Jim Crow segregation practices, African Americans moved northward in what is known as the Great Migration. Their arrival in America's urban centers, along with their immigrant counterparts, coincided with a pandemic outbreak of influenza. From 1918 to 1919, US agencies were disseminating public health information to members of new communities, each with a different culture and different language, in an effort to curb the destructive spread of the disease. As the immigrant population swelled and battled the outbreak of disease in urban cities in the North so did the ranks of black migrant newcomers from the South. Yet unlike many of the immigrant travelers, black migrants had to seek their fortune while also striving to stem extreme racial oppression. Despite these existential dilemmas, thousands of southern migrants filled the train stations of the South in pursuit of passage to northern cities. Noting in 1918 that "until the recent outbreaks in Germany, where under revolutionary conditions, a few lynchings have taken place, the United States has long been the only advanced nation whose government has tolerated lynching," John R. Shillady, secretary of the National Association for the Advancement of Colored People (NAACP), added further justification for southern blacks to seek the "cold-faced North [as] a kinder mistress" than the "lazy laughing South with blood on its mouth."[2]

THE PROMISED LAND OF DETROIT, MICHIGAN

The city of Detroit constituted the "better land" of opportunity for many African Americans. By 1918, southern newcomers to Detroit could gauge the effects of the influenza pandemic by the number of theaters, churches, and schools that were closed to prevent further spreading of the disease. With newspapers like the *Chicago Defender* publishing letters of African

Americans eager to leave the South, and other black newspapers like the *Pittsburgh Carrier* and the *Baltimore Afro-American* posting numerous network connections in northern areas for black migrants to gain employment, the threat of influenza was not enough to deter southern blacks from settling in Detroit and other northern cities. While the Great Migration of southern blacks into Detroit came between 1915 and 1929, African Americans actually migrated in two waves. The first wave occurred in response to Detroit's increased demand for labor from 1916 to 1917. The second was from 1924 to 1925, when the interwar years curtailed immigration. European immigration was thwarted during these years, so northern manufacturers attempting to fulfill government demands for manufactured products looked for alternative sources of cheap labor. Detroit especially had a high labor demand in this period, making industrialists pursue more and more black labor.[3] Thousands upon thousands of black migrants filed into Detroit seeking work with industrial employers: Michigan Central Railroad, Packard Motor Car Company, Michigan Steel Castings, and Detroit Stove Works.[4]

The Detroit Urban League reported that "Negro immigrants are arriving at the rate of 100 per day . . . coming of their own volition, attracted by the reports of extraordinary wages in Detroit and their migration is being stimulated by manufacturers in the city who have sent labor agents south."[5] The automotive industry was especially known for sending agents down south to recruit black laborers. Ford Motor Car Company, Dodge Brothers, and Packard Motor Car Company, for example, were known to send labor recruiters down south and held the reputation of being "companies [that] held the colored men in high regard" among those connected with the Detroit Urban League. Although the majority of southern migrants were employed as common laborers, a limited number of black migrant men were hired as semiskilled and skilled tradesmen. Female migrants in Detroit were employed as "domestics, day workers, and in laundries."[6]

Undeniably, employers often relied on racial stereotypes to justify placing African Americans in the "the longest and most grueling duties," claiming that "African-Americans were faster than anyone else in performing 'rhythmic' tasks."[7] Yet Detroit was still considered the land of opportunity. The automotive center of the world in 1914, the city became a locus of economic prosperity in the minds of black migrants. The major draw for European and African American newcomers alike was the "five-dollar day" promise Ford Motor Company issued on January 12, 1914. This was unimaginable to black workers, who in the South had earned far less than that in a week. As the words of one social worker state, "In Detroit, they made from six to eleven dollars a day. There are hundreds of Negroes in Detroit who are making more money in one day than they made in the South in one week."[8]

Thus with newspaper reports and industrial labor agents proclaiming the economic and social opportunities in cities like Detroit, southern black migrants headed north. In Detroit, the Michigan Central Station awed black southern migrants as they debarked and took in the four-story colonnade overshadowed by a series of decorative archways and sparkling chandeliers. As they moved through the doors of Michigan Central onto busy Michigan Avenue, they were accosted by the view of numerous hotels, boardinghouses, and more often than not, Rev. Dr. Robert L. Bradby and the members of Second Baptist.[9]

Reverend Bradby used the pulpit of Second Baptist Church to galvanize his congregation to hasten to the needs of Detroit's black newcomers. He and his members welcomed travel-weary migrants as they stepped off the platforms of Michigan Central and tried to navigate the large metropolis. As one church member of Second Baptist recalled, "During the First World War Reverend Bradby would have members of the community to meet the people coming from the South . . . to bring them in, to see that they had housing and food, and got them jobs."[10] For Bradby, Second Baptist was uniquely positioned to offer assistance to these southern strangers. Claiming that the black migrant was "in need of a church, which was to become the chief social center," Bradby "appointed committees to meet every in-coming train, to greet arrivals and offer assistance in the name of the church."[11] "Assistance in the name of the church," was for Reverend Bradby a divine call for Second Baptist to make God's presence a manifested reality in the life of the migrant, a reality that was realized through the garnering of food, housing, and employment for Detroit's newest black residents, hence the Kingdom of God. Such a task was monumental for Detroit's Second Baptist Church during this period. With an estimated one million black southerners migrating to northern cities from 1916 to 1929, Detroit, with its growing industrial culture, was a major draw for the southern migrant. Indeed, the US Department of Commerce, Bureau of the Census reported that in 1910, there were approximately 5,741 African Americans living in Detroit. By 1930, that number had increased to an overwhelming 120,066. The influx of black migrants into Detroit doubled the city's total population. In 1910, the Detroit census estimated a population of about 465,766. By 1918, the city's population had increased to around 800,000. Unforeseen challenges threatened to overcome the metropolis's resources as it tried to accommodate the massive needs of newcomers. Although food, clothing, and even jobs were readily provided through agencies such as the local black churches and the Detroit Urban League, housing for the city's growing black population became an enormous issue. Despite being the land of opportunity, African Americans in the city faced discriminatory housing practices. Detroit was a segregated city in terms of housing in 1918, and many of Detroit's black residents were already lodged in overcrowded residences in the "Negro District." St. Antoine, Hastings, Rowena, Macomb, Lafayette, Beaubien, and Rivard were streets where black migrants were squeezed in with older residents of Detroit's black community. Many lived in houses with four or five rooms; the houses were overcrowded and unsanitary, with no toilet and no bath.[12] Considered the "least desirable in the city," the district's bigoted landlords frequently overcharged on the rent, and city officials turned a blind eye to the need for new homes. Such massive demographic changes tended to weaken urban infrastructures in African American neighborhoods, which increased morbidity rates in black communities.[13]

Despite these challenges, urbanization allowed African Americans to pool resources and to expand Detroit's black neighborhoods. However, the movement of so many new residents into the city exacerbated racial tensions. The rapid invasion of immigrant newcomers made native-born whites resentful of European foreigners who competed for the same jobs and slowly invaded their surrounding neighborhoods. And the influx of African Americans settling alongside immigrant refugees made native-born whites scramble to maintain their hegemony in the city. Considered more degraded then their southern and eastern European immigrant counterparts, African Americans were seen as threats to decent white people. Fearful of African American "volatility, their carnality, [and] their utter incapacity to learn the lessons of civilized society,"[14] white members of church groups, merchants' associations, lodge halls, and white foremen and tradesmen united in a campaign to keep foreign-born competitors, and especially African Americans, from gaining access to high-quality factory jobs. With segregation operating as the driving force behind racial discrimination toward African Americans, housing became a pressing political issue for black Detroiters, who sought equity and equal citizenship under the claims of the US Constitution. Added to these pressures were the practices of white business owners, who despite their willingness to hire blacks for unskilled jobs, almost never hired them for skilled positions.

Despite job and housing discrimination toward African American newcomers in the city, black migrants still celebrated their arrival in Detroit, while older black Detroiters held mixed feelings about their southern neighbors bombarding the already overcrowded black districts. Many of them saw the new migrant as uneducated, uncouth, and unrefined. With older Detroiters already suffering under racist housing and employment practices, some feared that they would reify every black stereotype that existed in the white racist mind. Many migrants stepped off buses and trains as unskilled laborers, dressed in dirty overalls and makeshift dresses and with unkempt hair. Old Detroiters, those blacks who may have been in Detroit anytime from the city's founding through the late nineteenth century, complained about the new migrants, dirty and sweaty from working in Detroit mills, who boarded streetcars speaking in loud obnoxious voices.

RACE, CLASS, AND THE POLITICS OF RESPECTABILITY

At issue here for older black Detroiters was black respectability in public forums, namely, the city. For African Americans living in the early twentieth century, respectability was a way to avoid discrimination and violence. In Detroit, this form of "respectable blackness" was redefined over and over again from the 1910s to the 1930s in response to southern migrants' perceived lack of respectability. Such issues of respectability were often couched in the notions and rhetoric of "black uplift" ideology. Considered by some scholars as a "faulty construction that offered little protection during a difficult period,"[15] uplift ideology, with its historical notions of liberation and transcendence of worldly oppression, came to mean "self help, racial solidarity, temperance, thrift, chastity, social purity, patriarchal authority, and the accumulation of wealth"[16] by the turn of the twentieth century. Proffered by African American elites as they struggled to establish their equality in white hegemonic society, black uplift ideology revealed black elites' predisposition toward "class-bound argument[s] for black humanity [and] their attempt to rehabilitate the image of black people through class distinctions."[17] This method of black rehabilitation reflected one of the varied and often contested forms of racial uplift ideology. Working against broader versions of black uplift, which preferred collective struggle and advancement, African American elites tended to create an uplift ideology based on a racialized identity, one that was rooted in an "attenuated conception of bourgeois qualifications for rights and citizenship."[18] Ultimately, this brand of uplift ideology black elites embraced was grounded in a search for "moral authority" and recognition of a black humanity that was founded upon an agenda to "distinguish [African American elites] as bourgeois agents of civilization," distinctive and distant from the "undeveloped black majority."[19]

Christianity then, as it was practiced and ritualized in the local black church, became one of the primary tools by which African American elites sought to rehabilitate the horde of southern black migrants making their way to northern cities. Many African American pastors worked in tandem with local black elites in creating programs and services, which would help transform the black migrant's dress, demeanor, and behavior in the public forums of the larger society. Ministers in Detroit during the first waves of the Great Migration were called upon to combine resources and lend their help to local black elites in an effort to create a value system of bourgeois morality among black migrants. Such cultural politics, though seasoned with assumptions of racial differences, were the main forms of black uplift promoted by African American leaders in Detroit during this period. Reverend Bradby stood as a prime example of these types of race reformers as he aligned his influence and the power of his church alongside the Detroit Urban League in 1918.

THE DETROIT URBAN LEAGUE AND THE BLACK BAPTIST CHURCH IN DETROIT

That year, George Edmund Haynes, director of Negro Economics in the Department of Labor, conducted a survey on the conditions of southern migrants settling in Detroit. He reflected the sentiment of older residents living in the city. Outside of housing issues and job opportunities, older black residents of Detroit were also concerned that the southern migrants caused negative perceptions about all African Americans in the city. Previously, old Detroiters had enjoyed a level of acceptance from their white neighbors. By 1918, however, Haynes noted that white perspectives had changed as a result of black migration. He writes, "With the large increase in the number of Negroes and the coming of many of the less desirable type, there was a reaction of these older residents against a gradual tending toward segregation of all Negroes. There was also a class feeling growing out of their more favorable conditions."[20]

Overcrowded housing, unemployment, and the increase of the "less desirable type" of African American pushed agencies like the Detroit Urban League, and leaders like Haynes, to call for firmer agendas of black uplift and respectability. Haynes himself even declared that the well-being of every African

American was tied to the plight of the black worker, "especially those who are on trial in the industrial agencies of Detroit."[21] For Haynes, black workers were the testing ground of the legitimacy and respectability of Detroit's black community. For that reason alone he felt they must "make good" in the eyes of their white employers. Haynes, one of the founding fathers of the National Urban League, began to look to the local black church as a potential partner in the fight to establish black respectability in the eyes of both white and black Detroiters. His goal was to filter black uplift agendas for Detroit's newcomers through the lens of religion and the voices of Detroit's black religious elite. In 1918, Haynes issued a challenge that called for the implementation of dramatic social programs by Detroit local churches in order to address housing, unemployment, and issues of decency among the thousands of migrants pouring into Detroit. Haynes further delivered a direct charge to local black Baptist churches, stating, "This is largely the work of preachment from the pulpit and the platform. What a world of service is open here to the Negro churches!"[22] For Haynes, the main denomination positioned to school new migrants in the doctrines of respectability was the black Baptist church. Noting the fact that many migrants came "from states which were largely Baptistic in their religious faith, having religious affiliations, [which] were Baptists,"[23] Haynes provided guidelines and questions for local black Baptist churches on how best the "Christian church thru its members and organization [could] so extend its service to these people as to help them make the necessary adjustments . . . in obtaining those ethical and religious ideals which will make them an asset and not a liability to the community into which they have come."[24] In essence, Haynes's call to local black Baptist churches was a plea for Detroit's black religious institutions to transform the domestic spaces of black home life, which in Haynes's view, would reform the pressing issues facing black households. Thus if local black churches in Detroit, especially local black Baptist churches, could reform the black migrant community, then African Americans in Detroit would have proven their worth as productive citizens in the city, worthy of white acceptance and racial equality.[25]

Such lofty goals of racial uplift Haynes proffered had to contend with class tensions between Detroit's older and more established black middle class and mostly poor new southern migrants. Yet Haynes understood that if directives for service and social responsibility could be nourished by religious imperatives, black uplift efforts could possibly transcend petty class boundaries between migrants and the black bourgeoisie. Counting on Christian imperatives to undergird the call for racial reform and respectability by both black male and female leaders, Haynes's plea to local black churches teased out the fissures of religious fervor and devotion in Detroit's African American communities, thereby making black uplift efforts part and parcel of black Christian praxis.

Churches like Second Baptist, St. Matthew's Episcopal, Bethel African Methodist Episcopal, and Ebenezer African Methodist Episcopal were the most noted churches that met Haynes's challenge. These churches' congregations consisted of a vibrantly growing black middle class that was dedicated to raising the level of respectability among black migrants. These church men and women were the newly formed working classes that consisted of cooks, janitors, tailors, carpenters, laundresses, and factory workers; these folks made up Detroit's most elite black faith communities.[26] While Bethel and Ebenezer reflected the class status of Second Baptist, St. Matthew's Episcopal Church represented the upper echelons of black society. Located on the corner of St. Antoine and Elizabeth Streets, Sunday services at St. Matthew's held the attention of lawyers, doctors, and educated professionals, with many of the congregants priding themselves on their education and upper-class status. In fact, the members of St. Matthew's considered themselves as an "upstanding, courageous, intelligent, high type class of men."[27] The congregants of St. Matthew's believed they were the best and the brightest of Detroit's black society and endeavored to keep a distinctive boundary between themselves and those they considered beneath them in education and economic status. Haynes's call to transform the social attributes of the black migrant presented a challenge to the members of St. Matthew's, for how could a congregation "conscious of their role as community leaders and separate from the 'masses of the laboring classes'" attempt to meet Haynes's directives? Father Everard Daniel of St. Matthew's Episcopal Church, for example, was born in the Virgin Islands and was considered to be a very determined individual who shaped his career through educational achievements. A graduate of New York University and Union Theological Seminary, Daniel's Episcopalian connections and polished background, as well as that of his congregation, made class distinctions between the migrant and St. Matthew's parishioners extremely overt.[28] Despite these tremendous class differences, Rev. Robert W. Bagnall and Father Everard Daniel led the congregation of St. Matthew's to function within a Du Boisian concept of the "Talented Tenth" with regard to social uplift.[29]

While urban black Episcopal churches tended to include some of the highest social classes in the black community, the African Methodist

Episcopal (AME) and Baptist denominations reflected the rising black middle classes. The period of black migration throughout the early 1900s tended to create a cross-fertilization of class status in the AME and Baptist denominations, which consisted of poor migrants and the black working class. Church membership in the AME and Baptist denominations was a way for southern black migrants to raise their social and economic status. Although the level of social capital achieved through black church membership was somewhat fluid and transitory, many migrants sought out northern black Baptist churches as the first step toward raising their class status.

Heralded as the "home of strangers," Second Baptist became one of the first stops for black migrants coming into the Detroit. Reverend Bradby, working with Forrester B. Washington, the Detroit Urban League's first director in 1916, was one of the first ministers to open the doors of Second Baptist for the league's use of the church's auditorium for public meetings. The largest African American church in Detroit in 1916, Second Baptist constituted a direct line between the Detroit Urban League and the local black Baptist community for the black migrants. For many newcomers, "Second," was a familiar denomination to southern migrants seeking to recreate a sense of home in the new neighborhoods of the North. Indeed, local black Baptist churches have been one of the most enduring institutions among black southern communities. Jim Crow segregation codes fostered cultural institutions like the local black church to operate as places of refuge that were socially distant from the white community. As racial apartheid gained strength in the South during the interwar years, African Americans turned more fervently to their churches, so much so that on the "eve of the Great Migration, the church was the paramount focus of community life."[30]

With black Baptist membership primarily located in southern states and numbering over two million in 1906, the years of the Great Migration saw a large quantity of these congregants uproot their Baptist faith from southern pastures to northern streets. Between 1915 and 1925, it was quite common among migrant travelers to follow a pioneering pastor who had enjoined their congregations to settle with them up in the northern Canaan Lands of New York, Chicago, and Detroit. Readjusting to northern cities was often just a transplanting of the migrants' faith and denomination. The materializations of these faith resettlements stood on street corners and in houses transformed into makeshift "praise houses" or local storefronts churches. These new congregations grew in number as more and more migrants joined the rank and file of local black church congregations, many of them simply transferring their memberships on profession of faith in Jesus Christ, or by a letter of transfer written by the steady hand of their previous pastor. Places like Chicago, New York, Pittsburgh, and Philadelphia held membership rolls filled with migrants who had reestablished denominational ties with the AME church, the Baptist church, the Church of God in Christ, and other Holiness traditions.[31]

Among migrants, black Baptist churches in the North developed reputations as centers of refuge and aid—the "Moseses," if you will, that would help migrants settle in the new industrial "Promised Land." With many migrants entering Detroit absent of a pastoral connection, numerous southern newcomers "gravitated towards new messiahs in the North."[32] Between 1916 and 1921 many urban black churches experienced a dramatic increase in church membership. Olivet Baptist Church in Chicago, for example, which held a congregation of 600 in 1903, had more than tripled its membership during the first wave of the Great Migration, boasting 10,012 congregants by 1921. Although not as dramatic as Olivet Baptist Church, Second Baptist, like many churches in Detroit, doubled its membership during the Great Migration as well. In 1910, the first year of Bradby's tenure at the church, Second Baptist's membership was roughly 250 persons. Eighteen years later, the congregation had increased in size to a "total membership of 4,000" congregants by 1928.[33] The overall attraction of churches like Olivet and Second Baptist was due to the pastor and the congregations' ability to transform the very pews of the church into overnight shelters and housing facilities. Integral to the success of this transformation from "praise house" to makeshift "inn" was the networking support systems that black churchwomen established in these churches. Pastors would often call on black churchwomen to open their homes up for a night or two and give food and shelter to newly arrived migrant families. Union Baptist of Cincinnati, Ohio, for example, converted a lecture hall into a shelter for sixty-five migrant men a night, while other churches like Olivet Baptist Church in Chicago created over forty programs to assist migrants. While such a massive movement of southern black congregants into northern churches "presented fundamental problems to the black denominations with membership rolls weighted toward the South," established black churches in the North were forced to expand their ministries to accommodate the explosion of growth in their denominations, which often called for larger denominational structures. Thus Second Baptist Church of Detroit offered ministries reminiscent of its urban counterparts in other northern cities.[34]

MIGRANTS AND MINISTRY IN SECOND BAPTIST

Trusting their "shared religious and racial heritages with northern black Christians" to garner assistance, numerous migrant newcomers to Detroit sought out the ministries of the city's largest black Baptist church. For many, their first night's rest in the northern metropolis was spent literally on Second Baptist's church pews. Living up to its reputation, Second Baptist was truly the "home of strangers"[35] as numbers of black migrants found rest there for their bodies as well as solace for their souls. Like other urban black churches in the North during this period, Second Baptist had to hire assistants in order "to accommodate the overflowing crowds at [church] service[s]."[36] The Reverend Charles A. Hill was hired to help assist Reverend Bradby in his ministry to an expanding congregation. As a new associate minister, the Reverend Charles A. Hill would become a familiar face to migrant churchgoers; part of his job was to "assist new migrants in finding adequate housing and decent jobs."[37] Having grown up at Second Baptist, Reverend Hill had matured from a young boy who attended the church's Sunday school classes to a minister who worked closely with Bradby in the outreach ministries of the church. Appointed Sunday school superintendent of Second Baptist during his senior year of high school, Hill was able to groom his pastoral skills in the organizational structures of Second Baptist, making the church his "spiritual home" during his early years in ministry.[38] And as his spiritual home, Second Baptist, and Reverend Bradby in particular, laid the foundation for Hill to become a prominent pastor in his own right. He also became a powerful activist in the fight for unions among Detroit's black working class.

Although Hill and Bradby only spent a year together, Hill's life and subsequent leadership of Hartford Memorial Baptist Church, as well as his fight for black working-class equality, reflected the theological and political agendas of Bradby, albeit in a more progressive way. While in some ways Hill was more progressive in his reform efforts than Bradby, his actions reflected a version of Bradby's vision of the Kingdom of God. At the center of these actions was a political theology that understood the reality of God's presence in movements of social service and resistance against the oppressive forces of black disenfranchisement. The embodiment of this ideal "linked ideas about social transformation with an understanding of God's immanence, of his Kingdom as something that was a least partially realizable in this world."[39]

In attempting to accommodate the needs of black migrants populating his church pews, a desire that was reinforced by George Edmund Haynes's call to local black churches, Reverend Bradby implemented a feasible Kingdom of God, which was modeled through the very ministries of Second Baptist. For Bradby, the first step toward establishing this Kingdom was to confront a newcomer's needs at its onset—the initial moment the migrant debarked from Detroit's train station. Thus "every train coming into Detroit" from which migrants step off became a sacred space in which Reverend Bradby could execute the "program of the Kingdom of God,"[40] thereby solidifying the church's title as the "home of strangers" among Detroit's black migrants.[41]

Racial uplift was a central component of Bradby's conceptualization and implementation of the Kingdom of God, particularly as this theology became a form of Christian praxis in relationship to domestic home life. Among the multifaceted notions of uplifting the race, the idea of the home was a central component. During the Progressive Era, black discourse spoke of domestic spaces as spheres that could "purify" the environments of African Americans and thereby create the highest ideals of moral purity, thrift, and piety. As the idea of the African American home began to function as a sacred space within racial uplift discourses, domestic spheres took on multiple meanings as spaces that would (1) maintain the stability of black communities, (2) ensure the equality of African Americans alongside their white counterparts, and (3) establish a moral authority within the black race. Thus creating orderly homes and proper domestic life assumed dual significations within uplift efforts. Here, orderly black homes signified superior environments by which to nurture race progress; orderly homes also built strong black citizens who reflected the goals and ideals of Victorian bourgeois culture, which was highly valued by white Americans during the reform era.[42]

For Bradby then, implementing the Kingdom of God among Detroit's newcomers was synonymous with rehabilitating the home life of the local black migrant. With this divine directive in mind, Second Baptist created over thirty-five church auxiliaries dealing with everything from employment, hygiene, proper dress, and cooking to education.[43] Such ministerial programs for Detroit's migrant population on the part of Second Baptist were indicative of the Social Gospel's ontological worldview, which demanded that true Christians seek to reform "structural evil and corporate sin [through] salvation [and the ideology of] the Kingdom of God."[44] Reverend Bradby's social service programs that offered housing, skills in domestic life, and even education were, in essence, the minister's attempt at making the Kingdom of God a reality in the lives of Detroit migrants. In this respect, the church was not fully the witness of God in the world for Reverend Bradby, unless it constituted itself as a moral agent that sought to eradicate structural evils in the home and larger black community. Yet, for Bradby, operating as a moral agent in the African American community also required beneficial connections with the city's white elite.

With the rise of the NAACP in 1909, collaboration between liberal whites and highly educated blacks became crucial for many groups who attempted to reform society across the racial color line, including Second Baptist. During the summer of 1918, Second Baptist's influential minister met with W. P. Lovett, of the Detroit Citizens League, and Rev. H. C. Gleiss, superintendent of the Detroit Baptist Union, to discuss how to further accommodate black migrants entering Detroit, at an estimated "rate of about 2,000 or 2,500 per month."[45] The Advisory Council for Negro Work of Detroit Baptist Union consisted of fifty-six churches, all from the Baptist denominations—both black and white—in Detroit. Despite the interracial makeup of the council, the leadership consisted of an all-black faculty that established its headquarters at 1718 Russell Street.[46]

This group seemed to give a ray of hope in the face of the rise of racial tensions in the United States during this period. Despite interracial collaborations in cities like Detroit, northern urban areas were not exempt from racial violence. Between 1917 and 1919, America experienced an explosion of racial tensions in many of its cities as frustrations over urban crowding and competition for limited resources and jobs intensified. By the summer of 1919, race riots occurred in over twenty-six American cities, with a number of them ignited in northern and Midwest urban centers like East Saint Louis, Chicago, and Washington, DC. Racial tensions arose as whites sought to reinforce racial codes against black soldiers returning from the war, bent on fulfilling their constitutional rights, for which many of them fought and bled. Black veterans, in their attempt to reestablish their lives in American cities and towns, found themselves competing with whites in a limited job market. These pressures were compounded by the numerous instances in which whites fortified Jim Crow segregation laws. The tumultuous frictions between blacks and whites soon erupted in bloodshed throughout the summer of 1919.[47]

Although spared the carnage of race riots that year, Detroit had its share of racial friction, which would later ignite as more and more African

Americans settled in the city and threatened white control in Detroit's job and housing markets. By 1925, housing issues in the city would become the forefront of racial violence when an African American doctor by the name of Ossian Sweet attempt to move into an all-white neighborhood.

THE BAPTIST CHRISTIAN CENTER

Racial conflict and racial tension were major threads within Detroit's social fabric and would be for years to come, but the Advisory Council for Negro Work of Detroit Baptist Union worked in 1918 to create a locus of influence designed to "meet the social needs of the Negro migrant who came to Detroit . . . providing a place where the underprivileged and needy Negroes could be assisted . . . and secure employment." The council called this locus of influence the Baptist Christian Center (BCC). An extension of Second Baptist, the BCC operated as a vehicle for Christian socialization for newcomers and "a necessary extension of the traditional practice of Christian benevolence." Black churchwomen and men at the center believed they were called by God to "meet the social needs of the Negro migrant who came to Detroit."[48]

Between 1918 and 1919, the center focused on the needs of children, young females, and adults in an effort to transform the migrant into a respectable being. Hard work, thrift, sexual restraint, proper dress, and public conduct were identifiers of class status and privilege for blacks as well as whites. However, in the African American community these attributes were layered with another characteristic—that of race. Blacks who exemplified respectability were understood to be exhibiting an acceptable "blackness" in the eyes of the white community, one that affirmed the reality of black humanity and morality.[49] This brand of black uplift was couched in gendered terms that demanded migrants reform their "dress, demeanor, and deportment."[50] Black bourgeois respectability was gained by reforming the black female migrant and the black migrant child as a way to transform the larger black community. Claiming that "the child is the future disciple of the kingdom, related in a vital way to the purposes of God," Reverend Bradby equipped young migrant women and children in the rubrics of Christian respectability and service.[51]

Established, in part, in response to George Edmunds Haynes's call for Black Baptist churches to service Detroit's newcomers, the BCC also sought to address the Columbia-trained sociologist's findings on the demographical shifts of African Americans during the first wave of the Great Migration. As a result, the BCC was designed as a medium by which the local black church could aid those groups "less desirable" among the migrant population that needed "adjustments . . . in obtaining those ethical and religious ideals which will make them an asset and not a liability to the community into which they have come."[52] For Bradby, then, the BCC was a vibrant medium by which the Kingdom of God could emerge in the black community. Functioning as a form of black Christian cosmology, the Kingdom of God reflected one of the varied strategies black reformers employed in the name of domestic reform. Hence, "education was [understood] as a vital [goal] in developing capable people, and religion was critical in fostering moral fortitude." Both religion and education became prime goals in Reverend Bradby's ministries and operated as a theologically informed Christian praxis of black uplift.[53]

Although Second Baptist's reform efforts among the migrant population were parallel with that of the Urban League, the church's impetus was slightly more nuanced than that of the Urban League. While the Urban League sought to transform migrants based on the tenets of black uplift, Bradby's ordering of Second Baptist's ministries were more firmly grounded in the divine initiative to make the Kingdom of God an actuality in the migrant's experience.[54]

Thus the Kingdom of God was understood to be the ushering in of God's presence in and through public displays of bourgeois respectability. For Bradby, proper dress and public displays of good behavior were signs of the "Kingdom." Further, the ability to equip the migrant community with jobs, housing, and education was a manifestation of the Kingdom of God. This was social Christianity at its best, when it sought to counter the unrighteous white-racist perceptions of black humanity and at the same time empower that humanity to rise above its depressed socioeconomic conditions. This brand of social Christianity, as historian Ronald C. White argues, "was not simply spiritual, if that meant being invisible or coming at the end of history; it was not simply individual although personal commitment to the Lord of the Kingdom was preached; rather . . . the Kingdom [was] taking shape in the present world whenever men and women responded to its call for righteousness and love."[55] This was the type of "Kingdom" Bradby envisioned in Detroit when he embarked on setting up ministries for the migrant population. Here, Bradby hoped to display the immanence of God in all areas of the migrant's life. In this respect, the sacred blended with the secular in building the Kingdom of God. The ministry became what Social Gospel adherent Washington Gladden claimed "was a religion that laid hold upon life with both hands, and proposed, first and foremost, to realize the Kingdom of God in this world."[56] This connection between respectability and Bradby's vision of the Kingdom of God carried a double-edged sword for black southern migrants who on one hand were seen as vital members of God's kingdom in need of service, and on other were portrayed as flawed and even sinful in their cultural behavior. Southern migrants were understood as blemished individuals on some level, yet still worthy of redemption through the messages of the Gospel and the social uplift efforts of a black ministerial elite. The BCC, therefore, sought to transform migrant blacks into thrifty, well-behaved individuals who deserved all the rights of citizenship. As such, the center mirrored the same stratagems of other black ministries in its attempt to reclaim ideas of "blackness from white racist notions of black people."[57]

Whether migrants were aware of this "Kingdom" agenda is uncertain, but what is clear is that many migrants were attracted to the services the center offered. By the winter of 1918, a steady trickle of migrant families began to appear on the doorsteps of 1718 Russell Street ready to enroll in a number of classes whose instructors would teach them how to fit into northern society. By 1922, that steady trickle had become a flood with over five thousand migrants making their way to the center. Young men with Bibles in their hands were placed in courses titled "Athletics, Bible, and Theology." Mothers and young migrant women were taught courses on the "Care of Homes, Babies, and Personal Hygiene."[58] Migrant children were schooled in art and English.[59] On Thursdays, one could smell the aroma of macaroni drifting down the hall from the women's classroom. The women's voices were raised in unison reciting Bible passages from the Gospel of Mark, while the women waited for their first recipe to finish baking. Other women were enrolled in courses named "Health and Home Nursing and Elementary Handicraft." All these courses were intertwined with biblical teachings and scripture memorization. These teachings and domestic training were considered a necessary step in transforming the black migrant population into productive Christian citizens through the concepts of "home training."[60]

Many black churchwomen were crucial to the church's effectiveness among the migrant population. In fact, much of the rhetoric surrounding the BCC's call for reform was couched in the language of female respectability. This kind of discourse manifested itself in the curriculum of the center, which focused on domesticity, acceptable public appearance of women and children, and proper behavior in the workplace. Reverend Bradby, backed by the support of Second's black churchwomen, made sure that the center operated as a "settlement house, which had as its primary purpose the promotion of godliness among its members; but happily it seeks to do this through . . . practical activities."[61] Taking a lead from Haynes and other sociologists focused on reforming the migrant community, Reverend Bradby made domestic life a primary emphasis in Second Baptist's uplift efforts through the BCC. Such an emphasis signified a type of racial advancement and activism that was based in a Christian imperative to create a positive moral environment for black migrants.

This type of blending of biblical text with the tenets of respectability in the center reflected another dimension of black uplift. Here, religious imperatives were combined with black political strategies to enhance the overall representation and socioeconomic attributes of the black race. In short, black religious activism was very much a part of the nature of black uplift efforts. The structure of the courses and the mindset of the center reflected Bradby's concept of the Kingdom of God as a place where Christian doctrine ordered the everyday activities of its people. As a prominent leader of the center, Bradby believed that he was carrying out his Christian duty. He was constantly at the center; he could always be seen walking the hallways of the building, poking his head into classrooms, making sure things were running smoothly. Even seventeen years later, during the center's rededication ceremony on March 25, 1935, Bradby's voice, as the event's main speaker, bellowed over the noise made by the crowd gathered for the celebration.[62] Years later, affiliates of the BCC credited Bradby and Second Baptist for making "heroic efforts to cope with the situation. They organized themselves for institutional work. They put in play equipment and enlarged their staff."[63]

Sustaining Reverend Bradby all along were the strong support networks of black churchwomen who enabled the young pastor to create in Second Baptist a medium of exchange and empowerment on behalf of Detroit's black migrant. Through their efforts, BCC was one among a number of settlement houses connected with Second Baptist and the reverend. By 1919, the Big Sisters Auxiliary of Second Baptist had established another settlement house on the corner of St. Aubin and Antietam Streets that was especially for black migrant women. Adding to these endeavors, Second Baptist churchwomen also developed various church clubs and auxiliaries that met on Second Baptist's premises.

THE KINGDOM OF GOD, MASCULINITY, AND SECOND BAPTIST

With the turn of the twentieth century a New Protestantism based on a reconstructed image of Jesus emerged in the Social Gospel movement. By the

1920s, that reconstructed image had been embedded with a social-political agenda that understood the Christ figure as a "hearty carpenter-reformer . . . whose service, sacrifice, and love did not prevent him from being an assertive activist."[64] This new image was a far cry from the meek and mild Jesus figure portrayed in the nineteenth century; it spoke volumes to the populace's hunger to establish a masculine identity in a new age. The growing working-class population that lived in urban areas during the 1900s faced a plethora of challenges, and many found that traditional Victorian principles embedded in American Protestantism no longer aided them in overcoming societal problems. Thus ministers and activists seeking to address societal dilemmas caused by industrialization "reformulated the old Victorian morality" and pushed for a "New Protestantism," one that demanded two obligations from its Christian adherents—"to improve oneself, [and] the other . . . to improve society."[65]

At the crux of this intersection between reframed images of Jesus and new images of masculinity was, again, the concept of the Kingdom of God. During this period, numerous writings by Social Gospel adherents linked manhood and reform together with the Christian imperative to usher in God's Kingdom. For many, Jesus was a reformer with a "civic ideal" that had as "its goal 'the holy city descending from God out of heaven.'"[66] This conceptualization of the Jesus figure was a much more masculinized image, one that was in solidarity with the masses and not afraid to challenge abusive power structures. A revalorized Christ image of this nature made its way into the pews and pulpits of American Protestantism in the early twentieth century with the hopes of fostering "the best kind of manhood."[67] Many Protestant churches embraced this new image of Jesus, including local black churches. The fact that "African-American religious cultures played an important role in defining black manhood and [that] race played a role in contesting the definition of manhood,"[68] meant that the black religious community had embraced and even reformulated the rhetoric of the Social Gospel in order to meet the circumstances of the black experience. Clearly, Reverdy C. Ransom's Institutional Church in Chicago was a product of the Social Gospel reconstructed in light of race, and so were the ministries of Second Baptist of Detroit.

A man of his times, Bradby emulated the attitudes of Social Gospelers and their evolving ideas of manhood and masculinity. His involvement in particular ministries and clubs geared specifically to migrant men in his community stands as a window of analysis with regard to how other urban black congregations were mobilized to build upon the ideals of the Social Gospel and manhood, especially in reference to race. Reverend Bradby believed that the respectability of the black male migrant should also be established within Detroit society. Therefore, he pushed the men of Second Baptist to support and establish ministries solely designed to advance the respectability of the black male.

Within Second Baptist, Bradby pushed for groups such as the Men's Bible Class No. 1 (organized in 1911), the Men's Morning Bible Class, Alpha Class No. 9 (organized in 1919), Class "Starry" Eight (organized in 1917), and the Men's Usher Board (organized in 1916). The aforementioned groups were geared especially for black males in Second Baptist and offered black men a modicum of respectability and social capital in Second Baptist. These groups were, in some respects, a vision of Bradby's conceptualization of manhood. Pictures in the church's fortieth anniversary booklet display public forms of black male respectability. Members of the Men's Usher Board, for example, are seen wearing pressed double-breasted suits, polished leather shoes, and smart bowties. As one of the Detroit Urban League's closest affiliates, Second Baptist mirrored the Urban League's strategy of reform and respectability. Still, the primary impetus behind the church's social service programs and ministries was not just the pursuit of black respectability; it was the Kingdom and black uplift. Black male respectability was inextricably tied to establishment of the Kingdom of God. This masculinizing of the Kingdom of God and its manifestations in the world moved the struggle for black male equality in and out of class interests. While Bradby employed bourgeois respectability agendas throughout his ministries, he also mixed these agendas with the recognition that manhood was a God-given right for the African American male—a right inherent in the Kingdom of God.

Bradby's masculinizing of the Kingdom of God was not unlike that of his white counterparts in the Social Gospel movement. In 1911, just one year after Bradby had accepted the pastorate of Second Baptist, there was a nationwide drive to call men into social service and Christian action. The predominantly white Men and Religion Forward movement, as it was called, consisted of "all major denominations joined together to recruit men for the cause of Christian reform." With the "*Kingdom of God* the [central] focus of their message, they (the Men and Religion Forward Movement) challenged men and boys to devote their lives to its establishment on earth." Nine years later, Reverend Bradby would bring aspects of this movement into the various ministries of Second Baptist Church. In 1919, the educated, influential, and respectable of Detroit's black elite gathered together with Reverend Bradby to best see how to reform the dress and mannerisms of the black male migrant. Those in attendance were representatives from one of Second Baptist's men's group, as well as representatives from the Loyal Christian Brotherhood and the Young Negroes Progressive Association. All three groups pooled their efforts to further advance the directives of the Dress Well Club (DWC), a group organized two years prior in 1917 by Detroit's first Urban League director, Forrester B. Washington. A collaboration between Washington and the Young Negroes Progressive Association established the DWC. Although the founders of the DWC were men who sought to raise the level of black male respectability in society, the group used "feminine reform discourse" to neutralize embarrassing reactions caused by Detroit newcomers. With "'feminine' virtues of service, sacrifice, and love" made central components of masculinity after 1919, African American reformers mimicked their white male contemporaries as they embraced "language that appealed to earlier conceptions of manliness as rugged and ambitious." Most of the emphasis on respectability was geared toward men, but the DWC targeted migrant women as well. Stressing the importance of correct public behavior, dress, and personal appearance, the club was open to all blacks in Detroit. The one rule of the club was that its members had to carry a card listing sixteen guidelines to be observed at all times. These points emphasized "the most pressing behavioral problems in the black community of a non-criminal nature."[69]

THE DRESS WELL CLUB SIXTEEN POINTS

1. Dress well—don't wear dirty clothes on street cars, or flashy clothes.
2. Don't wear overalls on Sundays.
3. Don't sit barefooted in front of your house or loll around barefooted on Belle Isle.
4. Don't allow women to go out in bungalow aprons or boudoir caps.
5. Don't braid children's hair in knots, alleys, and canals.
6. Don't loaf—get a job at once.
7. Don't talk loud in public places.
8. Don't keep children out of school.
9. Don't send for family unless you have a job.
10. Don't think you can keep a job unless you are *sober*.

11. Don't fool with patent medicines.
12. Don't fail to be an *active* church member.
13. Don't buy on installment.
14. Start a savings account.
15. Don't spend all the money for pleasures.
16. Call on the Urban League if you need help.

Guidelines 1, 2, 6, 7, 9, and 10 of the sixteen points were especially directed toward African American men and their types of labor. Black males were often employed in the dirtiest of industrial jobs and were known to board streetcars filthy from foundry work, speaking in loud voices. With African American males frequently the first members of their families to settle in urban areas, many men would prematurely send for relatives on the promise of employment, only to be disappointed later. These situations often exacerbated the social service efforts of the Detroit Urban League and created massive overcrowding of already packed slums. Members and supporters of the DWC believed "These rules will help blacks make good, and keep down prejudice, race friction, and discrimination."[70] In this respect, the DWC constructed a black gendered self through guidelines reflected in Victorian American themes of "honesty, piety, self-control, and a commitment to the producer values of industry, thrift, punctuality, and sobriety." While clearly grounded in bourgeois notions of respectability, the guidelines spoke directly to black males, who depicted a manhood based in "independence, citizenship, engagement in the marketplace, mastery over self and the environment, and patriarchy."[71]

Reverend Bradby strongly encouraged membership in the DWC and even published some of the ideology of the DWC in the church's weekly newsletter, the *Second Baptist Herald*. A variety of black church members made the DWC one of the most striking examples of black Christian respectability and masculinity in Detroit. As head editor of the church's newspaper, the *Herald*, Bradby wrote powerful editorials and articles encouraging his members to adhere to the credos of thrift, respectability, and entrepreneurship. One article recites a member asking if going into business for oneself is a good idea. The *Herald* answers with an affirmative "yes, if you are able to work hard and save your money."[72] Publicly promoting a theologically based discourse of black uplift, respectability, and racial pride was, for Bradby, another way of establishing the Kingdom of God among black Detroiters. With Second Baptist's black uplift agendas revolving around gendered notions of the Kingdom of God the ministries and social discourse of Second Baptist spoke to the Progressive Era's metanarratives of reform and respectability.[73]

Thus Reverend Bradby's ideas were a reflection of the times, and like his contemporaries on both sides of the color line, Bradby wanted to Christianize the social order. Part of this desire to "Christianize the social order" placed Rev. Bradby within the Metropolitan Detroit Council of Churches (MDCC). Organized in 1919, the members of the MDCC believed themselves to be waging war against the evil forces of dance halls, burlesque theaters, alcohol, and movies. This sanctified vehicle of Christian political reform reflected the heart of the Social Gospel movement and organized over fourteen committees to deliver society from moral ruin. One of these fourteen committees, the Race Relations and International Goodwill Committee, was strongly connected to the activities of Second Baptist and its pastor, Reverend Bradby. In this group, both black and white church leaders sought to work with each other in order to reform the black migrants and save them from the evils of Detroit's "red-light" district. Second Baptist had already constituted a central component of this reform by virtue of its location on Detroit's east side, which was in the heart of the "red-light" district. An invitation was issued to Bradby and other black ministers in the city to join the Race Relations and International Goodwill Committee in combating Detroit's housing crisis, police brutality, racist news articles, and the "moral danger of the congestion of our colored sections."[74] Second Baptist's relationship with the MDCC not only expanded the church's ministries to migrants, but it also proved to be very beneficial for the church's finances. It was common knowledge that in an effort to support some of the church's reform agendas, the council often gave financial backing to some of Second's programs and centers. As one member stated, "At that time our church would receive large donations from the city council and other organizations to help migrants."[75]

Another vehicle born from Bradby's vision of the Kingdom and his drive to Christianize the masses was the institutional church he established in the city. Modeled after Reverdy C. Ransom's Institutional Church in Chicago, the Institutional Baptist Church, located at the corner of Hartford and Milford Streets, was created for newcomers settling in Detroit's west side. Rev. E. W. Edwards was the church's first pastor, and the fledgling congregation began to grow under the financial and ministerial support of Bradby and the Detroit Baptist Union. By 1920, the Institutional Baptist Church took on the new name of Hartford Avenue Baptist and gave homage to its "Mother" by appointing Rev. Charles A. Hill—Second Baptist's own assistant pastor—as its new pastor. The founding of Hartford Avenue Baptist was another step toward reaching Reverend Bradby's goal. Having trained its new pastor, Bradby knew that Hartford Avenue Baptist would carry on programs of black uplift and Christian teachings of respectability to the migrant families now settling on Detroit's west side. While Second Baptist was considered "the Mother of Hartford," the church was also the "mother" to many black churches created in Detroit.[76]

Bradby worked on both sides of the color line to meet the needs of his congregation and the surrounding migrant community, like other ministers of his day, and he used the sacred sphere of the church as a tool of secular resistance and even political action, which allowed him to negotiate the tumultuous waters of racial oppression. This aspect of the local black church and the example of Second Baptist points to the interconnectedness between the Social Gospel and the prophetic realities within the black Christian consciousness. Making the Kingdom of God a reality on earth was for Reverend Bradby essentially a divine imperative to reform society. However, his strategies for ushering in such a Kingdom drew disapproval from those who felt the minister too accommodating to white power structures.

TENSIONS AND CONFLICT: BRADBY'S RIVALS

While the Detroit Urban League and the black urban community sorely needed Reverend Bradby's ministry to the migrant community, the minister's relationships with white leaders brought scathing criticism from other sectors of Detroit's black community. As minister of the largest church in Detroit in the 1920s, Bradby stood in the "the upper echelon of common leadership" in the city. Highly connected with influential black leaders who were involved with Detroit's NAACP and the Detroit Urban League, Reverend Bradby rubbed shoulders with individuals like Rev. Robert Bagnall, John Dancy, and William Osby, African American men who had connections with white elites and were in positions of power to help shape the plight of Detroit's black newcomers.[77]

Rev. Robert Bagnall, then pastor of St. Matthew's Episcopal, worked in in the local and national offices of the NAACP, and he and Bradby often crossed paths as they worked on behalf of black Detroiters. As both men served as president of Detroit's NAACP office, Bradby and Bagnall also had working relationships with John Dancy, head of Detroit's Urban League, and William Osby, one of Second Baptist's trustees as well as a trustee at

Detroit's Dunbar Hospital. Influential men like Dancy, Osby, and Bagnall also represented extensive network ties to other prominent organizations that sought to advance the needs of black Detroiters. John Dancy, of the Detroit Urban League, "had ties to at least six different race-improvement agencies and organizations, including the state Negro Welfare Bureau, Alpha Phi Alpha fraternity, the YMCA, and the Detroit Federation of Settlements." Another influential group, the Detroit Council of Churches, also garnered the attention of both Dancy and Bradby in their reform efforts. Yet these social and political relationships were seen by some to compromise the very progress that Reverend Bradby claimed to achieve for his race.[78]

GARVEYISM AND DETROIT'S BLACK ELITE

Black nationalist and Universal Negro Improvement Association (UNIA) founder Marcus Garvey, for example, was extremely critical of ministers like Bradby, Dancy, and Osby. Founded in 1914 in Jamaica, the UNIA sought to build a vocational school modeled after the Tuskegee Institute, the first vocational college established for African Americans. Seeking funding for his school, Garvey came to America in March 1916 and moved the headquarters of the organization to Harlem. Endeavoring to uplift the race, Garvey's school implemented an educational program that focused on "psychological rejuvenation, with lectures on African history and poignant explanations of the economic determinants that . . . caused slavery and [the] oppression of black populations." Music and literary arts were also part of Garvey's educational program. Many in black society embraced Garvey's messages, causing the UNIA to expand its branches from New York to Chicago, Boston, Philadelphia, Los Angeles, and New Orleans. As his organization expanded, nationalism became the focus, which in Garvey's view constituted a "complete separation from the governance of the United States" and the creation of a separate "African Empire."[79]

Garvey's separatist agenda directly conflicted with the integrationist agendas of minister's like Bradby and race leaders like Du Bois. The mainstream of black reformers were looking to affirm their civil liberties under the constitution as citizens. Garvey's political agenda for a separate nation ignored the hard-won gains of the Thirteenth and Fourteenth Amendments, which emancipated African Americans and established blacks as citizens under the American Constitution. Race leaders in the twentieth century were wedded to the strategies that would affirm and solidify the civil liberties of black people in America. Garvey's position, therefore, was unconscionable to race leaders bent on claiming the same American rights to land, liberty, and happiness as their white neighbors.

Thus Garvey, driven by his separatist worldviews, considered such ministers as Reverend Bradby to be "Uncle Toms" who bowed to and served the whims of white power structures. With over five thousand members in the Detroit chapter of UNIA in 1922, Garveyites became the loudest critics of the ministerial black elite. With the Reverend A. D. Williams as the founder of the group's Detroit base, the UNIA was a striking symbol of black racial pride and nationalism in 1920. Parading down Detroit streets with red, black, and green flags, the group reflected the Harlem-based new Negro movement of the 1920s. Preaching a blend of black supremacy and self-help, Garveyism spurned the paternalistic offerings of white benefactors. Yet while Garveyism rejected the political alliances and strategies of ministers like Bradby, the group used the ideology of the bourgeoisie. Appealing to urban black professionals and businessmen, Garveyism in Detroit was led by "the black petite bourgeoisie."[80] This "petite bourgeoisie" crafted a discourse that reframed female uplift ideologies inherent in black reform with a more masculine language that expressed militancy and separatism. Marcus Garvey himself gave the most scathing criticisms of Detroit's black elite. Extremely critical of black leaders who often engaged in intraracial discrimination, a practice where African Americans discriminated against other African Americans based on skin color, Garvey was not afraid to publicly decry their hypocrisy.[81]

Pointing out the duplicity of Detroit leaders, Garvey claimed that Rev. Robert Bagnall, then pastor of St. Matthew's, only courted the lightest blacks as members. Garvey's experience at a Sunday night service in the church caught "Brother Bob" (Robert Bagnall) almost losing his balance in ascending to the pulpit when he chanced to see "such a face so near the holy of holies."[82] In retaliation, Bagnall termed Garvey a "Jamaican Negro of unmixed stock, squat, stocky . . . a lover of pomp and tawdry finery and garish display, a bully with his own folk but servile in the presence of the Klan, a sheer opportunist and a demagogic charlatan." Bagnall's criticism of Garvey and his connection with the Klu Klux Klan was the most overt insult to black race leaders like Bradby and Bagnall. Indeed, Garvey's 1922 meeting with the Ku Klux Klan signaled a betrayal of the black race on Garvey's part, despite Garvey's position that the UNIA and the Klan were natural allies. Indeed, Garvey's meeting with the Klu Klux Klan brought a formidable backlash from race leaders like A. Philip Randolph and W.E.B. Du Bois.[83]

Despite the backlash from black political elites, the influence of the UNIA would continue to grow under the guidance of F. Levi Lord. Born in Barbados, Lord nurtured Garveyism among the Detroit masses so well that the group was able to purchase property at 1516 Russell Street. Eventually, the Detroit UNIA would also buy five dollar shares in Garvey's Black Star Line, a steamship company founded and operated by Garvey. The Black Star Line operated from 1919 to 1922 and was built to fulfill Garvey's goals of international commerce between black communities across the African Diaspora. With stock in Garvey's Black Star Line and a growing number of supporters in the city, Detroit Garveyites created a number of small businesses. It was not uncommon to walk the streets of Detroit and see theaters, gas stations, restaurants, drugstores—and even a nurses' guild called the Black Cross—owned and supported by members of the UNIA.[84] Members of the UNIA were "largely working people from the ghetto—laborers, factory workers, laundresses, dressmakers. When they contributed to UNIA 'rehabilitation and expansion' programs, the donations were rarely more than a dollar, often much less."[85]

Tensions between ministers of local black churches and Garveyite leaders increased as UNIA leaders courted Detroit's black working classes. British Guiana native Joseph A. Craigen held the position of executive secretary of Detroit's UNIA. A friend and confidant of Marcus Garvey, Craigen was especially critical of Detroit churches. Appointed by Governor Frank Murphy to the Michigan Workmen's Compensation Commission, Craigen was able to move within and around white political circles while still maintaining his ties to Garveyism. The UNIA advocate used his position to criticize black religious leaders and the local black church. Writing in 1927, Craigen described the black church as a crippling agent among the black race. He declared, "To expect more churches to solve our problem is to ignore every lesson of history. . . . Standing erect we may demand, defy, dare, and do; on our knees, we can only confess to the world that we are a race of . . . cowering and whimpering slaves who give thanks for stones when we beg for bread."[86]

The reform efforts Craigen and Garvey attempted were limited in scope and separatist in their agendas, something many black leaders in the early twentieth century recognized. Further, Craigen's critique of the local black church ignored the long-standing history of resistance and empowerment the institution provided for African Americans. As the only independently run black institution that was afforded African Americans, the black church operated as the black community's "school . . . forum . . . political arena . . . social club . . . art gallery . . . conservatory of music, [and ultimately] sanctum, santorm."[87] In short, the black church has constituted one of the most influential "organizing principles"[88] around which African American life was structured.

Detroit Garveyites and groups like the Good Citizenship League ignored these attributes of the local black church and were plainly against the political tactics of ministers like Bradby and Bagnall. These groups reflected the tensions between the black middle class's support of bourgeois culture and the working class's desire for black nationalism. The tensions between these groups at times weakened the pervasive influence of Bagnall, Dancy, and Bradby.[89] Reverend Bradby and Second Baptist though, represented a cross-section of these tensions. While many members of Second Baptist were notably a part of the black middle class, the many migrants who assumed membership in the church and filled the attendance rolls in the church's numerous outreach programs were visibly part of Detroit's black working classes. Bradby's ministries at Second Baptist were designed to transform the migrant population into productive citizens who would enter the working population under the tutelage of his middle-class church leaders. Thus, while Bradby was definitely part of the black elite, his church was filled primarily with the rising black working classes. This sort of class differentiation in the church would create tensions as Detroit's working classes sought the benefits of unionism. By the early '30s, Bradby's own former assistant minister, Rev. Charles A. Hill, would eventually pull many of Second Baptist's working-class membership over to the pews of Hartford Avenue Baptist Church because of Hill's open support of unionism. The disjuncture between Second Baptist's middle class and the working classes would also create new and unexpected rivals to Bradby's power and influence. Other ministers and black leaders, disillusioned with the paternalistic relationships between white corporate elites and the black masses, would eventually pool their resources to topple the influence of Bradby, Bagnall, and even Dancy.

FRIENDS AND ACQUAINTANCES: BRADBY'S CONNECTIONS

Despite opposition from leaders of Detroit's UNIA and the Good Citizen-ship League, Bradby continued to build relationships with fellow ministers in Detroit. The Reverend W. H. Peck from Bethel AME church was a frequent visitor to Second Baptist on special occasions and anniversaries. And in 1927, even the Reverend Adam Clayton Powell of New York City made sure to participate in a dedicatory service in recognition of the new $79,000 annex to Second Baptist's church structure.[90]

Outside of prominent men, Reverend Bradby also maintained ties with Nannie Helen Burroughs, secretary of the National Baptist Women's Convention and founder and president of the National Training School for Women and Girls in Washington, DC. Burroughs corresponded with Bradby and visited Second Baptist on a number occasions, often making sure to send congratulatory letters on Bradby's pastoral anniversaries at the church. The Reverend L. K. Williams of Chicago, then president of the National Baptist Convention in 1927, was also an acquaintance of Reverend Bradby. In fact, Second Baptist played host to the National Baptist Convention (NBC) in September of 1927, marking the first time that the convention was held in a northern city. As one of the NBC's vice presidents, Reverend Bradby developed numerous networks with both male and female leaders in the upper echelons of the African American Baptist community. His influence and the various networks with black Baptists spanned from the local to the national and even international levels, as he maintain and nurtured Christian-based relationships with black Baptists in America and in Canada through his connections with the ARBA and NBC.[91]

CONCLUSION

In sum, the nature of Reverend Bradby's ministry in Detroit during the Great Migration is indicative of Ched Myer's concept of "conversion." If Myer claims that conversion is "predicated upon the judgment that our life constructs are fundamentally flawed when measured against the *Kingdom of God*," then Bradby, as he employed his understanding of the Kingdom, judged all Detroit society by this theological worldview.[92] Detroit, for African Americans living in the early decades of the twentieth century, with its atmosphere of segregation, discrimination, and enclaves of black poverty, clearly failed to live up to Social Gospel adherents' visions of the Kingdom of God. The plight of the city's black newcomers during the Great Migration certainly called for a "conversion" of Detroit's urban landscape in making the Kingdom of God a reality among African Americans. Thus Bradby, driven by the theological imperatives of the Kingdom, endeavored to meet the needs of Detroit's black newcomers by functioning within the "feasible limits"[93] of Social Gospel reform. In doing so, Second Baptist's nineteenth minister reinforced agendas of racial uplift with religious imperatives as he stood in the church's pulpit and led the congregation of Second Baptist in addressing the needs of Detroit's expanding black community.

Despite the almost nil existence of recorded sermons from Reverend Bradby, the titles of the few that were recorded in 1933 capture the minister's prime mandate in building the Kingdom. That year, Bradby preached a sermon series titled "Detroit's Confusion and God's Remedy." Here, directives were given to Second Baptist congregants and Detroit's newest black residents through messages titled "Business and Professional Responsibility," "Social Evils and Blockades to Culture," and "Racial Loyalty—What Is It?" Each of these sermons was built around the following questions: "Are you interested in a better city?" "Are you interested in finding a way out of our ills?" "Are you willing to look facts in the face?" and "Are you interested in 110,000 of us who struggle?" These sermons and the questions behind them reflected Reverend Bradby's call from the pulpit of Second Baptist to implement "an extensive program of education and social service to . . . their brethren from the South," and thereby establish the Kingdom of God as an attainable reality in the lives of Detroit's migrant community. Certainly, such a divinely inspired agenda made Second Baptist of Detroit really live up to its name, "home of strangers."[94]

3

THE POWER IN THE PEW

Rev. Robert L. Bradby and the
Black Churchwomen of Second Baptist

Congratulations upon the occasion of your anniversary as pastor of Second Baptist Church. I sincerely regret that I cannot be present to express my personal appreciation for the great work which you have done in Michigan. Your theology is modern in its construction and dress . . . your sermons sparkle with originality. . . . You are an unselfish leader with a far and clear vision like the ancient prophets. You seem to cherish a large ideal for the final perfection of the people to whom you minister. . . . You are courageous but kind—cultured but a good mixer—high minded but humble in spirit. Possessed with these powers you are panoplied for victorious battles against the evils in church and state. God Bless you.

Nannie H. Burroughs, November 7, 1925

In 1925, Nannie Helen Burroughs, one of the most celebrated members of the Women's Convention of the National Baptist Convention and the National Association for Colored Women, penned a letter to Detroit's most influential black minister in celebration of his fifteenth anniversary as pastor Second Baptist Church—Rev. Dr. Robert L. Bradby. A prominent activist for black equality in her own right, Burroughs observed that Second Baptist's nineteenth pastor displayed a "passionate enthusiasm for moral righteousness and social justice." As senior pastor of the largest black church in Detroit, Bradby used his pulpit and leadership skills to rally his congregation in extending a "helping hand" to the urban black community during the Great Migration. With over thirty-six auxiliaries and an extensive social outreach program, Second Baptist was driven by massive programs of social service in an effort to fulfill its pastor's "larger ideal" of establishing the Kingdom of God.[1]

Black churchwomen like Nannie Helen Burroughs found resonance with ministers like Bradby; these churchwomen measured the quality of a minister by his or her "commitment to social service."[2] Known for holding black churches to a higher standard of racial self-help than other organizations, Burroughs asserted that "no church should be allowed to stay in a community that does not positively improve community life."[3] Second Baptist was a church Burroughs could endorse and Reverend Bradby was a minister who Burroughs could approve of without reservation. His leadership of Second Baptist and the many social services afforded Detroit's black community modeled the type of church Burroughs applauded.[4] By 1943, Burroughs, who by this time had established herself as the founder and president of the National Training School for Women and Girls in Washington, DC, as well as the corresponding secretary of the Woman's Auxiliary of the National Baptist Convention, had reinforced her stamp of approval of Bradby's leadership by gracing the pulpit of Second Baptist in honor of his thirty-fifth anniversary as pastor. As part of the Woman's Day observance in celebration of Reverend Bradby's many years of service, her presence at Second Baptist was a high honor.[5]

Burroughs's presence was also a reminder to the aging minister of those who had helped him make his church such a success—the black churchwomen of Second Baptist. The women of Second Baptist constituted the foundation of Reverend Bradby's leadership and became the laborers in his vision of making the Kingdom of God a reality in the lives of Detroit's black community. Why and how the black churchwomen of Second Baptist enabled the church to offer so many vital resources to Detroit's migrant community is the focus of this chapter. This narrative also addresses how these same churchwomen laced the Social Gospel message of the Kingdom of God with the ideology of bourgeois respectability and black uplift in their efforts to advance their race and establish black womanhood.

In the 1920s, the churchwomen of Second Baptist swelled the membership rolls, many of them joining the Women's Division of the Metropolitan Baptist Association of Michigan (WDMBAM). Across denominations, "black women comprised the bulk of the black church population—representing anywhere from 65 to 90 percent of its members—they were a critical force in its development and support, and played a major role in the formation of public opinion."[6] Writing in 1920, W.E.B. Du Bois argued that "Black women (and women whose grandmothers were black) are today furnishing our teachers; they are the main pillars of those social settlements which we call churches, and they have with small doubt raised three-fourths of our church property."[7] The reason for such an increase in female participation is that "the church literally usurp[ed] the place of the home and became the social center of black life and the place where most of the community's interest were concentrated."[8] As the "home" of black life and culture became centered in the black church, African American women took up their place as the teachers, caregivers, and extended "mothers" of the black community. Writing in 1915, Burroughs proclaimed, "The Negro Church means the Negro woman. Without her, the race could not properly support five hundred churches in the whole world."[9]

By 1926, African American Baptist churches maintained a membership of 30,000 citywide. African Methodist Episcopal churches held 7,000 members in the city, while African Methodist Episcopal Zion churches held 1,600 congregants in Detroit. There were twenty-five black Baptist churches in Detroit, six African Methodist Episcopal churches, and only three African Methodist Episcopal Zion churches in Detroit during that year. Numbered among the African American Baptists in Detroit, Second Baptist boasted a membership of 4,000. If conservative estimates allow for 65 percent of Second Baptist's membership to consist of black churchwomen, then 2,600 black women filled the pews of Second Baptist and supported the mission of the church. Following the lead of their pastor, these women employed the teachings of the Social Gospel and became the grassroots laborers in establishing the Kingdom of God. At the core of their pursuits in manifesting this Kingdom was the transformation of the social, economic, and educational conditions affecting young black females. Carriers of the vision that Reverend Bradby had laid out, the black churchwomen of Second Baptist reflected the words of Nannie Burroughs: "A fact worthy of note is that in every reform in which the Negro woman has taken part, during the past fifty years, she has been as aggressive, progressive and dependable as those who inspired the reform or [led] it."[10]

As churchwomen at Second Baptist conceived the Kingdom of God, notions of bourgeois respectability were centered on transforming the persona of the black female migrant. Member Mary E. Cole wrote: "We have the opportunity to create in her (a young modern girl's) CHRISTIAN

IDEALS, so she will CREATE A CHRISTIAN CIVILIZATION. This is our privilege and our task."[11] Cole's call for the creation of a "Christian civilization" by black churchwomen was ultimately an agenda to make the Kingdom of God an actuality in the lives Detroit's black female population. This divine imperative held by the WDMBAM and Second Baptist's churchwomen was connected to a Christian praxis that tied racial uplift to their identity as black women. As such, the Kingdom of God became a gendered theology of black activism and Christian femininity in the minds of black churchwomen. Manifesting the Kingdom of God through programs of social service that bettered the socioeconomic conditions of black females was not just a form of racial advancement; it was a means of marking black womanhood.

JESUS AND GENDER AT SECOND BAPTIST

This image of black womanhood at Second Baptist was based on a modified image of the Christ figure. Here, Jesus was inclusive of female characteristics reframed in politically conscious agendas. Christ did not have the meek, lowly, and mild image traditionally ascribed to women; he was a confrontational figure, a mobilizer of the masses, and an outspoken proponent against injustice. Black churchwomen at Second Baptist, cognizant of the destructive forces of white supremacy against their race, embraced a theology that was constructed in the historical context of black discrimination and founded upon an eschatological view of God's in-breaking presence in the quotidian experiences of black folks. Here, black churchwomen believed that they were to be witnesses to, and ushers of, the very presence of God breaking into the ordinary experiences of black life, through public outcry against racial discrimination, creating services that countered black inequality, and reforming the black female image from white racist perceptions. Reflecting the dialectic between the priestly and prophetic, and the communal and the privatistic dynamics of black church culture, women-led church clubs, Bible studies, and church auxiliaries were priestly sacred spheres that also operated as formats for social capital and prophetic public political critique. When black churchwomen created sacred spaces where they could worship God, critique white racist culture, and mobilize networks to meet the needs of the black community, they constituted an eschatological witness to the coming of God in the black experience.[12]

THE KINGDOM OF GOD, CHURCHWOMEN, AND RESPECTABILITY

Living out this theology caused many churchwomen at Second Baptist to call themselves "workers" and "laborers," manifesting the very presence of

God and his Kingdom in the lives of their people. Thus attending to incarcerated women at Detroit's Wayne County Jail or reaching out to women at the Phyllis Wheatley Home was part of ushering in the reality of God in the lives of black women. As Second Baptist members Winifred Cooper and Pear Greene wrote, "This work was heartily entered into by consecrated workers of our church who hear the Master's call. . . . This has been a great joy and inspiration as we have seen those whom God has spared "even down to hoary hairs," and noted the keen joy they received from these services; we can truly say that God has never failed to manifest His presence in our midst, for which we praise Him. . . . May God ever bless us and them as we carry on in His name."[13]

With black churchwomen at Second Baptist creating "intricate layers of social uplift" on behalf of Detroit's African American community, a black feminine appropriation of the tenets of the Social Gospel took place, one that became anchored in Reverend Bradby's conceptual framework of the Kingdom of God and a bourgeois discourse of respectability that was geared toward women and young girls. For the women of Second Baptist, then, building black female respectability and resisting racial oppression were components of a larger drive to fulfill the divine commands of scripture and the messages of the Kingdom inherent in the Social Gospel.[14]

MINISTRIES TOWARD RESPECTABILITY AND CLASS

With groups like the Detroit Urban League, the Young Women's Christian Association (YWCA), and a number of middle-class women's clubs dominating black reform efforts in Detroit, Second Baptist became one of the harbingers in promoting a discourse of bourgeois respectability. Within such a discourse was a structured hierarchy between the "old settlers" and the "southern migrants" at Second Baptist. Old settlers represented those who had lived in Detroit prior to the Great Migration. Many of these men and women had made a stable living in Detroit's economy and now maintained leadership positions in most of the church's ministries. These church groups reflected Detroit's middle-class population and were seen as one step above the newer working classes—southern migrants. The status of the pastor of Second Baptist represented another "structured hierarchy," that of the black elite. This group exemplified W.E.B. Du Bois's concept of the Talented Tenth, a group of highly educated blacks that would inspire and lead the large masses of working-class blacks to respectability and equality.[15] As such, church clubs and institutions connected with Second Baptist, such as the Dress Well Club (DWC), the Baptist Christian Center (BCC), and even the Big Sisters' Auxiliary were clearly set up to parent the new migrant in the tenets of the Gospel as well as in respectability. This type of ecclesiastical paternalism was inspired by Reverend Bradby's concept of the Kingdom of God, but it also created class distinctions within the church as church officers and long-standing members in the church positioned themselves as leaders over their migrant neighbors. These classist goals were created within the sacred setting of the church, generating a discourse of bourgeois respectability that was intermingled with the tenets of the Social Gospel and its message of the Kingdom of God. Seen as the foremost representative of the black race, the black female was the frontline of the battlefield for black respectability. For black female reformers, the call to establish the Kingdom of God was exemplified through the creation of clubs and auxiliaries that taught and even "mothered" black females in how to display respectable behavior. These endeavors to "mother" the black female migrant took varied forms throughout the tenure of black churchwomen at Second Baptist.[16]

This type of ecclesiastical paternalism was based on a social salvation that reframed the image of the divine. Here, God was not the angry Jehovah, but a parental figure, one that "befriended man and surrendered to his moral creatures the agency to usher in his kingdom."[17] As "moral creatures" ushering in God's Kingdom, middle-class churchwomen at Second Baptist believed themselves to be divinely commissioned parents assigned by God to teach the "backward" migrant the correct way to demonstrate a respectable form of blackness. While these paternalistic attitudes may have exacerbated class tensions at times, middle-class churchwomen and migrant working-class women worked in tandem in social reform efforts that encouraged public displays of respectability. As the tenets of respectability became intertwined within the theology of the Kingdom of God and class distinctions at Second Baptist, respectability became a nuanced concept subject to the ever-changing view of scripture and black womanhood.[18]

Prior to Reverend Bradby's tenure, churchwomen like Etta Foster Taylor and Susie Ashby had been the forerunners of female respectability at Second Baptist. Following spiritual visions she had in 1901 and 1903, Taylor organized the Christian Industrial Club in 1904 in order to provide safe housing for young black women. Ten years later, Taylor and other churchwomen pooled their monies with the church and founded the Francis Harper Inn on December 14, 1914. The home was purchased in order to provide "a home for employed girls."[19]

As founder of the Earnest Well Workers Club in 1908, Ashby organized "a small group of Christian women understanding the aims of the Church." Church member Lillian Johnson, vice president of the club in 1940, encouraged the churchwomen of Second to uphold the mission of the group by "shar[ing] in the financial obligations of the Church and . . . help[ing] create a spirit of cooperation among the other members." Serving under the motto, "I am the Walking Lady, I am on my way to the Earnest Workers Club, Second Baptist Church. Please don't stop me; please give me a donation," Johnson and other women engaged in "fund-raising, charity events, and good will" for the various financial needs of the church. Both church clubs promoted an image of black womanhood that would carry over into the 1920s and 1930s in the church. Here, true black womanhood was exhibited with participation in the church's various ministries, devotion to God, steady employment, and if single, proper housing.[20]

By the 1920s, this Christian-based brand of female activism and respectability established by older churchwomen was in direct opposition to the displays of femininity seen in Detroit's newcomers. Female respectability at Second Baptist desired conservative forms of public behavior, proper dress, and active church service, behaviors that were in direct opposition to migrant women who appeared in public with dirty aprons, unkempt hair, and loud voices. The "old settlers" churchwomen like Taylor, Ashby, and Johnson viewed Detroit newcomers as "uncouth, rural, and naïve," and these perceptions "dominated much of the agenda of assimilation and reform during the Great Migration."[21]

Indubitably, many church clubs and groups were organized to teach black women how to cook, clean, set a dinner table, dress properly, and raise their children. Examples of "paternalistic mothering" by the black churchwomen of Second Baptist were also reflected in the establishment of two churchwomen's clubs, the Mother's Guild and the Mother's Club. The Mother's Guild was designed to teach and train women in the tenets of the Christian faith as well as offer good role models of Christian women to the black community. The Mother's Club meanwhile, which was organized in 1931 under the direction of congregant Mary Reid, was formed to provide churchwomen a space to support the ministries of the church as well as a space for discourse and activism that targeted women's needs. As such, the Mother's Club eventually evolved into the Second Baptist Women's Council in 1934. Both groups sought to enhance the attributes of the female migrant and her family through biblical teachings, domestic education, and proper displays

of public decorum. While not entirely motivated by the theology of the Kingdom of God, early black churchwomen's groups, like the aforementioned
clubs, were driven by Christian imperatives.[22]

During the early years of the Great Migration, these same Christian
imperatives were expanded and more structured in their lived praxis as black
churchwomen activities in Second Baptist became the foundation of the
church's reputation as the "home of strangers." With the women of Second
Baptist supporting over thirty auxiliaries in the church by the 1920s, many
of which were established and run by black women, the churchwomen of
Second Baptist signaled their dedication to Reverend Bradby's vision of the
Kingdom of God. At the center of this dedication was the home. In fact, the
homes of Second's churchwomen constituted one of the first meeting spaces
for some of the church's auxiliaries, thereby exemplifying the ways in which
black churchwomen, like Elizabeth Ecclestone and Cornelia Holland Lindsey
for example, were able to alter their domestic spheres into sacred mediums
of transformation and empowerment on behalf of Detroit's migrant community. Ecclestone and Lindsey were indicative of other churchwomen at
Second Baptist who desired to "help in the church wherever and whenever
needed." Accordingly, the churchwomen of Second Baptist filled the membership rolls of such groups as the Big Sister Auxiliary, the American Beauty
Club, the Silver Leaf Club, the Worthwhile Missionary Club, and the Christian Women Workers with the hope of ushering in the Kingdom on behalf of
the city's migrant masses. Established on May 1, 1931, the Worthwhile Missionary Club, for example, offered a variety of services from "visiting the sick
in hospitals and homes to taking gifts and programs to Marine veterans in
Fort Wayne, Dearborn and Battle Creek." The club members also visited pris-
oners in the city jail and patients at the Phyllis Wheatley Home for the Aged.
At the time of Reverend Bradby's death in 1946, the club even petitioned
for a street or school to bear Bradby's name. Other churchwomen clubs at
Second Baptist assisted in refurbishing the church's sanctuary from time to
time. The Silver Leaf Club, for example, "put carpet down the aisles of the
church, curtains in the pastor's study, [and] furnish[ed] the ladies' rest room"
under the motto "Nothing great is easy." Clubs like the American Beauty
Club and the Christian Women Workers Club were especially geared toward
the needs of black women. By virtue of its title, the American Beauty Club
redefined traditional perceptions of beauty, which were limited to Eurocen-
tric models. While sending cards to the sick and hosting fund-raising activities, the club also offered black women a space for acceptance and activism.

And whereas the Christian Women Workers Club's ultimate purpose was to "elevate standards of womanhood by promoting love, peace, and harmony," the Women's Council of Second Baptist was dedicated to "assist[ing] with youth programs, spiritually and financially."[23]

As Christian imperatives and the demands of racial reform pushed the women of Second Baptist to extend their social service and ministry deeper into the migrant community, other manifestations of their efforts to fulfill the goals of the Kingdom were realized in the fall of 1919. On November 25, 1919, the anxious voices Second Baptist's churchwomen could be heard throughout the sanctuary. They had all come at the behest of Reverend Bradby in order to discuss the ablest way to meet the needs of the migrant women flowing into Detroit by the hundreds. Sitting among the hundred or more women gathered at the meeting was church member Kate Johnson. As she listened to the commanding voice of her pastor, she and other church-women began to strategize how they could best support the conditions of migrant women and fulfill the divine mandate their pastor issued. By the close of the meeting, the women of Second Baptist had a plan and it took the form of a new black women's club within the church, the Big Sisters Auxil-iary. Elected as the club's first president, Kate Johnson was instrumental in mapping "out the work for the organization, meeting with the approval of all members." Under Johnson, fifteen subgroups were organized under the Big Sisters Auxiliary, creating a massive internal network of churchwomen dedicated to assisting black women migrants during the climax of the Great Migration.[24]

The establishment of the Big Sisters Auxiliary was a reflection of Bradby's theological and social concerns for black newcomers in Detroit. Bradby was especially anxious over the young women migrants becoming the target of houses of prostitution from the "red-light" district. Since Second Baptist was located on Detroit's east side and was part of the "red-light" district, Bradby made sure, through the efforts of black churchwomen, to direct the flow of young women away from Detroit's dangerous nightlife and to the doors of his church. Further, Bradby wanted to advance economic and social opportunities for these young women by giving them other alternatives than those offered by the "red-light" district. The Big Sisters Auxiliary aimed at "maintain[ing] a home for young women or such other help for the uplift of the Race," which was clearly an agenda for making the Kingdom of God a certainty among black migrant women. If Reverend Bradby writes in 1940 that the church is dedicated to making "a larger and more extensive program of the *Kingdom of God,*" then the establishment of the Big Sisters Home was one of his initial steps toward reaching this goal.[25] Black churchwomen like Kate Johnson rallied to Bradby's call and over the next four years oversaw the recruitment of more than four hundred "Christian women" who helped to raise five thousand dollars "for the purpose of buying a home on the corner of St. Aubin and Antietam Streets."[26] Under Johnson's leadership, the women of Second Baptist were able to purchase a $21,000 house, which stood as "a beacon-light for the protection of our girls." The black churchwomen of the Big Sisters Auxiliary established the home to "stand as a monument to our splendid women of Detroit." The Big Sisters Auxiliary used their settlement home not only as a place to provide housing for black women but also as a site for training in thrift, Christianity, and acceptable public behavior. Churchwomen like Johnson and others at Second Baptist were the mainstays of social service programs dedicated to Detroit's black community. And while these women were the very backbone of Second Baptist's presence and success in Detroit, they were positioned in a black ecclesiastical community that upheld traditional patriarchy structures and gendered divisions of social service. While public displays of leadership and power were imaged in the bodies of black males from the pulpit, the "long-arm" of the church was felt through the behind-the-scenes activities of black churchwomen.[27]

BAPTIST CHRISTIAN CENTER

These gendered prescriptions in the power structures of the church also bled into the nature of reform efforts toward the migrant community. The development of Second Baptist's Baptist Christian Center (BCC) was a primary example of how sexism was an unspoken reality in the reform efforts of the black Baptist church. Black women at Second Baptist adhered to traditionally prescribed gender roles and spaces. Throughout the existence of the church, black churchwomen never fully challenged the male-dominated pulpit or church organizations. Yet they did create social sacred spaces for themselves that sparked movements of black female equality and sisterhood alongside their male counterparts. These female-centered spaces allowed the black women of Second Baptist to assert their own views and establish a discourse reflective of their experience as women.

The BCC operated as a space for the black female voice, yet this space, like the church, was infused with levels of sexism. Although male and female migrants were targeted by the center, the majority of the center's efforts focused on the needs and reform of black women. The implication was that the behavior of black women migrants, more so than black men, could "make" or "break" the black community. Reverend Bradby, despite the progressive nature of his ministries, still held on to patriarchal prejudices, which viewed "women [as] the caretakers of home and neighborhood," and believed that women alone could make or break the respectable standing of the race as a whole. The majority of courses at the center were gender specific; they taught women domestic skills and feminine public decorum. In short, sexism was employed in the very makeup of the center's curriculum.[28]

Sexism in the BCC could also be seen in the leadership spaces afforded men and women. Black churchmen, for the most part, consistently taught black male migrants, whereas black churchwomen taught and mentored only black female migrants. Although women like Mary Reid and Kate Johnson were allowed to maintain leadership roles in the center and other organizations, these high-ranking positions were only permitted in regard to groups and institutions that were largely female centered. Missionary and church member Mary Louise Reid, for example, was the center's first director and oversaw the running of the third black settlement house connected with Second Baptist on behalf of migrant newcomers. The center's purpose was to minister to incoming migrants by assisting them in securing employment and training them in Christian principles. One of the primary groups the center targeted was young black females and mothers. Reid was responsible for instructing not only the children of migrants but also teaching the women in classes on cooking, sewing, gardening, music, Negro history, and housework. Many of her courses fell under the title "Domestic Science Class." A typical day for Reid consisted of teaching morning Bible class at the church, visiting a new member, making a house visit, and then holding cooking classes at the BCC between 7:00 p.m. and 8:00 p.m. Reid even ministered to black mothers with supposedly delinquent children. One 1927 journal entry in particular related Reid making a special visit to "police headquarters with a Mrs. Tate concerning her son." It appears that Reid filled in for Reverend Bradby when he could not make pastoral visits.[29]

Reverend Bradby's concern for the well-being of young migrant women and mothers made him a daily presence at the BCC. In a report on the activities of the center dated October 28–December 31, 1921, Bradby wrote of holding forty personal talks with mothers and girls. He went on to note that over 4,553 students, many of them women, were receiving training that year in some department of the center. Biblical rhetoric laced with "personal talks with mothers and girls" about the glories of morality, education, and domes-ticity was at the heart of the center's teachings and the subject of many home visits. This particular kind of discourse, which blended sacred theologies with social reform, emphasized the priestly and prophetic nature of black church reform, especially as it related to gender. Here, black churchwomen blended Christian teachings with the imperative for black female uplift in terms of training and education in domesticity, religious piety, and respon-sible behavior in society. Many of these lessons targeted the private sphere of the home, and the elements of homemaking were understood as sacred and secular tools that would raise the socioeconomic status of black women and usher in the reality of the Kingdom.[30]

Class issues and paternalism were embedded in the culture of the BCC, but middle-class churchwomen of Second Baptist felt it their duty to transform those migrant females with "little training or experience . . . utterly bewildered by the social surroundings . . . coming largely from rural regions of a primitive type civilization." Despite these pejorative and classist views held by Second Baptist's churchwomen of their migrant sisters in the faith, "training girls and young women and 'protecting' them from the dangers of the city were the stated duties of the 'mothers' in the Second Baptist Church." By 1927, the BCC looked like it was making the Kingdom of God a reality among migrant women. With over two thousand black females enrolled in courses, including several social workers and female teachers, the center became one of the most successful manifestations of racial advancement and black female uplift.[31]

Preaching sermons that motivated black churchwomen to establish the Kingdom of God through social outreach programs that met the needs of black female migrants was part of Bradby's sociopolitical agenda and success as a minister and leader. Sermon titles such as "The Detroit We've Made," "The Detroit as Headed," and the "The Detroit Which Can Be" were specially geared toward encouraging members to support ministries headed by black churchwomen on behalf of the migrant female. In 1929, the *Second Baptist Herald* mentioned all three sermons as being "promoted in the interest of the Big Sisters Home,"[32] demonstrating "the fine line that Bradby was able to walk between providing sermons and services that appealed to southern migrants [while] maintaining the respect of secular leaders."[33]

WOMEN, EDUCATION, AND CLASS AT SECOND BAPTIST (DETROIT STUDY CLUB)

The Baptist Training Union was another example of Bradby's ability to draw migrants to the doors of Second Baptist. Again, churchwomen were the power behind his efforts. For example, church member Mary E. Cole was appointed general director of the Baptist Training Union. In February 1933, Cole and other women worked alongside their male congregants in the training of new members in the fundamentals of Christian service. New congregants, especially migrant members, were trained in how to be upstanding participants in various church ministries. The Baptist Training Union operated along the same lines as the BCC and sought to extend the principles of Christian living and the messages of the Kingdom beyond the doors of the church and into the community. With the BCC and the Baptist Training Union expanding the ministries and membership of Second Baptist, churchwomen set about strengthening the educational opportunities the church offered. By 1931, providing intellectual stimulation to a congregation of 4,300 members was a daunting task, especially when the majority of the congregants were black women. Nevertheless, women like Lillian E. Johnson and Mary Etta Glenn rose to the task.[34]

On afternoons at Second Baptist, fellow church members could hear voices raised in discussion in the Detroit Study Club room. Among those debating themes like "Resolve That Christianity Is an Asset to Society" was church member Lillian E. Johnson, sister-in-law to Reverend Bradby.[35] Johnson's intellectual prowess in this particular debate was recorded in the club's thirtieth-anniversary booklet, which noted that she did believe that Christianity constituted an asset to society.[36] Johnson's stance mirrored Bradby's theology of the Kingdom of God and its fight against injustice. In another paper by Johnson, the issue of voting rights was discussed with an emphatic call for all women to vote. She wrote, "Running this government of ours is a joint job for both men and women. Now that we have our full civic and political rights, it is just as much our duty to see that the right people are elected to office."[37] For Johnson, Christianity and respectability were two sides of the same coin of female equality and black activism. As a member of the Detroit Study Club, Johnson was part of an elite group of middle-class women who were committed to "continual study and the need of being kept informed in progressive thinking in all educational fields in order to render a better job in whatever work they find themselves engaged."[38] Johnson, like other churchwomen connected with the group, was proud to hold membership in the Detroit Study Club. She wrote, "Of course I was glad to join a literary club and later was notified of my acceptance, the time and place of the next meeting." Making sure to rise early enough to finish "household duties [and] . . . partially prepare my husband's supper," Johnson recalled having to "bundle up my infant daughter, carry her around the corner to my mother's home, then rush off to the meeting."[39]

Membership in groups like the Detroit Study Club offered black women a level of status and prestige in the black community. Education had always been a marker of class and elevation in society, and the women of Second Baptist hoped to capitalize on this belief as they delivered papers and promoted intellectualism among their group. The Detroit Study Club offered respectability as well as class elevation to black churchwomen. This was especially true for female members newly incorporated into Second Baptist who sought to raise their social standing in society. Acceptance into clubs like the Detroit Study Club offered newly arrived female migrants an opportunity to join the culture of Detroit's black middle-class society. As such, churchwomen's clubs at Second Baptist were a cross-section of class interests geared toward respectability. Here middle-class women joined with working-class women to affirm the black female image and engage in female uplift ideology. By 1928, then, casual bystanders could look across at the doors of Second Baptist on certain afternoons and see Johnson, along with other neatly clothed black women, carrying the latest publication from Carter G. Woodson or black female authors such as novelist Jessie Fauset. In earlier days, these same women would have carried a copy of Robert Browning's poems, but in 1928 progressive ideology and racial uplift were the themes of the day, which were a "testament to the increased involvement of black women in political and civic affairs as well as their continued commitment to charity work and reform."[40]

Second Baptist member Mary Etta Glenn was a prime example of how migrant women who joined the ranks of Second Baptist could raise their social status. Arriving in 1917 from Bibb County, Georgia, Glenn came to Detroit with the prayers and hopes of her family. Guided by a strong faith in God and loving letters from her family, Glenn wrote, "I became a member of Second Baptist Church in September 1932. Became a member of the Deaconess Board two years later." Glenn's participation in the ministries of Second Baptist did not stop at the Deaconess Board. She also served as an active member in the Earnest Well Workers Club of Second Baptist, holding the positions of chairman and president. Later, Glenn would expand her service to Second Baptist by becoming the president of the Foreign Missionary Society and a member of Second Baptist's Altar Circle.[41] Her leadership skills in the ministries of Second would eventually place Glenn as the vice president of the Second Baptist Credit Union, the chairman of the Personnel

Committee, and the vice chairman of the Constitution & By-Laws Committee of Second Baptist Church.[42] Glenn's connection with all of the aforementioned church committees and clubs enabled her to transform her working-class migrant status into middle-class female respectability.

Adding educational achievements and engaging in intellectualism enabled Glenn to enhance her social status in the black community. As an active member of Second Baptist's local chapter of the Association for the Study of Negro Life and History,[43] Glenn worked to raise the intellectual consciousness of the church members and, in so doing, raised her own social status and level of respectability. She made sure that annual "sign-up" sheets caught the attention of church members as they vacated Second Baptist's sanctuary following morning services. Interested church members could write their names down to attend the latest lectures highlighting the achievements of Dr. Lorenzo Johnston Green and the father of African American history, Carter G. Woodson.[44]

Concerned over membership, Woodson corresponded regularly with Glenn, saying such things as, "We desire to thank you for whatever cooperation you may give, and to assure you that the results obtained from the effort will be productive of great good in prosecuting the study of the Negro scientifically that the race may not become a negligible factor in the thought of the world." Woodson became an almost constant presence at Second Baptist, whose members gathered on chilly afternoons around 4:00 p.m. to attend the latest lecture. Even Lillian Johnson came to hear the prolific speaker one winter evening on February 8, 1948.[45]

Glenn's efforts in the association helped link Reverend Bradby with some of the most powerful African American leaders of the early twentieth century, which in turn increased Bradby's influence and power in Detroit's urban community. For example, in 1943, Glenn worked as part of the convention committee for the Association for the Study of Negro Life and History. Glenn informed Bradby of the upcoming Negro History Convention in Detroit on October 29, 1943. Outstanding black leaders such as Mary McLeod Bethune and the national president of the Association for the Study of Negro Life and History, Carter G. Woodson, would be in attendance. Glenn reminded Reverend Bradby that even Charles Wesley, then-president of Wilberforce University, planned to attend this momentous event.

In preparation for the convention, Glenn asked for Bradby's assistance, writing, "if you would mention the time and place of the convention with any other facts which you may care to add . . . I've been shown many courtesies with undertaking but, I still NEED the 'emphasis' of the Pastor of Second Baptist." The correspondence between Bradby and Glenn points to tensions that often arose between Bradby and the churchwomen of Second Baptist. Glenn's initial letter, written with the capitalized "NEED," implied that other requests made to Bradby in the past had gone unheeded, thus necessitating another letter with added emphasis. In still another letter, Glenn wrote, "please help publicise this conference by announcing it to any group . . . and urge your congregation to attend the sessions." Glenn's subsequent letter to Bradby pleads her group's cause again, pointing out that Bradby had still not publicized the event properly.[46]

While Bradby was supportive of women-led ministries, he was not above exerting control over those who sought to dictate or control his actions from the pulpit. Patriarchy and its stronghold on public displays of black male leadership were part of Second Baptist's culture during the twentieth century. Reverend Bradby's reluctance or procrastination in announcing Glenn's programs from his pulpit may have been a type of passive-aggressive power play, which was not uncommon during his tenure at Second Baptist. Reverend Bradby did not take kindly to being dictated to, and the patriarchal culture at Second Baptist may have led its nineteenth pastor to disregard the desires of one of his female members, despite her noted leadership position in the church. Chapter 4 of this work highlights other instances of Bradby's attempt to control and manipulate those he felt were threats to his influence and power over the pulpit of Second Baptist and its congregation. Despite Bradby's lack of attention from the pulpit with regard to female leaders like Glenn, churchwomen continued to support and lead the ministries of Second Baptist, reflecting one of the presuppositions behind notions of black female respectability in the local black Baptist church—toleration of or accommodation to ecclesiastical forms of black patriarchy.

WOMEN'S DIVISION OF THE METROPOLITAN BAPTIST ASSOCIATION IN DETROIT AND THE KINGDOM

Black churchwomen in Detroit's Baptist community sought to busy themselves in the agendas of the Kingdom, and many took their efforts and labors to larger churchwomen groups within the African American Baptist faith. The participation of Second Baptist's women in the Seventh Annual Session of the Women's Division of the Metropolitan Baptist Association of Michigan (WDMBAM), for example, echoed a strong allegiance to expanding the messages of the Kingdom of God. Established as the sister organization to the

Metropolitan Baptist Association, the churchwomen of Second Baptist numbered prominently among the organization's membership in 1926. Bradby encouraged churchwomen such as Elizabeth Ecclestone, Irene Croxton, and Sadie Ewell to make a space for women in the association. Thus it was not uncommon for black male preachers of proper status and education to address the women's division of the association on such subjects as parenting, child rearing, and housekeeping. In fact, many black churchwomen's organizations that were connected with the Baptist denomination encouraged training in motherhood. While this emphasis reinforced traditional patriarchal structures, black churchwomen acquiesced to this male dominance in order to maintain solid family units and establish higher degrees of black female respectability.[47]

The WDMBAM invited the minister of Second Baptist to preach at their Seventh Annual Session on July 8, 1926. Reverend Bradby was encouraged to speak on the obligations of women to society and their family. As the state president of the Metropolitan Baptist Association, Bradby presented a sermon on the "struggles and hardships" the churchwomen "had undergone to try to build up" the association. Bradby encouraged the women to "consecrate" themselves "for the Master's work and get in closer touch with God."[48]

Part of the "Master's work" was addressing the needs and issues of black women in 1926. Slated as one of the convention speakers that year, Second Baptist church member Mary E. Cole presented a lecture titled "A Mother's Interest in a Modern Girl." In her address, Cole posed the question, "What about our girls with life, principle, moral, and soul . . . yes, our modern girls who must . . . shape the future generation, the girls who must cradle the future MINISTERS OF THE GOSPEL . . . yes, the girls who must give to the world the future—Booker T. Washington, L. K. Williams and Nannie H. Burroughs—what about them?" The question was presented as a challenge to practice a better form of motherhood within the black community. Cole encouraged the women at the convention to "Teach your girl the deadly harm there is in drinking and smoking . . . teach her that men admire modest girls instead of ruffians and flappers; they will play with a flapper, and marry a modest girl and make her happy." Here, modesty and proper displays of dress and behavior were calls to respectability. Cole's words demanded that black women take responsibility for the training and teaching of young girls in the lessons of piety and respectability. Piety, as it was linked with Christian education, was particularly important in birthing a respectable womanhood among young girls. As Cole wrote, "Every mother should in early childhood teach her girl Christian education. . . . Christian education means to know

Jesus Christ, to love Him, and to serve Him." Cole's admonitions were calls to black churchwomen to engage the young female population in "mothers' training," a practice that connected the uplift of the black race with a Christian praxis of motherhood, which in turn solidified black female respectability. This is clearly seen in the concluding proclamations of Cole's address. She writes:

> Mothers, if you desire your girls to be IDEALS, you must set the examples, you should stop just a moment to consider our future generation, our girls of today, whose lives depend on the TEMPER-ATE living of the mothers. If we are to save our modern girls, we must lower our skirts, wash SOME of the paint from our cheeks and lips, stop dancing, playing cards and getting intoxicated. Then we will have fewer marriages on style and fashion; less divorces on cruelty and non-support; happier homes; and healthier lives.[49]

Churchwomen's conceptualizations of black female respectability and womanhood were the complete opposite of a femininity that embraced heavily painted lips and refused to lower skirts while openly dancing, playing cards, and drinking. These were considered the vices that drove black female respectability from the minds of white society.[50]

SEXISM AND THE WOMEN'S DIVISION OF THE METROPOLITAN BAPTIST ASSOCIATION

While Cole's lecture lauded the benefits of proper motherhood in respect to racial uplift, churchwoman W. M. Banks exposed the tensions between black churchwomen and their pastors in the struggle to affirm black female respectability and equality. Empowered by the female-dominated context of the women's convention, Banks boldly stated how she and other women understood the role and responsibility of the pastor at their missionary meetings. In an address titled "A Pastor's Position or Interest in His Missionary Society," Banks asserted, "It is the position of the pastor to be in all of the meetings of the Missionary Society, be there to catch the women when they are about to fall, be there to give them the right advice at the right time (not merely to boss), to come as a lamb among wolves. But so often our pastors come (vice versa) as wolves among lambs, not thinking that it makes any difference"[51]

Cole's words imply an acceptance of the patriarchal hierarchy in black Baptist culture, but she does not condone total subservience to the dictates of black pastors. On the contrary, the arena of the Women's Division allowed black Baptist women to voice their discontent with black male pastors regarding their leadership in the Women's Missionary Society.

Complaining about the dictatorial stance of some pastors toward members of the Missionary Society, Cole asserts:

> Deputies [women representatives of the Missionary Society] were appointed to act in the absence of the body, some pastors don't seem to know what they are for. They think they were sent to boss, and the pastor readily tells them he knows what he wants done in his society and how to run it. . . . After the president of a Missionary Society studies hard the work and brings in new ideas and the work begins to grow . . . the pastor comes in with no vision and no interest in the work. You can imagine that is just like a cake with too much sugar (Sad).[52]

"A cake with too much sugar" not only is sad, but truly leaves a bad taste in the mouths of those who partake of it. Clearly, Banks and other female members found the ingredients of patriarchal attitudes and black male dominance of women in missionary outreach activities strongly distasteful. Giving voice to their discontent and even publishing their critiques of black ecclesiastical leadership in documented minutes demonstrated the power of black churchwomen in creating a sacred-political space in black church culture. Mrs. W. M. Banks certainly used the sacred-political space of the WDMBAM to assert her views of black female independence. Toward the end of her speech, Banks's tone becomes demanding as she states, "we need the co-operation of our pastors and that they will turn us loose and let us go, and we will assure you that the work will move on." Banks, like other black churchwomen, could accept black male leadership in the church as long as it was in their understanding of a masculine-designated sphere; for example, the pulpit. However, in areas where black churchwomen took ownership and control, black male dominance was resisted. Here, black male leadership was limited and tolerated only as a "cooperative" initiative among black women's groups like the WDMBAM.[53]

BLACK BAPTIST CHURCHWOMEN AND SYMBOLIC VIOLENCE

In certain ways these gendered stereotypes functioned as a means of what Pierre Bourdieu called "symbolic violence." For Bourdieu, symbolic violence is the way masculine domination is "imposed and suffered" relationally and symbolically. It is "a gentle violence, imperceptible and invisible even to its victims, exerted for the most part through the purely symbolic channels of communication and cognition (more precisely, misrecognition), recognition, or even feeling."[54] According to Bourdieu, masculine domination functions as a social relation that is recognized by the dominant (men) and the dominated (women) through conscious dialogue and socially constructed images infused with gendered spaces of power and powerlessness. Here, social relations based on the dominated and the dominant are seen as a normative state of being that manifests itself through "a language (or a pronunciation), a lifestyle (or a way of thinking, speaking and acting)—and, more generally, a distinctive property, whether emblem or stigma." One of the most powerful manifestations of this social relation is what Bourdieu calls "the symbolically perfectly arbitrary and non-predictive bodily property, skin colour." While this work does not have the space to formally address aspects of intraracism in African American church life, especially in regard to the varying way the skin colors of African Americans have been historically signified with meaning within and outside the black race, the author does indeed recognize that race, as it is signified through skin color, operates a symbolic manifestation of certain social relations, and because the connotation of skin color is socially constructed through class and gender perceptions, it is truly, an "arbitrary and non-predictive bodily property."[55]

From Bourdieu's perspective, black churchwomen were simultaneously victims and perpetrators of "symbolic violence" in black church culture. They were victims in that black male leadership in the church, especially from the pulpit, was taught and reinforced through social relations that masculinized scriptural mandates, which implied feminine inferiority and subordination. For example, in many black Baptist churches, the hegemonic masculine pulpit was never fully questioned or challenged from the feminine pew, but was actually promoted and advanced from feminine spheres. Masculine pastoral leadership was accepted and understood to be the standard means of God's presence and leadership in the black community. While there are some exceptions, the idea that God could lead the black community only through black male leadership was a normative view among men and women, and it is a view that persists even today in some black Baptist communities.

When Mrs. W. M. Banks challenged the control that black male ministers attempted to exert over the WDMBAM, she did not question their authority to be viable leaders of the church, she only challenged the way in which they attempted to insert their authority in a sphere designated by both sexes as solely feminine. Here, the black pastor is "out of bounds" because he attempts to usurp authority over a group—that is, women—that has already been given power, albeit limited power, by members of his own dominant group—men. Banks therefore represented women who had been victimized by masculine domination in that they defined their sphere of existence and authority based on the perceptions and designations of power bequeathed by black men. This reality was invisible and constituted a state of normalcy for many black Baptist churchwomen in the early twentieth century. Women-led auxiliaries, church clubs, and conventions wielded power and influence in their own right, but almost never challenged the right of males to exclusively control the top echelons of black church hierarchy. Again, Bourdieu's paradigm is salient here in that there are always pockets of resistance that transcend black male authority in the church and even redefine it from feminine-dominated spaces. However, this is more the exception than the rule in the black Baptist church.

Continuing with Bourdieu's paradigm, black churchwomen were also perpetrators of masculine domination. Victorian ideology, as it was appropriated and reproduced in black churchwomen's clubs and auxiliaries, operated dually as a vehicle of female subordination and resistance to white racist perceptions of black womanhood. Black women's clubs and church auxiliaries constituted spheres of social capital that were enacted through public displays of proper language, dress, behavior, and education. Yet public displays of dress, behavior, and education for black women were limited to contexts of domesticity and the home. These were gendered prescriptions of learning that limited the knowledge accessed by women to cooking, child rearing, cleaning, and homemaking. Thus black women's clubs functioned within a patriarchal perception of womanhood that was a by-product of Bourdieu's "symbolic violence."

A constituent of black patriarchal culture, Reverend Bradby also added to the "symbolic violence" against black churchwomen, consciously and sometimes unconsciously. While Bradby called for the mobilization of his church to confront racist measures in society, he invariably cast Second Baptist in a masculine image, one devoid of a feminine presence. For example, writing in the church's publication, the *Second Baptist Herald*, on August 4, 1929, bemoaning discriminatory practices levied against the members of his congregation, Bradby wrote, "In employment, we are the first to be laid off and the last to he hired. . . . There is but one way to meet the situation . . . for the manhood of our congregation to take the lead—each man deciding to act in the interest of all, using his influence to correct the evils that befall us."[56] In reality, black churchwomen often "read" themselves into such male-based proclamations and considered their participation as part of this masculine call to action. Nevertheless, published declarations from Reverend Bradby that used masculine images of Second Baptist excluded the majority of black churchwomen from political life and public leadership positions in church settings.

Although the women of Second Baptist maintained their loyalty and faith commitment to the church and their pastor's vision of establishing the Kingdom of God, there were a few who chose to resist and walk away from the black patriarchal limitations in the church. Second Baptist member Iola Turner was one such woman. Information about her background is limited, but church records note that after serving a number of years at Second Baptist, Turner ventured out of the confines of masculine domination to start her own church. Turner may have preferred a more ecstatic worship life than that afforded at Second Baptist. Reverend Bradby often encouraged self-restraint in worship. Hymns, anthems, and emotional restraint were the order of the day. Gospel music was rarely given license at the church. Storefront churches, however, embraced such music styles and openly engaged in ecstatic forms of praise such as dancing, rolling on the floor, groaning, and hysterical outbursts. The black elite of Detroit saw storefront churches as blemishes on bourgeois respectability. The unbridled worship styles and the open acceptance of black female leadership in storefront churches challenged traditional gender roles within sacred spaces of the black faith community, and hearkened back to what black urban elites considered "primitive" forms of rural southern-based religion. Unlike Turner, the majority of black churchwomen at Second Baptist opted to work and worship within the bounds of black male ecclesiastical authority, thereby "shap[ing] it (the church) into an institution for social as well as spiritual uplift." The vitality of Second Baptist was based upon the labors and faith commitment of black churchwomen. They were the cornerstones of Second Baptist's ability to flourish during the interwar years, and they worked hard to implement Bradby's vision of establishing the Kingdom of God, which in turn helped build and expand Detroit's ever-growing urban community.[57]

4

THE BLACK PREACHER AND
THE AUTOMOTIVE MOGUL

Rev. Robert L. Bradby and Ford Motor Company

Dear Mr. Sorenson [sic] . . . Everything is going along so smoothly and
has been for such a length of time that it seems to me as though we don't
want to have anything that would breed trouble. The statement on this
paper "these men to be exchanged for nine good white men," I am sure
is against your policy.

Rev. Robert L. Bradby, August 4, 1930

When Reverend Bradby's wrote "these men to be exchanged for nine good
white men, I am sure is against your policy," to Ford Motor Company's general manager Charles E. Sorensen, it was well over a year since the minister had successfully addressed an altercation at the company's River Rouge
Plant.[1] On the night of April 21, 1929, black bodies swayed to the rhythm of
the conveyor belt as sweaty arms strained under the weight of "the shakeout"
in an effort to remove yet another Ford model casting from its mold. The shift
was long and hard and breathing the fumes from the paint, mixed with the
hot air from the foundry, was even harder. In such a climate, tempers flared

easily. Fatigued and frustrated, Ford worker James Harris unleashed his anger and buried the shiny point of a blade deep in the body of one of his fellow coworkers. John Small, stabbed on the left side of his body, was rushed to Henry Ford Hospital in Detroit, while James Harris stood in jail at the Dearborn Police Station. The following morning, Rev. Robert L. Bradby casually penned the whole account to Ford Motor Company's chief general manager, Sorensen, in a brief letter.[2] Letters from Bradby's office to Henry Ford's general manager were a weekly, if not a daily, occurrence. The correspondence between Henry Ford, Charles E. Sorensen, and Reverend Bradby would last for over twenty-two years, thereby solidifying a relationship between the local black church and Ford's corner of the automotive industry for almost three decades. How was it that a black pastor from Detroit would shake hands with Henry Ford and his top man in 1919? What was in the power of the black pulpit that drew industrial giants like Henry Ford to pursue relations with the urban black church? And how did the black community respond to such relationships in light of the ever-growing struggle for economic and social equality? These questions are the major focus of this chapter as it addresses this extraordinary relationship between Second Baptist's nineteenth minister and Henry Ford during the interwar years.

HENRY FORD AND RACE

Living in the Progressive Era, Henry Ford embraced particular tenets of social reform and bourgeois respectability. The five-dollar-a-day minimum wage Ford established in 1914 was contingent upon how well a worker "abided by the rules and regulations of the system, which revolved around personal values, habits, and living conditions."[3] These attributes were in a large part based on middle-class virtues "including thrift, temperance, diligence, loyalty, Americanism, and family values."[4] Such values were institutionalized through various company policies at Ford Motor Company and were governed, studied, and implemented by Ford's Sociological Department.

The Sociological Department of Ford Motor, created in 1914, kept records on "the lifestyles and spending habits of each of Ford's hourly employees."[5] Reflective of Ford's beliefs in a "stable household, steady savings, and cleanliness," the department was staffed with investigators and interpreters who had the task of helping the Ford worker adjust to city life.[6] The department's first director, John R. Lee (1913–16), and his successor, the Very Reverend Samuel S. Marquis, former dean of the Episcopal cathedral of Detroit, were both hired to service laborers in terms of housing and even relationship issues in the home. On many occasions, investigators were given directives to help "broken families and confused immigrants, [often] moving families into satisfactory housing or by insisting that errant husbands break habits such as drinking and chasing women (at the risk of losing their jobs)."[7] Here, Henry Ford operated as a paternalistic employer to the hundreds of workers he employed.

When it came to issues of race and ethnicity, the Sociological Department at Ford Motor reflected the dominant ideology of its day. Although Anglo conformity was encouraged among nonwhite races employed by industrial companies, fears of miscegenation still circulated through industrial workplaces. Industrial employers often accepted and encouraged the assimilation and cooperation of "perceived intra-racial groups such as northern, eastern, and southern Europeans. However, interracial groups in the industrial units were shunned, especially where African Americans and whites might be forced to work together. Ford Motor Company was adept in exemplifying these policies, particularly in regards to the "housing of their European and non-European workers."[8] Leading sociologists of the day, like Paul Reinsch, Robert E. Park, and Ernest W. Burgess, described African American behavioral characteristics as "innate rather than socially constructed."[9] Park and Burgess presented African Americans as having "distinctive characteristics transmitted biologically," and Reinsch described the African race as inefficient in social action, and deficient in mechanical arts, relating that "the negro race has shown no tendency toward higher development." Both perspectives influenced how Ford Motor employed and positioned particular races in the company. According to Georgios Paris Loizides, "Indeed, company discourse and practices, to a great extent, reflected the social discourse of the Progressive period concerning race. . . . At the Ford Motor Company in particular, this idea took the form [of] 'the right man for the right job' . . . which meant that African American employees were relegated to the foundry, which offered the worst possible working conditions."[10]

While the Ford Sociological Department patterned its policies after such racial discourses, Henry Ford's actions toward Jews and blacks often contradicted some of the ideologies upon which he founded his Sociological Department. Ford's racial attitudes were complex, and at best, a convoluted mix of conservative and liberal views. Known as a staunch segregationist, Ford still poured thousand of dollars into black communities and worked closely with black intellectual elites. And though he was a strong anti-Semitic who decried "the Jew . . . [as] a mere huckster, a trader, [and someone] who doesn't want to produce, but to make something out of what somebody else produces," Ford posited that Jews "should be advanced along mechanical lines . . . [and] final judgment [of] the individual should be considered rather than the race as a whole."[11]

Ford's chameleon-like attitude toward race reflected the nuances of his personality. Described as "paradoxical, controversial, selfish, yet often generous, kindly, and compassionate," Henry Ford could not be "pigeon-holed" into one set of attitudes or characteristics.[12] Despite being an outspoken anti-Semitic, Ford still held close friendships with prominent Jews in Detroit. Albert Kahn, a Jewish architect, worked many years with Henry Ford and held the honor of designing all of Ford's factories until his death in 1942.[13] Rabbi Leo Franklin was Ford's neighbor on Edison Avenue, and the men enjoyed a strong friendship for many years. The automotive magnate also nurtured a friendship with George Washington Carver, and the two held a long-standing relationship, even to the point of Ford providing a substantial stream of revenue into Carver's research at Tuskegee Normal and Industrial Institute, presently known as Tuskegee University. Ford even hired graduates from Tuskegee and often sent Ford officials to inaugural events at the institute. Carver was allowed entrance into Ford's private home and often "visited Michigan to assist Ford in his research into nutritional uses for roadside vegetation."[14]

These friendships however, especially with his Jewish compatriots, left no compunction on Ford when in the spring of 1920 he published a ninety-one-week anti-Semitic campaign in his weekly magazine, the *Dearborn Independent*.[15] With a nationwide circulation of a quarter of a million in the 1920s, the *Dearborn Independent* was the voice of Henry Ford and a vehicle by which the mogul could publicly address criticisms against his company. From 1920 to 1922, the magazine devoted an article a week to Ford's racial epithets on the "role of the 'International Jew' in world affairs."[16] In these articles, excerpts were taken from the *Protocols of the Elders of Zion*, an anonymous document claiming to reveal the secret plans of Jews for world domination.[17] These articles were spun while the "auto king employed thousands of Jewish laborers in his plants."[18] Ford further capitalized on his anti-Semitic views by publishing a compilation of these articles into four brochures.[19] Each brochure reinstated the main themes touched upon in the ninety-one articles and had an international circulation.[20] Prominent Jews such as Bernard Baruch, Eugene Meyer, Paul Warburg, Oscar Straus, Flex Warburg, Albert Lasker, Otto Kahn, Julius Rosenwald, and Louis Marshall were named specifically in these articles; all of these men were successful in public service, banking, law, and commerce.[21] The publications even caught the attention of Baldur von Schirach, then student organizer of the Nazi Party under Hitler and later head of the National Socialist German Students' League.[22]

What could account for such a paradox in Ford's racial attitudes? It appears that Ford's attitude toward Jews and African Americans lay not in a denigration of their humanity but in certain character traits he found distasteful. Writing in 1919, Henry Ford declared, "We have learned to appreciate men as men, and to forget the discrimination of color, race, country, religion, fraternal orders, and everything else outside of human qualities and energy."[23] Carver, Khan, and Franklin exemplified character traits that Ford respected and valued yet failed to see universally in the African American and Jewish races.

What is clear here is that Henry Ford was unpredictable in his racial dealings and attitudes. This was certainly the case between Ford and Detroit's black urban community. For while he was not above exclaiming, "We are going out in society . . . to a nigger church," referencing his visits to St. Matthew's Episcopal Church, one of the first black Episcopal churches in Detroit, the automotive leader still allotted massive opportunities to African Americans in the pursuit of cheap labor and higher profits for his company.[24] Ford built schools and churches in black communities throughout Georgia and Michigan, and he employed hundreds of blacks as skilled laborers, foremen, and even salaried employees in his company. In fact, Ford was known to "court" blacks "assiduously . . . along with large numbers of handicapped employees and graduates of the Henry Ford Trade School." The questions surrounding his particular "courtship" of African Americans in Detroit and the nature of such interactions is what the following narrative seeks to answer.[25]

BRADBY, FORD MOTOR COMPANY, AND THE KINGDOM OF GOD

While Reverend Bradby's message of the Kingdom of God from the pulpit fed the soul, his desk often carried the message forward in practical terms, especially in regard to providing economic sustenance among Detroit's black community. For Bradby, the proof of his calling was in securing mediums of economic stability within his congregation. Although many opportunities to fulfill this divine mandate would fall into Reverend Bradby's hands, a luncheon invitation issued by Henry Ford proved to be the most transformative measure in shaping modes of economic mobility among the black Detroiters. As a leader among his growing congregation, Bradby functioned in what activist A. Phillip Randolph termed the "Old Crowd" of black leaders—"a group subsidized by the Old Crowd of White Americans which viciously opposes every demand made by organized labor for an opportunity to live a better life."[26] Race leaders like Randolph "thought the tactics of the Old Crowd of black leaders perpetuated servile relations between black and white Americans," yet Bradby looked upon his relationship with Ford as an opportunity to fulfill his Christian mandate of establishing the Kingdom and uplifting the black race.[27] As the rising labor movement began to take shape in the early 1930s and 1940s, churches like Second Baptist eventually became a point of contention with regard to unionism.[28] Prior to the rise of unions, ministers like Bradby were considered race leaders who used the opportunities white benefactors opened to them. With de facto segregation and the prevailing view of black inferiority confronting African Americans in the early twentieth century, the most viable avenue afforded for black ministers to counter the tide of black oppression was in the relationships they nurtured with white elites. Such relationships were often the only means of racial uplift obtainable for black elites during the Progressive Era, when African Americans "had few friends and more than enough enemies."[29] Representative of the "Old Crowd" type of black leadership, and though openly contested by other race leaders like Marcus Garvey and A. Philip Randolph, black leaders who catered to white elites were implementing a feasible means of black self-help and empowerment in the 1920s. Racist attitudes and segregation policies left few doors open for black economic opportunity and social mobility. Leaders like Reverend Bradby essentially paved the way for Randolph's "New Crowd" to push for more advanced levels of freedom and black equality. In this respect, Bradby, like other ministers in the city, capitalized on the desires of the automotive industry in order to advance the economic status of Detroit's black community.

Father Everard W. Daniel of St. Matthew's Episcopal Church in Detroit, for example, drew Ford's attention as he searched Detroit's black neighborhoods for cheap labor sources. Daniel appeared to have had a closer relationship to Henry Ford than to Bradby. Ford published articles that noted, "he and Daniel had developed a warm personal relationship. Ford, an Episcopalian, donated funds for St. Matthew's parish house, as well as annually attending at least one service at the church . . . on numerous occasions Ford asked him to represent the company at formal ceremonies, including the installation of presidents of black colleges."[30] Both Bradby and Daniel "greatly valued their ties to the Ford family which enabled them to dictate the nature of community building" in Detroit's black urban areas.[31] For A. Phillip Randolph, ministers like Bradby and Daniel were the quintessential "Old Negro," men "lulled into a false sense of security with political spoils and patronage" from whites. Despite these negative perceptions, Bradby and Daniel were placed in a position to revolutionize the racial presence in Detroit's automotive industry for years to come. African Americans were the new face of the automotive laboring classes in Detroit, and their wages fed the socioeconomic milieu of the black community.[32]

For Reverend Bradby, his relationship with the Ford Motor Company positioned him as an *in-between* figure. Bradby was *in between* the last bastions of race leaders who courted white paternalism as a form of black advancement, and black activists who disdained these types of top-down relationships between power whites and working-class blacks. The latter group of black activist constituted yet another form of black uplift, one that contested older visions of black uplift that depended on white benevolence. In industry, these new race leaders upheld unionism and threatened the "old guard" of white paternalism. Thus as Reverend Bradby moved forward in his agenda of the Kingdom, he was caught *in between* white industrial elites and the black working classes, and *in between* the local black church and the Detroit's automotive industrial world. All these *in-between* positions in which Bradby moved helped shape Detroit's urban spaces and constituted another hermeneutic of how the Kingdom of God operated within new forms of black uplift ideology.

NEW OPPORTUNITIES

With the influx of southern black migrants into Detroit's industries came the rise and expansion of black urban communities. Black churches like Second Baptist used the power of the pulpit and the influence of their ministers to create innovative avenues of black employment, thereby expanding Detroit's urban population and its black working classes.

With its minister pushing the Social Gospel message of the Kingdom in connection to black uplift, Second Baptist became a gateway for the black migrant to enter Detroit's industrial working class. The year 1919 marked the season for such an entry and demonstrated how the sacred space of the black church could penetrate the secular spheres of Detroit's automotive industry. Five years prior, Ford had done the unthinkable by establishing the Five Dollar a Day Plan in January 1914.[33] The next month, word had spread like wildfire of the first African American employed at Ford Motor Company—William Perry. Hired in February 1914, William Perry walked the grounds of

Ford's Highland Park plant until his death in 1940. Perry's hire began a succession of black hires at Ford. By 1916, Ford had employed fifty more black laborers among his 32,702 employees. The "Negro Experiment" was working at Ford, and the automotive giant wanted to keep up the progress. Ford had opened the Henry Ford Trade School in 1916 that enrolled blacks as well as whites. However, by 1918, the automotive inventor was desperately seeking ways to alleviate the prevailing labor shortage caused by World War I and the cessation of European immigration. Automobile firms were prevented from soliciting foreign sources of labor, as they had done in the past. The massive influx of African Americans into the major urban centers of the North caught Henry Ford's attention.[34] The automotive mogul's response to Detroit's growing African American population was a watershed moment in black labor relations, especially when the majority of African Americans were excluded from working in industrial companies. Jim Crow laws and racist sentiment in the North kept many African Americans out of the predominantly white industrial labor classes. By the middle of 1918, Henry Ford's Five Dollar a Day Plan and his willingness to hire unskilled African Americans drew a black labor force of over one thousand strong. Black Ford employees were listed as 1,059 that year, and the number continued to grow.[35]

While numerous black migrants helped relieve the labor shortage, they also created racial tensions in the workplace. These tensions were primarily between black workers and southern white workers as well as Poles, Italians, Hungarians, Russians, and other European workers—groups that added to the racial conflict at the plants. Racism among all ethnic groups at automotive plants in Highland Park and Dearborn seemed to slow Ford Motor Company's production down. Ford grew weary of these tumultuous happenings and strategized for ways to alleviate work-related conflicts. As 1918 progressed, the name of Reverend Bradby caught the auto magnate's ears. Ford had heard of Bradby and Second Baptist from the well-known Employers Association of Detroit. Known for working with organizations like the Employers Association of Detroit and the Detroit Urban League, Second Baptist nurtured such alliances in an effort to recruit black southern labor for Detroit.

SECOND BAPTIST AND DETROIT'S URBAN LEAGUE

While the Employers Association of Detroit worked in connection with the Detroit Urban League and even subsidized the salary of the league's industrial secretary, Bradby held church meetings in which workers learned how to be more efficient in maintaining their jobs. In return, Second Baptist and the Urban League supplied the Employers Association with black labor. The Urban League encouraged black southerners to seek the comforts of Detroit industries through public statements and agents sent to the South. Rolling through the streets of Detroit in the wee hours of the morning, trucks owned by the Urban League would cruise through black neighborhoods offering jobs at some of the major industrial plants in Detroit. By mid-morning, Detroit residents could open newspapers such as the *Detroit Free Press* and the *Detroit Tribune* and read editorials by Forrester Washington about the high wages black workers were afforded in the automotive industry.[36] Briefly serving as the director of the Urban League from 1916 to 1918, Washington's leadership was succeeded by John L. Dancy, who served as director of the organization for over forty years.[37]

By 1917 the Detroit Urban League had elevated over 10,800 blacks to Detroit's working class. With such a success rate, the league openly advertised its ability to employ African Americans in flyers that read, "We furnish carefully selected skilled and unskilled colored men and women for factories, foundries, theatres, department stores, domestic service, etc. We make better workmen by caring for them outside of their work; we provide hundreds with homes, establish wholesome recreation, through community dances, athletics, etc., for colored new-comers."[38] Most flyers and leaflets the Detroit Urban League produced stated that its employment program was social in nature and was "supported by a joint committee of white and colored citizens and the Employers' Association, with the purpose of making the Negro a self-supporting citizen and an asset to the city of Detroit rather than [a] liability."[39] The Urban League further boasted of its ability to produce the right kind of black citizen in Detroit, one that would lend respectability and efficiency to the industrious society. These were the type of workers that appealed to Henry Ford, especially when daily conflict between blacks and whites too often slowed production. Tensions were severest between recently hired black migrants and southern white workers. As African Americans filled the rank and file of Ford laborers, "the firm experienced difficulty in adjusting its workers, both white and colored, to the new employment procedure." Viewed as "overly aggressive toward white workers," African Americans became the bane of discontent in the company's working culture. White workers, especially, resented the influx of greater numbers of blacks into the plants. Charles Sorensen, Ford's executive manager, was so troubled by the "fist fights and stabbings" that he made inquiries "as to Negro leadership in Detroit." Hearing of a prominent black minister who held strong connections to the Urban League's director, Sorensen's attention was drawn to Second Baptist's nineteenth pastor. The best type of worker would certainly be one handpicked by a minister who could hold his congregants in stronger accountability toward the actions of brotherly love and Christian morals. Sending Reverend Bradby an invitation to lunch with Henry Ford and his top officials was a matter of course for Sorensen.[40]

THE MEETING

After walking into Charles Sorensen's office one day in 1919, Bradby focused on a jumble of knives, guns, and other makeshift weapons in Sorensen's desk drawer.[41] The weapons had been confiscated from some of Ford's black autoworkers. Ford, also in Sorensen's office, and Sorensen were at their wits end about how to curb the violence between black and white workers at the River Rouge Plant. White workers had become disgruntled with the increase in African American workers.[42] Inviting Reverend Bradby into the fray was an innovative move for Henry Ford and Sorensen, who were "concerned about the inefficiency of some workers, and the frequency of bloody fights within the plant between black and white workers, and among blacks themselves." As "Ford personally outlined to Bradby his desire to recruit carefully selected Negro workmen," Reverend Bradby, looking at the weapons in the drawer, asked, "How long do you keep a man before you wash your hands of him?" Ford replied, "We're here to save the devil." Under such a challenging declaration, Bradby and Ford cultivated a relationship that would further transform the racial makeup of Ford Motor Company.[43]

Reverend Bradby offered to recommend only the "highest type" of "Negroes" to Sorensen, and his connection with Ford enabled Second Baptist "to do some very definite things for a large number of the members of our group." Those "members of our group," of course, were the migrant newcomers flowing into Detroit's urban community. As Second Baptist member Frank L. Morris states, "Fortunately he [Bradby] had the personal friendship of Henry Ford and was placed in [a] very favorable position to secure jobs for many of these migrants. Hundreds were beneficiaries of these efforts, which became known throughout the Southland, making Rev. Bradby a very popular person, a popularity that continued throughout his lifetime." Another member, Mildren Dillard Croff, noted that Reverend Bradby not only provided migrants with jobs at Ford, but he also gained

Baptist Christian Center graduation, 1924

Reverend Bradby's last sermon, 1946

Second Baptist Vacation Bible School, 1919

Second Baptist Church members and Bradby, 1923

Second Baptist Church, 1923

Ushers of Second Baptist Church, 1923

Reverend Bradby's family: children Robert, Katherine, Martha, and Bernice, and wife, Marion Louise (Taliaferro) Bradby

Reverend Bradby and the churchwomen of Second Baptist Church of Detroit

Bradby at his desk

Reverend Bradby

them employment at other factories. Unlike most industrial companies in Detroit, Ford provided Bradby with his own personal pass to "all the firm's buildings." Bradby spent numerous hours walking the Highland Park and River Rouge Plants "settl[ing] differences between Negroes and whites and among the Negroes themselves, [with] many of the men [giving] him their weapons." Writing Sorensen in 1926, Bradby proudly stated that "not even a fight, nor a cut, or a disturbance" had taken place "in over two years."[44]

CORPORATE PATERNALISM AND THE KINGDOM OF GOD

If this move by Henry Ford was "a strategy of corporate paternalism grounded in black community dependency,"[45] Reverend Bradby was either unaware or unconcerned about the paternalism in which Ford was propagating. Ultimately, Bradby endeavored to use his connection with Henry Ford to fulfill his divine mandate of making the Kingdom of God an actuality through what initially appeared to be an economic gain for Detroit's black community. Reverend Bradby may have courted Ford's brand of paternalism in order to gain concessions for his people and bring about his vision of the Kingdom. Therefore, if Bradby and the Second Baptist Church functioned as "the gates to the Kingdom of Ford," then economically, the "Kingdom of Ford" was a means to an end—the Kingdom of God. For Reverend Bradby, the connection with Ford enabled thousands of black migrants to transform their social and economic status. This move on Bradby's part also created racial uplift among black workers. Promoting the idea of race consciousness among black laborers, Bradby insisted that black employees "be 'steady workers' so as to improve the worthiness of colored industrial workers."[46] This ideology was especially appealing to Sorensen and Henry Ford, as both men had experienced black employees working until payday, and then completely walking off the job.

It is no surprise, then, that by 1919, Reverend Bradby had become a permanent fixture in Ford's African American employee relations. As rumors spread as far as the Deep South of a northern black minister who could guarantee a job at Ford Motor Company, the pews of Second Baptist swelled with the influx of black newcomers, looking for their "Moses" to lead them to the "Promised Land" of economic security with the flick of his pen. Bradby's recommendations to Ford created a level of respectability among blacks in the Detroit community. African Americans were proud to hold a city or factory job, especially at Ford. Sunday church services in Detroit offered opportune venues for black workers to exhibit their newfound status and establish respectability among those in their community. On most Sunday mornings at Second Baptist, church members entering the sanctuary were wearing their Ford badges.[47] Even the church ushers of Second stood wearing brightly polished badges upon the lapel of their uniforms. Others could look among those sitting along church pews and see any number of armbands with the Ford insignia stitched smartly on the fabric. Many migrants who obtained jobs through Reverend Bradby signed their names to Second Baptist's membership rolls and poured a portion of their earnings into the church's tithing basket. It was rumored that those who received a recommendation from Bradby and thereby obtained employment at Ford, were impressed upon to maintain an active membership at Second Baptist and to give regular financial contributions.[48]

Holding a job at Ford Motor Company or having any form of employment was a sign of status at Second Baptist as well as in Detroit's black community. One of the most prestigious Ford badges worn by a black worker had a star in the design. But African Americans at Ford Motor would not wear such a badge until 1934, when James C. Price, a black man sponsored by Ford's manufacturing executive Charles E. Sorensen, was given the honor.[49] James C. Price was handpicked by Charles E. Sorensen to work at Ford Motor Company. While working as a tailor from 1905 to 1910, Price caught the patronage of numerous Ford executives, including Sorensen. Price, enticed by Ford's five-dollar-a-day minimum wage, pressed Sorensen for a job. Sorensen agreed, with the words "Jim you're going to be the first colored man here to get a job that means something. I'm going to put you in charge of a tool crib. If anyone abuses, insults, or humiliates you, I want you to come to me." Price's badge and others like them designated salaried employees of Ford Motor Company. Price's appointment in 1934 constituted the first African American to be honored with such a status on Ford's payroll.[50]

Ford worker Horace L. Sheffield wrote of the status and respect accorded to one of Ford Motor Company's star men. "Back in those days, everybody knew that a man who had a star on his badge was a 'real wheel.' The powers of a 'star-man' were so considerable, or believed to be, until the mere mention that one was in the area was enough to get everyone on their toes." Remembering Ford's most prominent "star man," Jim Price, Sheffield wrote, "He was in charge of Ford Motor Company's entire abrasives department and I shall never forget the warm feeling of pride that use [sic] to envelop me whenever he came through the shop." Figures like Price invoked positive images of black masculinity and black male respectability in Detroit's African American community.[51]

Like Sheffield, Reverend Bradby was fully aware of this fact and openly promoted employment as one of the marks of respectability. The *Second Baptist Herald*, the church's weekly newsletter, gave front-page recognition to this fact, reporting, "It is a matter of record that the policy of Ford Company is to employ a fair percentage of colored employees. We rejoice in the spirit as shown here. This rejoicing carries with it the hope that the conduct of our laborers will be such as to increase the employed ratio."[52] Bradby rejoiced in his Ford connection, and other members of the black community echoed their pleasure as well. Reflecting on thirty years of service at Ford Motor Company, Sheffield wrote of Henry Ford's benevolence as a supporter of the United Auto Workers, stating, "it occurred to me that there was another aspect of Henry Ford's greatness that has been woefully overlooked . . . he had achieved a good measure of fair employment practices in the shop."[53]

Looking upon Henry Ford as one of the means by which to establish the Kingdom of God, Reverend Bradby used his status and influence at Second Baptist to funnel African Americans into Detroit's automotive industry. After 1919 and through the 1930s, general manager Charles E. Sorensen and Bradby developed such a positive relationship that Bradby wrote a personal letter of thanks and appreciation to Sorensen and Henry Ford for employing so many of his members. He wrote, "I want you to know how happy we all are to know the attitude of the Ford Motor Company toward the unfortunate members of our group. I think it is one of the most outstanding pieces of work that has been done in the attitude of the company to people in Inkster."[54]

Considered by some scholars to be the "most extreme example of Henry Ford's paternalism,"[55] Inkster was originally a small black settlement adjacent to Dearborn established in the mid-1920s. Backed by the payroll of Ford Motor Company, fifty-two black families attempted to make a better life for themselves under Henry Ford's patronage. By 1931, this small black community was suffering financial difficulty due to the Great Depression. The American Red Cross appealed to the Ford Motor Company to assist the floundering community. Henry Ford heeded the call for help and on Christmas Eve 1931 opened a commissary in the village that provided affordable food, clothing, fuel, and other supplies on credit. A shoe repair shop, medical clinic, and dental facility were opened as well. Ford also arranged to pay off any delinquent utilities, rental contracts, and tax obligations of Inskter's black community. Even loans and insurance policies were made available to the settlement's black inhabitants. Those who took advantage of Ford's provisions were hired at Ford's River Rouge Plant and paid one dollar a day in cash, with the rest of their earnings laid aside to pay off expenditures accrued through credit. While some members in Detroit's black community were uneasy with Ford's patronage of the struggling Inkster community, many African Americans continued to view Ford Motor Company as a benevolent benefactor. And though the latter perspective gave more acceptance to Bradby's relationship with Henry Ford, it also created a certain suspicion about the minister's agenda in capitalizing on such a powerful connection. These suspicions had taken root back in 1927 when Ford laid off over 1,500 black workers when he discontinued the Model T.[56]

REACTIONS TO THE FORD-BRADBY RELATIONSHIP

Despite the job opportunities Bradby garnered for Detroit's black community, some saw his tactics as suspect and questioned his motives in promoting labor relations between the black community and Ford. Many Detroiters claimed that he pushed blacks to work at Ford in order to increase church membership rolls as well as lining his pockets.[57] Reverend Bradby's critics were right in this respect. Special gifts from Henry Ford seem to have benefited the personal life of the minister more than his congregants at times. Henry Ford and Charles E. Sorensen often showed their appreciation for Bradby's help in the form of coal shipments to the church and theater tickets to popular Detroit performances.[58] This type of benevolence by Ford not only reinforced Bradby's drive to help recruit cheap black labor for the company, it also predisposed Second Baptist's minister to become a loyal customer and advertiser of Ford Motor's products. In a letter written on April 25, 1934, Reverend Bradby wrote, "The matter about which I want to write you is the car. I suppose you know that I am the proud possessor of a '34 V8 Deluxe Model. . . . I wish you might see the number of V8s that have already been purchased by our group and that can be seen any Sunday morning parked around our church."[59]

Clearly, Reverend Bradby was not ashamed to boast that he and many of his members were consumers of Ford Motor cars. Such declarations made directly to Sorensen may have been attempts to gain more favor from the industrial magnate. At the conclusion of his letter to Sorensen, Bradby writes, "At least six or seven of my friends have followed my example, and two others have told me this week that they are placing their order soon for one. The secretary of my Trustee Board is turning in a Chrysler to get a Ford, and two of our local ministers are trading in their cars." Sorensen's response to Bradby's letter read, "We are certainly pleased to know that you are obtaining such wonderful results from your V-8."[60]

BRADBY, HENRY FORD, AND THE GREAT DEPRESSION

The Great Depression deepened people's criticism of Reverend Bradby's relationship with Ford Motor, and slowly tensions arose between Bradby, Sorensen, and Henry Ford. Despite these growing tensions, Bradby continued to work with the Ford Company offering black Detroiters a small level of stability during this era. Writing to Bradby in 1932, Thomas H. Jairison pleads, "I am out of work and buying the home my son occupies, and he has been laid off from the Ford Motor Car Co. since last June. He has 6 children under 12 years of age. . . . I would appreciate a job with the Ford Motor Car Co. and pledge my experience, cooperation, and loyalty to the Company and its material and moral interest."[61]

Reverend Bradby received numerous letters of this kind during this period. The Great Depression created tremendous economic instability in Detroit, especially among the black community. Black churches like Second Baptist felt the strain of the economy upon their outreach ministry efforts, but Bradby continued to try and gain employment for blacks at Ford Motor.[62] Writing Donald Marshall, Ford's first black personnel director, in 1932, Bradby recommended an African American man named James Gaffney, stating, "This man, James Gaffney, is the man about whom I was talking to you yesterday special. . . . I was wondering since he has been off so long, he is such a fine chap . . . if you could not place Gaffney. . . . Mr. Sorensen's secretary asked me to send his record through and I did that."[63]

For African Americans living in Detroit during the Great Depression, layoffs became the rule of the day, even at Ford Motor. Replacing the Model T Ford with the Model A Ford led to numerous layoffs of black workers at the company. By 1929, 20 percent of Detroit's black community was still supported by Ford jobs. Attempting to delay further layoffs and restore jobs to those in his congregation who had been laid off, Bradby was tenacious in pointing out to Ford and Dodge Motor Car executives that they were "really . . . laying off some men whom I am sure if you could see them you would be convinced that they are among the very best employees you have. . . . And just now at this point of the depression when employment is almost an impossibility.[64]

In his plea to C. J. Winniegar, superintendent of the Personnel Department at Ford Motor, Reverend Bradby made sure to argue that he had nothing to gain personally from his requests, claiming, "He does not happen to be a member of my congregation so there is nothing selfish in my solicitations."

For newcomers to Detroit as well as for old timers, Bradby's recommendation constituted a direct medium for African Americans to enter and reenter the industrial working class, thereby creating both a means of economic survival and advancement for blacks during the Great Depression.[65]

Ford, still tied to courting the local black church for cheap labor, made sure to keep Reverend Bradby and Second Baptist afloat by supplementing some of the church's expenditures from time to time. On September 15, 1930, Bradby penned a letter to Sorensen, stating,

> I find my work and my organization in such a serious situation. A very large percent of the people of my organization have been out of work, and I am facing a winter that is to be very difficult. What I am trying to do is to lay enough coal to guarantee operation in this Winter. It takes about one hundred twenty-five tons. The price is five dollars and seventy-five cents a ton. And I am just writing a few of my friends, believing that because they know of my work and the work of this organization in all lines of interest for city and state, that will help.[66]

Sorensen's response was to forward the letter to Henry Ford with the words, "The Bradby preacher of the colored folks church have been a great help to us could we deliver 50 tons of coal?"[67] By October 7, Ford employee Russel Gnau had sent department communications to Sorensen's office confirming coal deliveries to Second Baptist Church.

> Please deliver 50 tons Pocahontas Mine Run and Lump Steam Coal to the Second Baptist Church, 442 Monroe, Ave, Detroit, Michigan. Instruct the truck driver to drive around the rear of the building, at the above address, and be sure that the quantity of coal delivered does not exceed 15 tons at any one delivery. The above is charged to the Welfare Department.

A month and a half later, Gnau wrote,

> This morning we delivered seventeen tons of coal to the Second Baptist Church, 441 Monroe Ave Detroit, making a total of fifty tons and eleven hundred pounds, in accordance with your communication of October 7. Mr. Bradby has indicated that he will talk to you about further deliveries.[68]

The following morning, Reverend Bradby's letter of thanks read, "I drop this note to express to you my very deep appreciation for your kindly consideration of my request. I have no words that are adequate to express to you just what this has meant to us. I trust however that I may be able to continue in such a way as to merit your friendship."[69]

By 1934, the vendors in Detroit's Greektown could look down Monroe Street to see Reverend Bradby stepping out of his new '34 V8 Deluxe Model Ford at exactly 9:00 a.m. in front of Second Baptist. Vendors set their clocks by Bradby's arrival and started the business of the day on it. On most occasions, the moment Bradby parked his car, mobs of migrant men who had gathered on the steps of the church hours earlier greeted him with desperate pleas for one of his coveted recommendations for employment at Ford Motor Company. Writing Sorensen in 1934, Bradby related, "I want to thank you for the opportunity of sending some men out during these days. I have tried to be careful and selected some whom I think very high type fellows. They have mobbed me almost every morning, but I have finally got by. I have not sent out so many. I don't want to overdo it."[70] Throughout the Great Depression era, Reverend Bradby was still able to maintain an amicable relationship with Ford and Sorensen. Despite the unevenness of the relationship between Bradby, Second Baptist, and Henry Ford, this triangular relationship transcended secular and sacred boundaries in its inception and operation. Second Baptist was at once a sacred institution promoting the Gospel of Jesus Christ and a secular institution that operated as a black employment agency, thrusting migrants into the industrial spheres of Detroit's economy, which were major steps in establishing the Kingdom of God for Bradby. Regardless of the impetus behind it, this relationship expanded the ability of Second Baptist Church to transcend its sacred boundaries and positively impact Detroit's urban black community on a socioeconomic level not experienced in the past. A letter written to Reverend Bradby by Sorensen, celebrating Bradby's fifteenth pastoral anniversary, conveyed as much: "the contact you have had with us in the industrial work in our plant, is one of the angles that I like to see attached to the work of a pastor, because it certainly gives him a broader opportunity to help his congregation."[71]

COMPETITION

Reverend Bradby, however, was not the only minister Ford contacted to recruit black workers. Father Everard W. Daniel of St. Matthew's Episcopal Church was also an associate of Ford Motor Company.[72] Daniel was the parish priest of Ford Motor's first black personnel director, Donald Marshall. Marshall was a vestryman at St. Matthew's Parish and worked with Daniel to recruit black labor for Ford Motor Company. Marshall was one of the first black policemen in Detroit and was well known in the city for his bravery. Henry Ford recruited the young officer to his Service Department in 1923. Ambitious, Marshall rose quickly through the ranks and achieved a supervisory position; he hired and fired black personnel at Ford. With the title of special investigator, Marshall, along with a white employee named Harry Bennett, oversaw the black workers with a strong arm. Harry Bennett, "nominally the head of personnel" at Ford Motor Company, was in charge of the Ford Service Department. His reputation as a "bully" was backed by his power to employ undercover investigators, "tough-looking former athletes—'thugs'"—to keep an eye on "any employee who was known to be a member of a union—or worse, who discussed unionization on or off the Ford premises." Under Ford's blessing, Bennett was even known to have "planted men in most departments to listen [to] and watch the other employees." Both Marshall and Bennett concentrated their efforts in converting ex-convicts, boxers, and gangsters into respectable laborers.[73] Marshall's power was unprecedented for an African American at the company, and the former police officer was well aware of this fact. Reverend Bradby's relationship with Sorensen and Ford did not sit well with Marshall and became a source of conflict between the two men and their respective churches. Notwithstanding these power conflicts, Bradby's and Daniel's recommendations continued to cement the black working community's relationship with Ford Motor Company.[74]

Ford days were sometimes full of irony as black clergymen presented their Ford passes and strolled into the foundries of Ford's Highland Park and River Rouge Plants.[75] Each minister was allowed access to the Ford plant based on his ability to maneuver back and forth between the color line of black and white. In some ways, Reverend Bradby and Father Daniel were the proverbial "blessed peacemakers" of racial conflict given power by the godly hand of Henry Ford. Although both ministers operated in this capacity, it was Bradby who first roamed the halls of Ford plants.[76] Such a precedent sparked competition between Bradby and Daniel and created strife between their respective churches, especially between Reverend Bradby and St. Matthew's member Donald Marshall. The deepening years of the Great Depression exacerbated these strains and would eventually affect Bradby's relationship with Henry Ford.[77]

HARSH REALITIES AT FORD MOTOR COMPANY

While Reverend Bradby's connection with Ford helped direct the flow of black labor into Ford Motor Company, this advantageous triangular relationship was bittersweet at best for black workers at Ford. Bradby's success in resisting black poverty on a small level could not eradicate racial inequalities inherent in Ford's hiring policies and treatment of black workers. Many African American families benefited from working at Ford, but they paid for these benefits at an extreme cost to their mental and physical health. Charles Denby, a black worker living in Detroit in the mid-1920s, for example, wrote in his journal:

> I never wanted to work at Ford. And I never did work there. Everyone talked about it, they said it was the house of murder. . . . Every worker could identify Ford workers on the streetcars going home at night. You'd see twenty asleep on cars and everyone would say, "Ford workers." Many times the conductors looked over the car and shook a man to tell him it was his stop. On Sunday Ford workers would sleep on the way to church. . . . But everybody knew Ford was a "man-killing" place. That always frightened me. I tried to stay away.[78]

Denby's recollections reflected the harsh realities of working at Ford. Many black laborers at Ford were put in the most undesirable positions at the company. In 1926, the mayor's Inter-Racial Committee Report, under the direction of Forrester B. Washington, published a survey on the African American experience in Detroit. Members of the mayor's Inter-Racial Committee included influential white and black elites such as Rev. Reinhold Niebuhr, pastor of Bethel Evangelical Church; Bishop William T. Vernon, pastor of African Methodist Episcopal Church; and Donald J. Marshall, employment officer, Ford Motor Company. Under the committee's direction, the survey published that year recorded that Ford Motor Company employed approximately six thousand black men and no black females. The majority of the six thousand men were employed as unskilled manual laborers.[79] Typically, these unskilled jobs were the most undesirable and dangerous in the plant. Black workers were given the most grueling jobs, under the racist notion that blacks were faster than whites and performed tasks rhythmically.[80]

The attitude of most white officials at Ford Motor toward African American workers was a determining factor in black job placement. Herman Feldman and

Bruno Lasker's study in 1931 notes the particular attitude of certain white officials toward African American workers. They write,

> Sometimes the distinctions made between Negroes and whites in this respect are brutal, for one investigator reports: "I asked if Negroes were not employed anywhere in the plant. He said, 'Yes, some jobs white folks will not do; so they have to take niggers in, particularly in duco work, spraying paint on car bodies. This soon kills a white man.' I inquired if it never killed Negroes. 'Oh yes,' he replied. 'It shortens their lives, it cuts them down but they're just niggers.'"[81]

The sentiment of the investigator exposes the underlying perceptions of white laborers toward black workers at Ford and the rationale for placing black personnel in the most hazardous working conditions at the plants. Ford used 55 percent of its black workers in two of the toughest jobs in the foundry—the reels and the shakeout. And though Ford hired more black foremen than any other manufacturer at the time, the majority of black laborers were still placed in the dreaded foundries of the plant, which had a "notoriously high death rate." According to the report Louis I. Dublin and Robert J. Vane of the Metropolitan Life Insurance Company conducted: "Fumes, dust, and especially sudden and extreme variations of temperature are highly conducive to the contraction of respiratory diseases. . . . The dust count on some foundry jobs is almost unbelievable. . . . The shakeout, an operation in which the casting is removed from the mold, is by far the worst in this respect. . . . The heat, however, is intense. This operation, of which there are sever[al] variations, was performed exclusively by Negroes in those plants visited."[82] Skilled black laborers obtained positions as bricklayers, crane operators, mechanics, tool and die workers, and even electricians.[83]

Even with the harshness of the labor and the incredibly dangerous working conditions, Reverend Bradby continued to recommend black workers to Ford in an effort to better their living conditions. The demands of black migrants soliciting Bradby's support reinforced his notion that he was helping them. In 1930, for example, an African American named Dock Hornbuckle wrote Bradby, stating, "I called the church this morning but could not get you. Ford Motor Co. has started to hiring and I want you to get me on there please. . . . I wish you would get me on at Ford's Plant. Thanking you in advance for this favor."[84]

Although the work was "back-breaking" and housing was poor, black Detroiters were afforded a level of economic freedom unattainable for members of black communities in the South. These gains were paradoxical at best, given Ford's known wage discrimination against black workers. Despite this type of racial limitation, Ford's wages for blacks exceeded earnings in the South and elsewhere in Detroit. Southern newcomers to the city were especially desirous of Ford jobs, even with the difficulties and danger connected with the foundries. Many newcomers were black men bent on sustaining their growing families. Thomas N. Maloney and Warren C. Whatley's study of Detroit's labor markets posits, "Not all black Detroiters could stay away, especially those who were young, married, and settling down to raise a family. Locked out of the better-paying and less-effort-intensive jobs that were open to married white Detroiters and facing financial needs that kept them from taking the poorer-paying but less-strenuous service sector jobs, married black Detroiters were driven to Ford in large numbers."[85]

Maloney and Whatley's assertion is well taken. Racial exclusionary practices among other white employers in Detroit played right into Ford's sense of paternalism and impolitic social perspectives, which often resulted in deeper forms of racial discrimination. For example, Maloney and Whatley also argue that from the mid-1920s on, black workers who were confined to the dangerous jobs in the foundry lost their compensating wage differential after the department became a "black department." Along with actively recruiting black male workers in 1916, the automotive mogul also hired over nine thousand disabled workers and more than six hundred ex-convicts.[86]

HENRY FORD—"A THROW-BACK TO THE OLD FEUDAL BARONS"

Henry Ford's idiosyncrasies and avid anti-Semitism made one newspaper call the magnate "at heart a throw-back to the old feudal barons, [saying] he sought to dictate the entire life of his workers and would brook no opposition," yet men like Reverend Bradby and Claude Harvard did not necessarily hold the same views as some of Ford's naysayers. A black graduate of Henry Ford Trade School, Harvard's skill in perfecting Ford Motor machines placed him in close proximity to the automotive inventor. The young black man was even called upon to work with Ford as "part of the Ford Rotunda display, which was a highlight of the 1933 Chicago World's Fair." Henry Ford was duly impressed with Harvard's skill, so much so that he put him in "personal charge of instruction of Henry II and Edsel in the skill of machine tool and die." Harvard eventually left "the Ford 'inner circle' and later involved himself in the work of training tool and die workers during the war." Before Harvard departed from Ford, he had patented twenty-nine inventions for the automobile maker and even managed to introduce Ford to agricultural chemist George Washington Carver. From this connection developed "a relationship which later became a highly personal one, and influenced the lives and works of both men." Harvard became the spokesperson for the Ford Motor Company at Tuskegee Institute and went on to build a close relationship with Carver himself.[87]

Henry Ford's connection with innovative black leaders like Harvard and Carver may have inferred to ministers such as Reverend Bradby that Ford, despite his racist tendencies, was willing to support the black community. Ford's establishment of the George Washington Carver School in Richmond Hill, Georgia, in 1939 had certainly sparked hope for black Americans living in the Jim Crow South.[88] Influenced by his growing relationship with Carver, Henry Ford named the school after his friend and dedicated its enrollment solely to black children. While this act strengthened black support of Henry Ford, other black Detroiters held mixed feelings about the man. Charles Voorhess wrote: "Mr. Ford did have some desire to help the colored when he built the George Washington Carver School down there. . . . On the question of amalgamation of the colored and the whites, I think he remained pretty much neutral. If anything, he was in favor of separation and segregation. I think he felt the colored people could be educated and used to better advantage, and that they could fit in their own place, but not as an amalgamation with the white people. That was my idea from seeing him operate."[89]

Ford advocated both racial separatism and white paternalism. If Ford claimed that "the white man holds one end of the log [and] the colored man holds the other," then Bradby, like other black leaders who attempted to unite with Henry Ford, sought to hold the other side of the "Ford log" for Detroit's growing black community.[90] The recommendation system was one of the few avenues presented to black leaders in advancing the needs of Detroit's black society, and Bradby used what was afforded to him at the time.[91] Yet racial tensions and horrid work conditions at Ford Motor Company made Bradby's grip on the "Ford log" somewhat difficult. Disgruntled by these issues, many black laborers began to enlist the aid of labor unions over that of local black ministers like Reverend Bradby. This move by black workers in Detroit was unprecedented. As early as 1921, Detroit labor unions were segregated. Racism ran high in Detroit during the 1920s. The Ku Klux Klan's (KKK) membership in the city rocketed to 32,000 in 1923. Burnings of crosses in front of Detroit's County Building were the rule of the day. The KKK's influence even reached to the mayoral elections the following year. Backed by the KKK in the mayoral election of 1924, Charles Bowles ran openly as a Klan sympathizer, initially winning the election by seven thousand votes. However, upon a recount demanded by John William Smith, Bowles's opponent and known Klan enemy, the election commission ruled that any write-in vote for Bowles that was misspelled was null and void. The commission's ruling eventuated in Bowles being summarily kicked out of office within seven months of beginning his term, and the election of 1924 signaled the intensity of white supremacist sentiment in the city. Even Detroit's police department was prejudiced by Klan sentiment, especially from the time period "between January 1925 to June 1926, [when area] police killed 25 blacks in Detroit, [compared to] New York City, with a black population three times greater, [where] police killed [only] three black citizens during the same period." These pressures made black Detroiters wary of white collaboration, especially in the arena of black working rights.[92]

PROBLEMS IN THE PROMISED LAND IN THE 1930S

Yet the short life expectancy of black workers the automotive company employed pushed them to take a second look at white labor unions. White labor unions had overtly discriminated against black workers in the 1920s, but the late 1930s and early 1940s seemed to push both black and white workers at Ford to unite, albeit on a very small scale. Both groups were fed up with unbearable working conditions. Over the years, reports flowed from the Ford plant concerning the life expectancy of black laborers. According to one account, "The figures show that in Detroit . . . 246 Negro workers die of pneumonia every time 80.2 workers with a normal life die; that Negroes die of tuberculosis every time 40.1 persons die who have lived a normal life . . . bad working conditions in the foundry and in the open hearth—and in other back-breaking departments of the Ford Motor Company—have contributed much to death and disease in the Negro community."[93]

All of these conditions began to push black workers closer to uniting with white labor unions. This move would also create problems for black leaders who had for years bought into the white economic paternalism industrial corporations offered. As one of those leaders, Reverend Bradby stood as an *in-between* figure in the push for unionism in the late 1930s. He stood between Henry Ford and the black community and he also stood between the "old guard" that wanted to maintain the status quo of white paternalistic relations and those that embraced an activism that no longer needed the favor of white industrial elites.

CAUGHT IN THE MIDDLE: BRADBY AND THE ELECTION OF 1931

The mayoral election of 1931 was under way and Detroit's circuit court judge, Frank Murphy, was running for mayor. Officials at the Ford Motor Company were against Murphy and supposedly anyone who voted in support of him. Black employees heard rumors that anyone who failed to vote the way Ford desired would forfeit their job. Worried congregants, in fear of losing their employment at the Ford Motor Company, brought their concerns to Reverend Bradby. In response, Second Baptist's minister set up a church meeting where he could address his congregation's rising fears. A close acquaintance with Frank Murphy, "Rev. Bradby took a decisive stand supporting Murphy in defiance of Ford's interests." However, this move did not necessarily "trump Bradby's loyalty to Henry Ford," but rather reflected a more nuanced approach in Bradby's brand of racial uplift. First and foremost, Reverend Bradby was committed to the principles of Christianity and his vision of the Kingdom of God; second to that was the minister's resilient fidelity to the stability and well-being of Detroit's African American community. His relationship with Christianity and the African American race took precedence over any other relationship Second Baptist's most prominent minister would garner during his years in Detroit.[94] Seeking to stabilize both relationships, Bradby stood before his membership on September 28, 1931, and related that he had just come from a meeting with Ford's top officials. These men, he assured his congregation, claimed that the rumors were lies. Bradby posited that he was not speaking for himself, but on the very authority of Ford Motor's chief executive, Charles E. Sorensen. Attempting to prove his sincerity, Bradby noted that he spent three hours with Ford officials, pointing out the dangerous ramifications of firing black workers who supported Murphy's election as mayor. He writes, "I plainly told him that he as a leading citizen of America would not want to drive the Negro that far back into slavery." Henry Ford's, or more likely Sorensen's, response was that the company did indeed want the cooperation of the black workers in this matter, but "we know we can't get it that way . . . we are willing to go to the last inch for their support, but . . . we are not seeking to use our influence as a big stick over the heads of anybody." Bradby related these sentiments to his congregation, somewhat alleviating his congregants' fears for a while.[95]

However, by November of that year, Frank Murphy had won the mayoral election and Reverend Bradby was nervous and hurt as he read the words, "And they boast of the fact that they have silenced you at the Ford plant because you supported Murphy. And Marshall used the expression that you lied like a dog." An anonymous friend had sent the letter that now rested in Bradby's hands. The individual had attended a worship service at St. Matthew's Episcopal Church the day before and noted the comments of two key speakers that Sunday morning—Father Everard W. Daniel and Donald Marshall, fellow laborers with Bradby in the vineyard of Ford Motor Company's black recruiting strategies. Added to these insults by Daniel and Marshall was Bradby's shock to find that black workers who supported Frank Murphy were jobless. For Bradby, this could not have been the desire of Sorensen and the other officials who had assured him of Henry Ford's fairness. Writing to Mayor Murphy, Reverend Bradby pleaded, "I am sure that neither Mr. Ford nor Mr. Edsel Ford have any knowledge of the treatment that is being accorded to Negroes in his company because they voted for you. . . . But I know of many instances where colored men are being turned out from the Ford Motor Company just because they are supposed to have supported you. I can furnish the names of individuals who have been told that they were dismissed because they were disloyal to the best interests of the company."[96]

In Reverend Bradby's mind, Marshall was to blame for this outrage, primarily because Marshall was openly anti-Murphy. Marshall publicly attacked Second Baptist's minister for insinuating himself into the business affairs of the company, and he claimed that Bradby had been the recipient of bribes from Henry Ford. Reverend Bradby, frustrated and disappointed in the breakdown of communication between Marshall and himself, penned a letter to Marshall, first apologizing to the black Ford executive for addressing him at his home, and then vehemently denouncing every accusation levied against himself and his church. Marshall claimed that Bradby had taken bribes from Ford in the form of coal shipments for over nine years, that Second Baptist's membership was built up through Ford's influence, and that Bradby had openly slandered Father Daniel of St. Matthew's Episcopal Church, Marshall's own pastor. Marshall further accused Bradby of even starting a petition at Ford to get him fired from his position as employment officer.[97]

While Marshall's assertion may have had some grounds, Reverend Bradby adamantly denied all of these claims, declaring, "Of course my church was the same size it is now before I even started to cooperate with you. The fifty ton[s] I received from [you] this year I gave them a check for at cost [and] I never said anything about Father Daniel except to say that I respected his sternness and positiveness." Marshall's biggest claim was that Bradby tried to get him fired. Reverend Bradby argued: "Now with regard to the petition. May I say to you very humbly and very earnestly that I knew nothing of it and under no condition would I be party to it. It is rather hard for you to believe, but if they were bringing pressure on you to lose your job, I would be one of the men to defend you." Bradby's elaborate response to Marshall is filtered with tones of reconciliation and even anxiousness to stay on an even keel with one of Ford Motor's main employment officers for African Americans. He attempted to assuage Marshall's anger with the words, "Ford Motor Company can live without any of us. It might be a struggle but we would without them. But we do want to give our best support to their organization [i.e., Ford Motor Company] because of certain fine things that they are willing to do and are doing without discrimination."[98]

Reverend Bradby, caught *in between* the black community and Ford Motor Company, did not want to lose Ford's patronage; to do so was to shut down his vision of racial uplift and the building of the Kingdom. Yet the conflict between Bradby and Marshall mirrored the growing hostilities developing between black workers and Ford Motor Company, and also exhibited the control Henry Ford wielded over particular black churches through black employment officers like Donald Marshall.[99] The election of 1931 alone began to make African American workers more conscious of a need to unite with unions in an effort to better protect their jobs and their right to vote. This growing consciousness among black workers and the racial frictions at Ford were omens of things to come between Bradby and Henry Ford.[100]

ENEMIES IN THE MIDST

The combination of Ford's layoffs of African American workers and the effects of the Great Depression made black workers eager to join in the push for unions at Ford Motor Company. Yet for ministers like Reverend Bradby and Father Daniel, white paternalism had worked in the past to uplift the African American community and they saw no reason why it could not work in the future. This perspective somewhat blinded both ministers' ability to recognize the black working-class's growing fascination with unionism. As a result, the two pastors fell under growing criticism from sectors of Detroit's black community. The rise of black trade unionism made black Detroiters begin to question the fairness of their relationship with Ford Motor Company. Outspoken leaders inside and outside of the black Christian community began to criticize Bradby's and Daniel's Ford connections. Rev. Horace A. White, pastor of Plymouth Congregational Church, was extremely vocal in his negative opinions of ministers like Bradby. White, who arrived in Detroit in 1936, embraced a perspective of the Social Gospel that rejected power relationships between rich white benefactors and working-class blacks. As a graduate of Oberlin College's Divinity School, White believed part of his calling as a minister was tied to fighting for black labor rights. Asserting that "the Negro should not stand on the outside and look in; but should step in and join the union," White was not afraid to directly confront individuals like Donald Marshall. An outspoken advocate of labor rights, the Congregational minister was not above criticizing the conservative stance of his fellow clergymen in Detroit. Without specifically naming Reverend Bradby and Father Daniel, White penned an article in the *Christian Century* with the words, "In spite of what the preachers have been saying, the Negro workers of Detroit no longer believe that the crumbs from the tables of the controllers of industry are better than a man's place in the line of march of American workers, with head high and shoulders back in the struggle for economic justice."[101]

DIFFERING OPINIONS

While White was not the only black minister who called for labor union support, he was the most outspoken against ministers like Bradby and Daniel. Other ministers who were in line with White's views in Detroit were Rev. Charles A. Hill of Hartford Memorial Baptist, who was also Bradby's former associate minister, Father Malcolm C. Dade of St. Cyprian Episcopalian Church, and Rev. William Peck of Bethel AME Church. The latter minister, though a friend of Bradby, refused to join in friendly relations with Ford. Yet Peck was an activist on behalf of the black community just as much as was Reverend Bradby.

Like White, Peck was a graduate of Oberlin College Seminary and came to Detroit six years prior to White. After accepting the pastorate of Bethel AME Church in 1930, Peck strategized with other black ministers and leaders about ways to address socioeconomic challenges inherent in the black community. Building an association of black businessmen and professionals was one way that Peck sought to alleviate the sufferings of members of his community. His planning resulted in the Booker T. Washington Trade Association (BTWTA) in 1931, which was designed to encourage the black community's support of black-owned businesses. Working with the Housewives' League under the direction of Reverend Peck's wife,

Fannie, the BTWTA provided another source of empowerment and economic stability to Detroit's African American community. Father Malcolm Dade joined Peck and White and became an activist. Dade publicly rejected an alliance with Henry Ford, as did Peck and White. Dade, who was a staunch Episcopalian, earned his graduate degrees from Lincoln University and the Episcopal Theological Seminary in Cambridge, Massachusetts. Dade was often at a loss as to why African Americans held memberships in both St. Cyprian and St. Matthew's in order to maintain good standing at Ford Motor Company. In answer, one of the church's members told Dade, "I belong to St. Matthew's Men's Club because of Mr. Marshall. All the men who belong to St. Matthew's Men's Club have some sort of tie-in with Mr. Marshall and Father Daniel, and through them you have to buy a car and also you're assured of work and continuing to work at the Ford Company." Father Dade believed that "the good Lord" had guided him in avoiding the "trap" of the church-company alliance.[102]

White, Dade, Peck, and Hill embodied the secular and sacred aspects of black church life. Each minister believed in creating economic stability within the black community through reform efforts that mixed black uplift with the tenets of the Social Gospel. Yet their methods were very different from those of ministers like Reverend Bradby and Father Daniel. Whereas Bradby and Daniel saw white alliances as spaces for black empowerment, ministers like Peck, Hill, White, and Dade were wary of white patronage and saw black reliance on white patronage as slowing the progress and advancement of their people.

Rev. Charles Hill especially held this view. His response to the rise of unions at Ford Motor Company, compared with that of Reverend Bradby, is particularly telling. Although Hill served under Bradby at Second Baptist, he was more influenced by his tenure at Bethel AME under Reverend Peck. Hill's sense of calling and activism leaned more toward the strategies of Peck than those of his former mentor and friend, Reverend Bradby. The tensions between Detroit black ministers over the issue of unions and Ford patronage were added to the ever-increasing racial conflicts between white and black workers. As white union organizers pushed industries for higher wages and better working conditions, they became furious with black migrants who sought immediate employment in the midst of unionist strikes, thereby making it increasingly harder for unions to demand concessions from automotive giants like Ford.[103]

THE POLITICS OF ACCOMMODATION AND RESISTANCE

By the mid-1930s, the triangular relationship that had worked so well in the past was filled with tension. Black churches, Henry Ford, and the African American community were unsure of how to deal with one another in light of unionist agendas. Reverend Bradby found himself at the center of this tumultuous triangle. He was torn by his loyalty to the black community, his friendship with Henry Ford, and what he thought God's Kingdom warranted in the best interests of his people. For over fifteen years, Bradby and Henry Ford had a mutual relationship from which both parties had benefited. The rise of black unionism created an imbalance in the relationship. Ford felt threatened by unionism, and Bradby was confused as to what steps to take next. A scathing article by Rev. Horace A. White captured the dilemma of ministers like Bradby. Writing in 1938, White declared,

> Labor in this capital of the motor industry has waked up. What is even more surprising, Negro labor has waked up. And the Negro minister, to whom the aroused worker naturally turns for leadership and support, is caught unprepared. He is in most cases utterly bewildered. And in the few instances where he is not bewildered, he is likely to find when he begins to take action that this church, where he thought was the one institution belonging to the Negro, is actually the property of the big white industrialists.[104]

White's words reflected the growing acceptance of unionism within Detroit's black community in the late 1930s. When the United Auto Workers (UAW) came to Detroit in 1936, only a few black workers participated in the sit-down strikes in Detroit. By June of 1937, however, the UAW had attracted a massive following among Detroit black workers due to its policy on racial equality. Jack B. Kennedy, head of the Ford unionization drive, announced at a meeting at Union Hall that "Negroes have been assured their rights by their inclusion on all important committees of the union, [one of] complete equality with white workers."[105]

This racial equality policy was the catalyst for the push for black unionism by some of Detroit's African American leaders and Ford workers. The policy was also the beginning of the end for the Bradby-Ford relationship. In the words of Second Baptist historian Nathaniel Leach, "Necessity brought Rev. Bradby and Ford together; unionism caused them to stray apart."[106] Leach further argued that "Reverend Bradby could not afford to displease Henry

Ford. So he tried to be neutral." However, in the beginning of the conflict, Bradby attempted to remain loyal to Henry Ford when he threatened to boycott the NAACP's Twenty-Eighth Annual Conference in Detroit that year, if UAW president Homer Martin took the podium.[107]

COMMUNISM AND BRADBY

One year later, Reverend Bradby's grand gesture on behalf of Henry Ford proved short-lived when A. Phillip Randolph, an avid supporter of communism and unionism, was slated to come to Detroit. Randolph was a successful union organizer for Chicago's black Pullman porters, and he was considered one of the most militant and intelligent leaders among African Americans. Invited to speak at Second Baptist in 1938, Randolph was called to "the largest church [in Detroit] . . . for the meeting." Still the largest church in 1938, Second Baptist Church was known for its large sanctuary. Randolph held national prominence and Reverend Bradby did not want to close his sanctuary to a fellow race leader and thereby jeopardize his credibility among his members. Yet less than twenty-four hours after the news of Randolph's arrival was known in the city, "men in the church who worked in the factory were threatened by their bosses in the factories that if they permitted Mr. Randolph to speak, they would be laid off and their minister would not have the privilege of securing them another job." Reverend Bradby was unmoved and was said to have "stuck to his guns," but at what cost? The action would eventually compromise Bradby's standing with Henry Ford and jeopardize the economic welfare of some of his members. After the Randolph event, "some of [the] men were dismissed and told that they were dismissed because they allowed the speech to be made in the church." Reverend Bradby supported Randolph's leadership, but the move caused him to fall out of favor with Henry Ford. By 1939, Bradby's recommendation power no longer held the same weight at Ford Motor Company. While this move cost Bradby his influence at Ford, it also revealed part of the minister's struggle to adopt his vision of God's Kingdom to the ever-changing landscape of black activism in Detroit.[108]

Twenty years before, Reverend Bradby had a strong vision of how to build the Kingdom of God in Detroit's black community. The rise of unionism and the new black progressivism threw Second Baptist's savvy minister into a quandary as to how to conceptualize the Kingdom of God in this new form of black uplift. Added to this dilemma was how Reverend Bradby embraced leaders who rejected white paternalism. Opening his church to A.

Phillip Randolph was a bold move for Bradby, and may have been an indication of how his perception of the Kingdom had changed by 1939. These variations in Bradby's theology could have been due to more progressive forms of black activism, which sought to disengage from white paternalistic power structures. Another reason for this change could have been his frustration at Ford and Sorensen for allowing some of his church members to be fired for attending Randolph's lecture. Regardless of the reasons, it was clear that by the 1940s, Bradby was slowly changing his perceptions of black uplift and his vision of what it meant to establish the Kingdom of God in relation to Ford Motor Company.

While not openly Christian in his proclamations, Randolph was accustomed to using the church to build his support networks. Bradby's strategy of using sacred spaces to energize the black community to engage in social service programs and agendas to uplift the black community revealed his conception of how the Kingdom of God should work in the lives of black people. The Kingdom was tied to social, economic, and political advancement of the black race. It was made realizable through social service programs that brought money, food, and housing to the black community. It was not out of character then for Reverend Bradby to embrace the speeches of Randolph, even if he knew the race leader disdained relationships like the one Bradby maintained with Ford.

Reverend Bradby's support of Randolph's presence in Detroit also indicates that the minister was not afraid of those who openly supported communist agendas. Like other leaders of his time, Bradby did not view communism in the same way that many white Americans viewed communism in the early twentieth century. The UAW and other groups that held ties to communist groups were seen as stepping-stones to black equality. For example, Reverend Peck and Bradby maintained friendly relations throughout their pastorates. Bradby presented talks at the BTWTA, and Peck was often cited in Second Baptist's annual anniversary booklets congratulating Bradby on his accomplishments. These types of interactions between Bradby and those thought to have ties with the Communist Party were not unusual. However, relationships with communist-inspired black organizations and leaders like Randolph would eventually lead to the termination of the already tenuous relationship between Reverend Bradby and Henry Ford. In actuality, Bradby's loss of influence with Ford stemmed more from the bullying tactics of Ford officials than his tolerance of race leaders like Randolph. It was routine for black Ford officials like Donald Marshall to threaten and fire black workers who voted in support of unions. Marshall was certainly not above discrediting the recommendation system at those churches that allowed UAW speakers to address their congregations. Ministers like Bradby and Daniel felt the brunt of Ford's fear of unionism, and it was a "bitter [pill to swallow among] those preachers whose members wore their Ford badges to church with great pride."[109]

The African American community initially looked to ministers like Bradby and Daniel to set the tone of how to respond to such actions at Ford. For up until the 1930s, the black community had been unanimously supportive of Henry Ford and openly shunned unions. By the late 1930s, however, opinions had changed. Black congregants began to see the loss of Bradby's and Daniel's power. Further, when ministers proclaimed the goodness Henry Ford showed toward African Americans, these congregants questioned their credibility as pastors and sacred leaders.[110]

REVEREND CHARLES A. HILL

By 1930, Reverend Hill had become one of the leading spokespersons for black unionism in Detroit. Since leaving Second Baptist in 1920 to pastor Hartford Avenue (now Memorial) Baptist Church, Hill had established himself as one of Detroit's leading prounion ministerial activists. By 1936, Hill had grown in stature and was openly hosting union meetings in Detroit. If Bradby represented the "Old Guard," Hill represented the "new crowd of activists, [and] much more closely aligned with grassroots and working-class politics, [that] emerged from the economic turmoil of the Depression and the social dynamics of the migration."[111] The sociopolitical stance of both ministers reflected variations in the function of the "priestly-prophetic" dialectic of the local black church and its culture. If the "priestly" dialectic within local black churches was demonstrated in the care for congregation and community, then the prophetic dialectic within the black faith community consisted of a "forthright resistance to racism and other modes of exploitation and oppression."[112] This dialectic between the "priestly" and "prophetic" orientations of the local black church, with its fluidity between conservative agendas of accommodation and radical programs of resistance, was and is indicative of black existential understandings of God as a present reality, in struggle with, and empowering those who believe "that trouble don't last always." Here, accommodationism and conservatism both operate as a form of black uplift and resistance in that both forms of activism strives either psychologically, or even socially, to reinsert black humanity as a viable entity in the economic and sociopolitical realities of white society. For example, though Reverend Bradby may have accommodated the power structures of white patronage, he resisted white racist opinions that African Americans could not be viable workers in the automotive industry. Using the sacred space of the church, Bradby created a space of resistance to white racist assumptions about black work ethics and respectability. Albeit in a limited way, black workers walking the Ford automotive plants were living examples of black capability, humanity, and equality with white workers. Maneuvering blacks into some of the worst jobs at the Ford plant could not negate the fact that whites had first filled those distasteful jobs. Thus, Second Baptist provided African Americans a *seat* in the economic spaces of white society, thereby demonstrating that the black working class was just as viable as the white working class.

This act of resistance was based in the priestly understanding of the establishing of the Kingdom of God. If the "prophetic represented a forthright resistance to racism and other modes of exploitation and oppression," then the foundation of priestly conceptualizations as they function within the tenets of the Social Gospel were embraced by black preachers who sought to usher in the presence of God and uplift the race. The prophetic, then, is a continuation of the priestly in more expressive and innovative forms. Resistance against oppression is inherent in both concepts, yet one, "the prophetic," is more vocal and finds new ways for expression based on the gains garnered by the more conservative resistance efforts of the priestly.

In other words, Reverend Bradby's actions with Ford Motor Company, though seen as accommodative by some scholars, were in actuality actions of resistance. These actions in turn laid a foundation for the more radical resistance efforts of ministers like Rev. Charles Hill. Both conceptualized what I term a *sacred resistance* toward black oppression, one that combined hybrid notions of accommodation, radicalism, and gradualism. This type of accommodationist resistance constituted the form of sacred resistance that became the foundation for Bradby's and Hill's black political and economic action. Bradby considered uplifting the black race part of his calling as a minister, and so did Hill. Uplifting the black race meant taking the sacred realities inherent in the black church and in the faith of Jesus Christ to the street, where African Americans dealt with white oppression. God had called black preachers not only to speak the Gospel but also to reform society and fight against racism wherever it reared its ugly head. The two men had the same goal, but they served their communities in different ways, and their different strategies brought them into conflict, blinding them to the goal they shared.

While Bradby remained loyal to Ford and silent on the subject of unionism, his protégé, Hill, was being threatened by Ford's Donald Marshall, who told Hill he would "fire every black in the neighborhood if he allowed the UAW" to hold meetings in his church. Reverend Bradby, on the other hand, was antiunion, especially "regarding back-to-work by Blacks to break such strikes and conflicts as the 1937 Battle of the Overpass at Ford's, 1939 strike at Chrysler Motor Company, and the 1943 strike at Packard Motor Car Company."[113]

Throughout the years, Reverend Bradby made it a point not to exacerbate tensions at Ford, and he went as far as to proclaim Ford's generosity and benevolence to the black community. In 1941, Bradby was presented as one of the main speakers at a pro-Ford banquet hosted by Donald Marshall and Willis Ward. During the banquet, Reverend Bradby declared, "If Henry Ford hires one colored for every ten whites, I am for him first, last, and always. It will be a sad day for us if the Ford Company changes its policy."[114] Donald Marshall attempted to solidify Ford's support by issuing a veiled threat to "black ministers that their future was tied to Ford's victory over the union."[115] The banquet was effective in gaining some level of support for Ford just two days before union leaders had planned a "Ford walk-out." Backed by the public endorsement of the Interdenominational Ministers Alliance, Henry Ford's position seemed secure.[116] As time went on, however, Ford began using harsher strikebreaking tactics, and support of Ford's position began to wane, especially when Ford began hiring black farmers to take the places of white laborers during strikes.[117]

As a result, other black ministers in Detroit, such as Horace White and Malcolm Dade, were now joining Reverend Hill and pulling many other ministers with them. As the tide began to change, "even Bradby failed to deliver his customary public defense of Ford and maintained uncharacteristic silence" in the face of Ford's strikebreaking tactics. The UAW finally swayed black opinion to their cause. Further, the union's promise to fight for black workers' rights and equality on the job drew not only the support of black workers but also the support of black leaders who had traditionally been against unionism. The endorsement of so many African American leaders, especially ministers, played a key part in the growing prounion sentiment among black Detroiters. And as the UAW made greater strides at Ford Motor Company, Reverend Bradby began to settle into a slow acceptance of black unionism and his waning influence at Ford.[118]

In retrospect, some scholars paint ministers like Reverend Bradby as black leaders who failed to keep up with the times and found themselves perplexed when African Americans began to push past traditional means of empowerment. However, by the start of World War II, Bradby's awareness of black progress through the UAW was becoming more evident. For example, when the Baptist Ministers Conference issued two statements in support of Ford, Bradby's name was conspicuously absent from the statement. Still wavering in his stance toward the UAW, Bradby continued to strive for higher levels of black equality in his community. The 1940s were paradoxical times for Bradby in terms of his political activism. Establishing the Kingdom of God in the 1940s became a convoluted journey for the minister. Reverend Hill had been Second Baptist's former associate minister and Reverend Bradby's protégé, but his activism on behalf of black unionism had caused Bradby to rethink his former position on the subject. Bradby's twenty-three-year tie to Henry Ford and Charles Sorensen hung like a cloud over his relationship with new black leaders like Hill. In 1942, Bradby called for the members of Second Baptist not to back Reverend Hill's endorsement for the Detroit branch of the NAACP's presidency. Instead, he joined the Fair Employment Practices Committee (FEPC) in his continued effort to help African American women gain the same employment opportunities as black men. Bradby saw no contradiction between his denial of Hill's leadership and his participation in the FEPC on behalf of the same people Hill sought to help.

BRADBY, FORD MOTOR COMPANY, AND BLACK WOMEN WORKERS

Establishing the Kingdom of God for Bradby, despite his rejection of the "New Guard" of black leadership, remained tied to resisting oppressive structures and gaining employment opportunities for the black community. In 1942, the Ford Willow Run plant excluded black women in their hiring of female labor. Joining the FEPC, Bradby, along with other black and white leaders from the Detroit FEPC Council, approached one of Ford's top officials, Harry Bennett, about changing the company's hiring policies regarding black women. According to August Meier and Elliott Rudwick, Bennett patronizingly praised Bradby "for his early 'constructive influence' on Rouge's Negro workers, noting how the company 'didn't have near as many knifings as they used to.'"[119] Despite Bennett's sarcasm, Bradby and the FEPC received a cursory promise that "Negro females would be hired, as soon as Negro groups, whose sole interests are political, stop their agitation."[120]

Bennett's response reflected Reverend Bradby's unsteady relationship with Henry Ford and positioned the minister closer in line with union sympathizers. While Bradby tried to walk a "middle ground" between

Ford and those in the black community who pushed for labor unions, his silence on the subject eventually caused Ford and Sorensen to see Second Baptist's minister as a supporter of labor unions. Bradby's continued silence, combined with his activism in the FEPC, would eventually point to the slow but steady unification of the "Old Guard" and the "New Guard" in the fight for black equality in the automotive industry. As time passed following the Ford strike of 1941, relationships between black and white unions "would be replaced by united efforts to secure forceful action from the war manpower agencies and the FEPC." Prior to the Ford strike of 1941, African Americans had no reason to fully trust unions. The UAW still maintained members who were not completely open to blacks and saw them as an unwanted entity with the group. African Americans began to join the UAW in larger numbers, but the tenuous relationship between black and white workers in the UAW and the larger Detroit community was reflected two years later in the riots of 1943.[121]

CONCLUSION

Until 1941, Bradby's "Old Guard" politics had worked well for Detroit's black community. However, with the violence between blacks and whites during the riots of 1943, it was clear to Detroit's African American community, and to Reverend Bradby, that black folks had many obstacles to skirt as they gained equality in the city's industrial sphere. Although Bradby realized the power of the resistance white patronage could wield against racial oppression, he also understood that if he was to be successful in establishing the Kingdom of God in the lives of black Detroiters, he had to carefully carve out a space of empowerment and agency within the limitations of the white racist system. Bradby's loyalty to the welfare and empowerment of African Americans, and to his faith in the reality and acting presence of God through the salvific messages inherent in Jesus Christ, were two commitments that went above and beyond his allegiance to white patrons like Charles Sorensen, Henry Ford, and Frank Murphy.

Nevertheless, the networks of black labor and white patronage that Reverend Bradby helped to weave, while tenuous and unequal, offered members of the black community the ability to move further up the ladders of socioeconomic and political equality. The result was the rise of a new black working class in Detroit that would transform the sociopolitical milieu of the city's automotive industry for years to come. Leaders like Reverend Bradby opened the door so that more progressive leaders like Rev. Charles A. Hill could continue to fight for black equality in the workplace. As both types of leaders were needed to break the realities of racial oppression, activists like Reverend Bradby afforded their successors a better chance to run the race of black equality without the hand of white patronage. For Bradby, forging a relationship with Henry Ford was ultimately one of the greatest steps he took in establishing the Kingdom of God in his community, and it demonstrated the power of the sacred to shape sociopolitical and economic realities.

The Bradby-Ford relationship also demonstrates the nature of black activism and its varying degrees of radicalism in the fight for equality. Movements of conservatism and accommodation were intertwined with pockets of radicalism in Detroit. The transformation of the racial makeup of workers in the automotive industry in early twentieth-century Detroit was certainly a manifestation of black uplift based in the sacred theology of the Kingdom of God. Employment at Ford enabled many in Bradby's congregation and the surrounding black community to build better homes, make more money than they had in the South, acquire higher levels of education, and raise their social status. These gains were manifestations of the presence of the Kingdom of God and signs of black uplift. Bradby, as an *in-between* figure—between former modes of black activism and new strategies of black empowerment, between the black church and the black community, between Ford and Detroit's black workers—was able to stand as a medium of racial uplift for his people. His pulpit and the message of the Kingdom helped redefine the nature of industrial relations in Detroit's black community and added another facet to the making of urban Detroit in the twentieth century.

THE BLACK PULPIT, POLITICS, AND ESTABLISHING THE KINGDOM OF GOD

Rev. Robert L. Bradby used the power of his pulpit to spark viable manifestations of the Kingdom of God in the lives of southern migrants, and his efforts behind the pulpit also garnered the minister other mediums by which he could institute these sacred paradigms. Inspired by the tenets of the Social Gospel movement and its Kingdom rhetoric, Reverend Bradby entered Detroit's political scene through the influence of Detroit's largest local black church, Second Baptist. At the turn of the twentieth century, the Social Gospel writings of Washington Gladden and Walter Rauschenbusch permeated the political landscape of American consciousness. During this period, a "new age of politics" emerged, one that went far beyond former notions of progressivism to include such values as an "expanded sense of social responsibility and public welfare, governmental regulation of business in the interest of democracy, and greater popular participation in government." Such a transformation within progressivism resulted from the influence of the Social Gospel. Those who embraced the Social Gospel believed that society had a moral obligation to confront and overcome the problems of its culture. Reformers made demands on government on behalf of families "buffeted by industrialization and the urban environment." With Christian principles directing their activism, many reformers "helped to create the 'politics morality' that marked American political culture after 1900."[1]

Due to the priestly/prophetic dialectic of the local black church, African Americans were accustomed to having the only sustainable institution available to them operate in the same way that progressives were now demanding of their government. Local black churches had traditionally felt a sense of responsibility for the economic and social welfare of their members. Racial segregation and discrimination continued to be a point of contention and led to resistance among black religious leaders in America. However, the rhetoric of progressivism—as it was undergirded by the tenets of the Social Gospel—further heightened the local black church's sense of moral obligation to its community. As a result, its ministers began to model their social service programs along the lines of those provided by the government, thereby creating conditions for black economic growth and stability based on what they understood as a divine moral obligation. Solidified by progressive political rhetoric that created an "arena for right action—a bully pulpit to defend public morality," politics, as it was practiced in the early 1900s, used Christian metaphors and sacred language to promote moral responsibility. Twenty-eighth president of the United States and leader of the Progressive Movement, Woodrow Wilson, for example, demanded that "'ministers of reform'. . . use the machinery of government to build the kingdom of God on earth [and thereby] Christianize the social order . . . sav[ing] the nation."[2]

This call to "Christianize the social order" was supported by "social gospelers [who] supported progressive politics, believing that it would usher in the kingdom of God." Building on the writings of Social Gospel proponents, progressive politics echoed the proclamations of Washington Gladden and Samuel Zane Batten that "if the kingdom of heaven ever comes to your city, it will come through the City Hall" and sought to establish "a social order in which the great ideals of the kingdom shall be realized." Here, the state and other civic institutions stood as harbingers of the Kingdom of God. If Social Gospelers believed that the "State" and "City Hall" were vehicles of transformation that ushered in the Kingdom, then African American leaders who were living in the same period certainly understood this concept. The early twentieth century witnessed the founding of numerous black organizations that operated under the Christian imperative of moral responsibility. The formation of such groups as the National Negro Business League (1900); the National League for the Protection of Colored Women, which merged into the National Urban League (1905); and the National Association for the Advancement of Colored People (1909) were all founded on the concept of moral responsibility and social outreach to African Americans.[3]

In 1910, Reverend Bradby, nineteenth pastor of Second Baptist Church in Detroit, was no different from his earlier counterpart, Reverdy C. Ransom, forty-eighth bishop of the African Methodist Episcopal Church, who had founded Chicago's Institutional Church and Social Settlement ten years prior. Both ministers modeled their churches and outreach programs on the Social Gospel initiative of establishing the Kingdom of God in their respective communities. Like Ransom, Bradby understood the mission for establishing the Kingdom of God to be directly linked to political involvement. This chapter highlights Reverend Bradby's strivings to make the Kingdom of God a reality in Detroit through his connection with such civic organizations as the National Association for the Advancement of Colored People (NAACP), and through grassroots mobilization activities surrounding seminal court cases like that of the Ossian Sweet case of 1925 and the Scottsboro Boys trials of the 1930s.

BRADBY, THE NAACP, AND BUILDING THE KINGDOM

Walter White held the title of acting secretary of the NAACP in 1925. His letter of recognition to Reverend Bradby was no surprise to the forty-eight-year-old minister. Writing with a sense of relief and gratification, White told Bradby of the good news he had just heard from William Pickens, field secretary of the association. "I am gratified beyond words to hear . . . that you have been elected the President of the reorganized Detroit Branch. The condition in Detroit has given me no little worry as I knew that we had there splendid material for a large strong and efficient branch." White's words to Reverend Bradby were telling. Four years after the founding of the NAACP in New York in 1909, the Detroit branch sparked and then floundered under the leadership of William Osby, Father Robert W. Bagnall, and attorney William Hayes McKinney, the branch's first three presidents.[4] NAACP meetings at Detroit's St. Matthew's Episcopal Church on St. Antoine and Elizabeth held more empty pews than members. By 1925, the Detroit branch's membership rolls were almost nonexistent, as was its effectiveness. White's letter to Bradby was full of hope and praise for the branch's new leader. "In my opinion you are the key man to make the Association all that it should be in Detroit, and I am sure that your dynamic personality, your splendid enthusiasm, and your earnest advocacy of the cause will result in the branch becoming as it use to be, one of the strongest in the Association."[5]

James Weldon Johnson, field secretary to the national organizer of the association, also believed Bradby was the man to fill the empty leadership shoes in Detroit's NAACP branch. The national press release from the headquarters of the NAACP practically said as much on March 6, 1925. The release read, "The reorganized branch has elected as its new President, the Rev. Robert L. Bradby. . . . Dr. Bradby has been an earnest worker in the interests of the NAACP for many years, and under his leadership it is expected that the Detroit Branch will make great strides." By 1925, Reverend Bradby had truly made a name for himself in the Detroit community and beyond. His ability to expand the membership in his church from two hundred members in 1910 to three thousand members in 1925 astonished even the white elites of Detroit. Adding to his reputation was how he led Second Baptist Church into raising $80,000 to cover damages from two church fires, an unprecedented amount raised by a black congregation in that era. Alongside these feats were his numerous positions in influential organizations throughout Detroit. In the spring of 1925, Bradby walked the streets of Detroit as a prominent member of the boards of the Urban League, the Dunbar Hospital, the Phyllis Wheatley Home for the Aged, and the St. Antoine Street branch of the Young Men's Christian Association. Always the entrepreneur, Reverend Bradby was even the vice president of the black-owned Liberty Life Insurance Company. Maintaining his Baptist connections, Bradby also held leadership positions within the larger body of the denomination; he was the president of the Chain Lake Baptist Association and the superintendent of Color Work among Baptists in Michigan.[6]

The NAACP sought to capitalize on Reverend Bradby's influential connections in Detroit as well as on his ability to draw his three-thousand-member congregation into the membership rolls of the Detroit branch. Robert W. Bagnall, director of branches of the NAACP, wrote to Bradby: "The Second Baptist Church alone ought to furnish 3000 members for the Association, and sure will do so if you stress the matter insistently." In turn, Reverend Bradby sought to use his new position to expand his influence for himself as well as for the rights of black Detroiters. While Bradby was clearly motivated by a personal drive for power and influence, he was also dedicated to Social Gospel tenets promoting the economic, social, and political well-being of members of the black community. Numerous letters on behalf of church members and acquaintances confronting racial discrimination and mistreatment attest to this fact. Involvement with the NAACP offered Bradby an opportunity to fulfill his personal goals as well as his agenda for advancing the Kingdom of God among his race.[7]

RISING ENEMIES

There is evidence that Reverend Bradby had been vying for position and influence in Detroit's NAACP since 1921, and many in the organization had noticed his maneuvering. In a letter to Walter White in 1921, W. Hayes McKinney, acting attorney for the Detroit branch, complained about remarks Reverend Bradby made during a meeting of local ministers to raise money for the defense of Thomas Ray, a recent migrant from Georgia who was accused of murdering his landlord in June of 1920 and was eventually captured near the Canadian border.[8] As Ray's defense lawyer, McKinney was annoyed that Bradby "made a speech to the effect that he was not satisfied himself with the distribution of this 'large sum of money,' the major portion of which was raised in his church; that he felt that Willis & Hinton only should be the attorneys to represent Ray and that the ministers should give the firm their unanimous support in this matter." Clearly, Reverend Bradby sought to sway the other ministers in the meeting to his opinion not only of the defense team on the current case, but also to the fact that he had raised the most money and should have the most say in the matter. White's response to McKinney's letter was to invite Reverend Bradby to be one of the association's main speakers for its upcoming convention. The move caused McKinney some concern and pushed him to write, "It may be that these protestations were made in order to obtain the most coveted honor of being one of the speakers at the convention." McKinney further argued that he was not alone in his opinion of Bradby. The Detroit local branch executives ultimately questioned whether Bradby was loyal to the NAACP or to his own ego. Reverend Bradby's support of the Willis & Hinton defense team was seen as "siding with the enemy," and McKinney was unsure if he could trust "one who would throw the support of the ministers to an avowed enemy of the Association." For McKinney, Reverend Bradby was "hardly the proper person to be the local representative speaker at its convention." In a bold move, McKinney closed his correspondence to White with the following plea, "that unless Rev. Bradby shows by deeds . . . that he will stand by the Association, this Branch ask that the decision of placing Rev. Bradby on the program as a speaker at the Convention be held in abeyance until there are some further expected early developments in the matter."[9]

McKinney's letter sparked White to write Reverend Bradby: "Will you be good enough to advise me regarding statements made by you. . . . I understand that a meeting was held on Wednesday, April 20, between the ministers and the executive committee of the Association."[10] Bradby wrote a lengthy response, which continued: "dissatisfaction with the method in which the branch has expended money raised for the defense of Thomas Ray . . . and his opinion that the firm of Willis and Hinton has done a great deal in this case and deserves some consideration and remuneration." White wrote Bradby back with the words, "We are glad at any time to have honest disagreement with either the National Office or any of our branches, for it is only in that fashion that we can be effective and efficient as we would like to be."[11]

This "honest disagreement" between Reverend Bradby and the national office of the NAACP was a sign of things to come. Bradby was not one to be controlled. A case in point was the interesting position of the NAACP Detroit branch's secretary, Mrs. Lillian E. Johnson. While acting secretary of this branch, Johnson was also an active member of Reverend Bradby's congregation at Second Baptist. Johnson held committee memberships in Second Baptist's Earnest Well Workers and was one of the principal members of the Detroit Study Club, another organization that included a large number of Second's churchwomen. Johnson's position as a loyal member of Reverend Bradby's church and as the secretary for the NAACP's Detroit branch may have afforded Bradby an inside seat in the executive committee of the association, making him privy to the internal actions of the group as well as discriminatory events happening in Detroit. Bradby may have even been maneuvering himself into the leadership of the branch long before his official appointment to the organization.[12]

Yet for all of Reverend Bradby's maneuverings, he still had the progress of the African American race in mind. A report written by Lillian Johnson in the fall of 1921 recorded Bradby's activism on behalf of the black community. "We are enclosing clipping from our daily paper regarding the fight to the present showing of the 'Birth of a Nation,' in Detroit. Rev. R. L. Bradby went personally to the Mayor of the City the week previous to the date for the showing of this film, who took the matter up with the Police commissioner with the result that the showing of the picture was forbidden." Outcry against D. W. Griffith's Birth of a Nation, released in 1915, was heard throughout African American communities across the nation due to the film's racist depictions of African Americans, which reified derogatory black stereotypes afresh in the minds of white society.[13]

Approaching discriminatory businesses and even school districts on occasion was not something new for Reverend Bradby. He had always made it a point to confront racism in Detroit wherever it reared its ugly head. For years, Bradby functioned as a race man of sorts in Detroit. Connecting himself more fully with the Detroit chapter of the NAACP would enable him to fulfill that capacity to a greater degree. By the summer of 1922, Bradby had made inquiries to the director of branches, Robert W. Bagnall, for volunteer opportunities in the organization. Specifically, Bradby pushed to gain more control over the organization by offering "to do volunteer organization work for the Association." Bagnall deflected Bradby's advance by authorizing him to do "work for the Association in the territory of the Great Lakes, until the time of the meeting of the Board in September." In September 1922, Reverend Bradby's formal appointment to the Detroit branch would be considered. It would be another three years before Second Baptist's minister could ascend to the position he truly desired in the organization. While he waited, he bided his time as an active member of the organization. By March 1925, Bradby was poised to confront racial discrimination as the fourth president of the Detroit chapter of the NAACP, yet his position in the association would prove to be one filled with internal tensions between himself and the national officers of organization.[14]

BRADBY, SECOND BAPTIST CHURCH, AND THE NAACP

In the first years of Reverend Bradby's leadership of the Detroit chapter of the NAACP, the very location of the branch reflected the dialectical relationship between the priestly and the prophetic strains of the local black church. From 1925 to 1927, Second Baptist Church was the home of the Detroit branch of NAACP with many of Reverend Bradby's congregants holding dual memberships in both the church and the association. During these years, it was not unusual for Walter White or James Weldon Johnson to receive letters from Bradby written on Second Baptist's letterhead. For two years, the political arm of Detroit's NAACP was headquartered in Bradby's church office and guided by his Social Gospel vision of establishing the Kingdom of God. Having a local office of the NAACP placed in the sacred sphere of a black church was not considered unusual. It was a normal course of action that reflected the dialectical nature of African American religious culture.[15] In the spring of 1925, Reverend Bradby sat in his church office, twenty days after the first press release of his presidency, and penned a letter to Robert W. Bagnall, stating, "I have your letter and wish to express my appreciation for your encouraging words. Truly I think our branch here is destined to be a very splendid organization, as it was under your administration."[16]

One of Reverend Bradby's first actions as head of the Detroit NAACP branch was to establish a membership drive. Any member of the Detroit branch who brought in more than two hundred new participants was awarded a paid trip to Denver.[17] Bradby's second action was the organization of the Detroit branch's first NAACP Baby Contest in April of that year. Local black newspapers, such as the *Detroit Independent*, ran pictures of the city's African American babies entered in the competition with the words, "The N.A.A.C.P. Baby Contest to be given April 17 at Second Baptist Church for the purpose of raising the Detroit quota to be sent to the National Office for the carrying on of the national work."[18] And of course Bradby's name was listed first among those donating prizes for the event. The Baby Contest was a success, with the Detroit branch raising $780.37. Seventy-five percent of the proceeds went to the national office—$515.34, the largest contribution sent since the branch's founding in 1912.[19]

April was a busy month for Second Baptist's pastor and the NAACP. Along with his membership drive, Reverend Bradby challenged the Jane and Jim Crow policies of Detroit's public facilities. Cited again in the *Detroit Independent*, Bradby proclaimed: "We will open the swimming pools in all the schools and Community houses in Detroit, financed by this city if it costs a thousand dollars. We will see that the law is carried out and freedom given to our youths or they might as well prepare for a long battle in court."[20] By the end of May, the *Detroit Independent* declared that "Under the leadership of Rev. Bradby, the N.A.A.C.P. has stormed the citadel of race prejudice and discrimination . . . we feel grateful to Rev. Bradby, the N.A.A.C.P. Branch, of which he is head, the attorneys in the cases, and the fine cooperation of citizens at large."[21]

By June 1925, correspondence between Reverend Bradby, Walter White, Wayne County Circuit Court judge Ira W. Jayne, and the NAACP's national secretary, James Weldon Johnson, occurred almost weekly.[22] For the most part, communication among these men remained cordial, but as the Michigan summer slowly gave way to the cold winds of fall, tensions formed between the men, especially between Bradby, Johnson, and White. The first point of friction was over money and its proper distribution. It appeared that Bradby did not always agree with the 7 percent cut the national office took from the Detroit branch's earnings. In Bradby's view, a larger percentage of the contributions the Detroit branch raised should be kept in the local treasury.[23]

Another point of contention that long frustrated Johnson and White, even before Reverend Bradby's presidency, was how the Detroit branch handled contributions. The local and national branches did not always work together in processing member contributions. Contributions made to the Detroit branch were not always forwarded to the national office in a timely manner. Too often donors received two separate letters requesting support—one from the Detroit local branch and one from the national office in New York. As a result, many supporters, both black and white, stopped sending money to the Detroit branch altogether. By the end of June that year, Johnson's desk was flooded with contributions sent directly to him from Detroit supporters who had bypassed the local branch. Uneasy about the new leadership in the Detroit branch, Johnson wrote Wayne County Circuit Court judge Ira W. Jayne, a member of the national board of the NAACP, concerning Bradby. "You are fully aware of the origin of these contributions . . . we are inclined to feel that Dr. Bradby does not have a clear idea of the distinction between contributions of the National work and branch memberships and contributions coming through the Branch."[24] Jayne's response to Johnson was to steer clear of directly confronting Bradby on the matter. "I feel that I have no jurisdiction, as the lawyers say . . . I hope you and Dr. Bradby, to whom I am sending a copy of this letter, will each use your usual diplomatic ability in once and for all arriving at a happy solution of this not unsolvable problem."[25]

A peaceful solution to this issue would be delayed as the stifling heat of Detroit's July tickled the tempers of both blacks and whites. For most African Americans the only place away from the hot sun was in Detroit's Black Bottom, a piece of shade already overcrowded with massive numbers of African Americans. Black Bottom was located in the eastern part of downtown Detroit in the heart of the area between Hastings and St. Antoine Streets. Visitors to the area would swear they had entered an eclectic land where immigrants from Germany and Russia sprinkled the sidewalks with sounds of the motherland. A short walk farther down St. Antoine Street, bystanders could see unkempt apartment buildings filled to capacity with black migrants. Between 1916 and 1917, the influx of black migrants into Black Bottom would gradually push their immigrant neighbors farther away from Detroit's downtown area. By 1925, Black Bottom was home to black laborers, waiters, shoeshine boys, and domestics. Even prosperous black doctors and lawyers had homes in this densely populated area.[26] Many of these black migrants and professionals were either acquainted, affiliated, or members of Second Baptist Church of Detroit. Reverend Bradby, president of Detroit's NAACP, drew many in Black Bottom into the pews of his church and the membership rolls of the Detroit branch.

BRADBY AND THE OSSIAN SWEET CASE OF 1925

While the membership rolls of Detroit's NAACP began to grow with the names of Second Baptist's church members, Reverend Bradby continued to receive daily correspondence from the national offices of the NAACP. On July 22, 1925, Johnson's letter rested in Bradby's hand. The national secretary's inquiry concerned the housing situation in Detroit. "We have been following the press comments on the housing situation in Detroit. We should like to get an opinion from you on the status of the whole situation and upon what you think can be done by the local Branch and the National Office to remedy and change it."[27]

Reverend Bradby described how incredibly difficult the housing situation in Detroit was for black residents. While there were many houses available for purchase, most of them were in predominantly white districts that were hostile to blacks. Bradby even noted that the police department provided no assistance to black homeowners who moved into these districts. "Our police department seems very favorable to the mob spirit and very prejudice to our group. Our Mayor seems very, very undecided and our newspapers in most parts very one-sided and of course, that side is not in our favor."[28] Bradby's report to Johnson carried the sad tone of truth. Even officials in Detroit's Highland Park area were known to order blacks off the streets because they were in white neighborhoods. Bradby did note that for some black residents who "stuck through these things it has finally adjusted itself, but where there has been a disposition to get away from the situation because of threats it has only bred situations of like nature." These "situations of like nature" were mass riots that sometimes occurred in white neighborhoods whose residents were determined to keep blacks out of the vicinity. The only place that allowed black homeownership was Detroit's Black Bottom. White real estate agents maintained a strong policy of black exclusion from any neighborhood outside Black Bottom. Exclusion from white neighborhoods and the deliberate depreciation of black homes by local white realtors worked to limit socioeconomic opportunities for blacks. The housing situation in Detroit would eventually cause Reverend Bradby to stand face to face with the top officials of the national NAACP, sometimes in collaboration and at other times in confrontation. His pulpit would carry the voices of James Weldon Johnson, Walter White, and even the acclaimed lawyer Clarence Darrow, thereby once again transforming the sacred sphere of Second Baptist into a political one. Bradby's connection with these men would also push him more directly into the public arena of the race struggle.[29]

A glimmer of these powerful relations was seen almost three years prior, in 1922, when Reverend Bradby, along with other board members of Liberty Life Insurance, hired a young doctor named Ossian Sweet as its premier medical examiner. The position offered the young physician a steady income and the organization a respectable doctor. Working for one of Detroit's first black-owned insurance companies, Reverend Bradby and Sweet's paths were sure to cross. And their paths did cross, three years later, when the men stood face to face with prison bars between them at Detroit's Wayne County Jail. As the summer of 1925 progressed, James Weldon Johnson and Reverend Bradby could feel the rising racial tensions in Detroit. The cool winds of September did nothing to quell the disgruntled tempers of Detroit residents. When the month's temperatures dropped, Bradby heard the news that Dr. Ossian Sweet and his wife, Gladys, had just returned from Vienna. Working as a successful doctor for the last four years in Detroit's Black Bottom had earned the young doctor a profitable income, and touring Europe was one of the perks of his position. His money and vocation had earned the thirty-one-year-old doctor a pristine reputation in Detroit's black community. As a graduate of Wilberforce and Howard Universities, Sweet walked the streets of Detroit with confidence and recognition.[30]

Although he was a friend of Reverend Bradby, Sweet and his family spent their Sunday mornings at St. Matthew's. Coupling his prestigious church membership with his involvement in the Kappa Alpha Psi Fraternity, Sweet positioned himself as a "very highly respected" and "law-abiding citizen." With all his accolades, Sweet wanted his home to reflect his accomplishments. He purchased a house just a few miles from Detroit's Black Bottom, at 2905 Garland Avenue, well situated in a white middle-class neighborhood, which suited his new position and reputation in the city. Sweet had learned of the house from a former patient, and he liked the fact that the bungalow sat on a corner lot and intersected with Charlevoix Avenue, a main thoroughfare. The young doctor felt fortunate to have purchased the house from Mrs. Marie Smith and her husband, Ed. Marie was white and Ed was a "colored real estate dealer," yet the couple passed for white to everyone on Garland Avenue. Passing for white was easy for the Smiths, especially since Ed Smith's brother was the sergeant of detectives in the Detroit Police Department. The two brothers' appearance never alerted their white neighbors to the blackness of their ancestry. With the generous financing of the Smiths, Sweet laid down $4,000 in cash for the house, while the balance was made up in monthly installments. With such an easy purchase, Sweet must have felt that his new home was just the right blessing for his wife and new baby girl.[31]

As Sweet prepared for his move in September, Reverend Bradby was busy using the power of his pulpit and his position as Detroit's NAACP president to speak out against the crimes the white residents of Detroit's west side perpetrated. His former associate minister, Rev. Charles Hill, had called upon Second Baptist members and the black community to fight for black equality in homeownership through the court systems. The call brought forth a volley of criticism from the white public. One of the most scathing remarks was leveled at Second Baptist itself in one of Detroit's prominent newspapers. An editorial in Detroit's *Saturday Night* challenged the remarks of Hill, implying that the Second Baptist community and other black residents preferred a race riot to giving up one of their legal rights. Writing to William Pickens, field secretary of the NAACP, Reverend Bradby declared, "I think the colored people of Detroit should answer this editor in no ambiguous terms and let him know that we prefer a half-dozen race riots to the loss of any one right that he might mention."[32]

Bradby's fiery response reflected the sentiment of most black residents in Detroit. Many of them were tired of the Klan rallies and the never-ending police brutality in Detroit. Between January 1 and September 1, 1925, the black community witnessed the shooting of at least fifty-five of its members by Detroit police officers. Out of the fifty-five who were shot, black Detroiters would stand at twenty gravesites of those who had died as a result of their wounds. The black community was growing angrier by the moment and the atrocities in Detroit's housing market did nothing to comfort seething black minds.[33]

While the Sweets were aware of these tensions, their elation over the purchase of their new home overshadowed any fears they may have had about moving to Garland Avenue. However, midway into their moving day, trouble began to brew. The morning started with the usual moving of boxes and such, except as the Sweets were unpacking, police sergeant Clayton Williams made an unexpected call, introducing himself with the warning that he was there to protect their property. Such a startling welcome message was a sign of things to come. Later that night, as the unpacking was coming to an end, word had spread throughout the predominantly white neighborhood that a black family had moved in. On the second day of the Sweets' residency, Ossian Sweet went off to work as usual, only momentarily reminded of Sergeant Williams's warning and the unsettling memory of a crowd of disgruntled white neighbors gathered in front of his lawn the night before. By five o'clock that evening dinner was cooking on the stove in the Sweets new home. Sweet and his friends, Charles Washington and Hewitt Watson, were playing a game of bridge on the front porch. Every now and then the group would look up to see if Otis, Sweet's brother, and William Davis, a friend of

Sweet's from Washington, DC, had arrived by taxi. Mrs. Sweet called for help in the kitchen and the game was stopped for a bit, but not before notice of a continually growing crowd of white residents that stood only feet away from the Sweets' front door. By the time preparations were being made for dessert, loud screams filled the air, followed by people throwing rocks onto the roof, and angry demands directing the crowd to encircle the house. Sweet, his family, and his friends watched as a crack in the crowd was made just as his brother, Otis, emerged from a taxi, with Davis following. Racial epithets blanketed the air as Sweet opened his front door to Otis and Davis. Inside the house, Henry took hold of a rifle while Washington and Watson withdrew their revolvers. The crowd had completely surrounded the house by now and rocks were being thrown through the Sweets' windows. Sweet and those with him had had enough and fired warning shots from the house. Violence erupted and when it was all over, Eric Houghberg had been shot in the leg and another of the Sweets' new neighbors, Leon Breiner, lay dead of his wounds. Immediately Detroit's Inspector Schuknecht entered the Sweets' house with five other officers and promptly arrested Sweet as well as each of his family members under the charge of premeditated murder.[34]

Thus, on the evening of their second day in their new home, the Sweets' elation had turn to fear and regret. When the news filtered through the offices of Detroit's NAACP, local officers were hurriedly pushing through the doors of Second Baptist. In September of 1925, the church was still the main headquarters of the local branch, yet its president was out of town.[35]

In 1925, the National Baptist Convention, USA, was held in Baltimore, Maryland, September 10–11, and Reverend Bradby was in attendance. On September 11, James Weldon Johnson opened his morning newspaper and immediately fired off a telegram to Bradby requesting the "fullest information possible" on the Ossian Sweet matter.[36] Vice president Moses L. Walker answered Johnson's telegram in Bradby's absence. After the arraignment of the entire Sweet family, Walker and attorney W. Hayes McKinney, chairman of the chapter's legal redress committee, rethought trying to handle things without the national office and requested White's presence in Detroit "immediately."[37]

Reverend Bradby's brief absence would reveal the personality and power conflicts within and between the Detroit local branch and the national branch of the NAACP. When he pushed through the doors of his church office days later, he found his power and position threatened by members of his own local branch as well as certain members of the national branch.

The interaction between Bradby, his vice president, Moses L. Walker, and occasionally even Walter White revealed a personality accustomed to power, influence, and prestige—three things Bradby was not always willing to share with his fellow black leaders.

After September 12, 1925, correspondence between the local office and the national branch of the NAACP tripled daily. Telegrams were sent almost four times a day between officers from Detroit and New York. W. Hayes McKinney hurriedly wrote James Weldon Johnson of the events of September 9, 1925. "Dr. Sweet, his wife, two brothers, and six others were arrested, put in jail, and denied privilege of seeing Counsel. Warrants issued, mean-while, for all ten persons, including the wife of Dr. Sweet, charging mur-der. Arraigned this morning. All denied bail."[38] Four days later, the Detroit chapter of the NAACP had sprung into action. Reverend Bradby returned from his trip to find that his church had been used for the first meeting of the NAACP in support of the Sweets, an event planned without his input or supervision.[39] Described as a "wide-awake and honest" man, vice president Moses L. Walker stood in the pulpit of Second Baptist Church on September 13, 1925, and looked out over a massive crowd that overflowed the pews of the church and spilled out onto Monroe Street. Walker told the crowd that the "problem under discussion was national in scope and affected every colored person in the United States." Reminding the audience that the Detroit chap-ter of the NAACP was supported by some of the most influential race leaders in the nation, Walker exclaimed, "The national association stands behind us in this battle and will stand behind it to the last ditch." W. Hayes McKinney added his words to Walker's and declared, "We have met for the purpose of defending and advancing our property rights. We do not want the mind of our people enflamed, but should look at the problem from the standpoint of Confucius who said: 'Let me live this life each day, so that I can look back and say that I have harmed no one.'"[40]

The next day Walter White, secretary of the national branch of the NAACP, sent a lengthy letter to James Weldon Johnson telling him of the success of the Detroit chapter's first meeting for the Sweet case. In the details of his corre-spondence, the national branch's opinion of Reverend Bradby's leadership is vividly displayed. "It is fortunate Bradby wasn't here for Walker did a bang-up job." The "bang-up job" that White refers to is the establishment of the Sweet Defense Fund under a chairmanship that excluded Reverend Bradby. White continued, "He [Walker] saw to it that a disbursing committee was appointed of which he is chairman. The money raised thus far has been placed in a special and separate bank account known as the 'N.A.A.C.P. Special Sweet Defense Fund.'" That night, the meeting at Second Baptist raised over $700 for the Sweet defense. With Bradby out of town, White was assured that there would be no argument over how the local and national branches should manage the money. White was familiar with the nature of Bradby's leadership. He knew that in the past, Bradby did not always follow the dictates of the national branch and usually made decisions without even consulting them. Tension between Bradby and the national branch always seemed to arise over the distribution of money. While the national branch appreciated the numbers that Reverend Bradby's influence could bring to the NAACP, they were frustrated over his refusal to govern the Detroit branch under the leadership of the national branch of the association. At times, "Bradby ran the Detroit division of the NAACP just like he governed Second Baptist . . . after all, the local office was located in his own church." This aspect of Bradby's leadership even frustrated members of Detroit's local branch. The Sweet case exposed these dynamics even more. In an unprecedented move, Reverend Bradby attempted to establish another defense fund for the Sweet case, one completely under his authority. In a frantic letter to White, Walker wrote, "I understand that Bradby plans asking the mass meeting next Sunday to create an emergency fund placed at his disposal . . . just the situation we have planned to avoid, is going to arise, and this Committee will be compelled to relieve itself of the responsibility placed on by the Executive Committee, and which has been endorsed by the Public." Walker believed Bradby's actions were motivated by envy. Continuing his letter to White, Walker claimed, "The whole thing is a feeling of jealousy on his part. There was quite an ovation when my name was mentioned in the meeting Sunday, which of course I am not seeking. Write to Bradby at once, speak to him generally about the situation here. . . . He will fall for all you can hand him."[41]

It is clear that Walker felt that Bradby was power hungry, insecure, and a bit gullible. While Walker was convinced that Bradby's tactics jeopardized the standing of the organization, he was careful not to directly confront one of Detroit's most powerful ministers without garnering a number of supporters. "I think your letter to Bradby will take care of the matter referred to you, if not, I have several strong supporters who will." These letters between the NAACP local chapters' vice president and Walter White were sent in secret, reflecting the internal conflicts within the Detroit organization.[42]

In response to Walker's letter, White agreed to comply with Walker's wishes. White's letter to Walker arrived in the offices of Second Baptist on the weekend of September 19, 1925. Having recently returned from the National Baptist Convention, Bradby looked over his morning mail and noticed mail from the NAACP's national office addressed to his vice president. Whether through insecurity or his drive for power, Bradby opened the letter. Sometime the next day, Reverend Bradby sent his own message to Walker by casually handing the opened letter to him. Four days later, Walker expressed his anxiety over Bradby's tactics to gain control. "Yours of the 19th was handed me Sunday by Bradby after having been opened and read by him. It is well that you did not say anything you did not want him to know. I suggest you send my mail to my home . . . as he is a very jealous nature and is afraid that something might be said that would be of a praiseworthy nature about some one else." Walker's letter revealed how the members of the local and national branch of the NAACP worked to limit Bradby's personal control and influence in the organization.[43]

These tensions between Bradby and the local and national branches of the NAACP also uncovered common misconceptions about the unity among race leaders in the early twentieth century. "Race men" were black male leaders who sought to confront the tide of racism rising throughout the American cultural landscape. These individuals sought to establish equality for African Americans through collective organization, but many had to sometimes confront internal favoritism, arrogant egos, and personal agendas.[44]

Bradby's ego may have been bruised by the events of September 13, but the minister did not let his rivals thwart his support of the Sweets. Throughout the following weeks, Bradby made himself one of the strongest spokespersons for the Sweet Fund. Using the massive influence of Second Baptist, Bradby urged his large membership to empty their pockets on behalf of the Sweets. On Sunday afternoons, Second Baptist was filled to capacity with church members and fellow supporters of the Sweet defense. Pledges from $5 to $150 came from devoted congregants and sympathetic organizations.[45]

SACRED SPACES AND BLACK PROTEST

As September skies faded into October, the black Protestant church in Detroit joined in the struggle to support the right of one black man to protect his property under the Constitution. Sundays in the fall of 1925 became days of worship *and* protest. Local ministers, chairpersons of local lodges, and members of fraternal organizations crammed into church pews and consolidated their money and support. Meetings organized by the Detroit NAACP were held weekly at some of the city's most prominent black churches. Organizations listed in attendance at the meetings of Detroit's NAACP in 1925 were Prince Hall Lodge F.&A.M., Mt. Sinai Lodge No. 18, K. of P. Mosaic Temple, American Woodmen, Young Men's Club, Idle Hour Service Club, St. John C.M.E. Church, Workingmen's Club, Young Men's Progressive League. D.A.C. Waiters, Detroit District of A.M.E. Churches, Calvary Baptist Church, Knights of Ethiopia, St. Matthew's Episcopal Church, and Greater Bethel church. The words of one newspaper article capture the grassroots power embedded in the movement of Detroit's black community. "Every organization in the city, including the N.A.A.C.P., the Knights of Ethiopia, U.N.I.A., churches, fraternities, and entire Detroit has turned their money and attention to his case of the martyrs of our city."[46] Local newspapers often alluded to the Christian setting of these massive gatherings. As the *Detroit Independent* noted, the Sweets had now become "martyrs" in the minds of black Detroiters, and it was the duty of every black Christian to gather in the house of God on the Lord's Day and sing the hymn of protest on behalf of God's incarcerated people—the Sweets. The words of Walter White mirrored the sentiment prevalent in the minds of black Detroiters and the larger black community: "The national office is behind the fight and we will do everything we can to secure the full justice for the . . . martyrs."[47]

Major churches such as Second Baptist, Hartford Memorial, St. John's C.M.E, St. Matthew's Episcopal, Macedonia Baptist, Scott M.E., Morning Star Baptist, St. Paul A.M.E., and Greater Bethel A.M.E. were some of the principal gathering places around Detroit for fund-raising and strategizing among black leaders. Representatives from major government and local institutions such as the Detroit Urban League, the Michigan People's Finance Corporation, and the Detroit Young Men's Christian Association made their way to the doors of these churches on Sunday afternoons. Black support even came from beyond the Detroit city limits. Prominent black colleges such as Spellman and Morehouse even sent representatives to these sacred spaces of protest.[48]

Committees were formed at these gatherings to address the needs of Ossian Sweet's family and friends. Funds were raised not only to furnish the Sweet defense team but also to support the personal obligations of the defendants. Notable ministers, such as Rev. Joseph Gomez, pastor of Greater Bethel, and Rev. Charles Hill of Hartford Baptist Church, gave enthusiastic speeches urging listeners to provide food, clothing, and even funds to pay off debts owed by those in custody. The A.M.E. Ministerial Union of Detroit even called for the second Sunday in October to be named "The Sweet Fund Day." The group declared, "Every A.M.E. church in the city and surroundings will put on a drive for funds to assist in fighting the case. It is hoped that a large sum will be the result of this effort."[49]

The sacred space of the local black church reinforced the depiction of the Sweets as martyrs and the Christian duty of black Detroiters. Almost every major rally in support of the Sweets was held in the sanctuaries of black churches. These sacred spaces of black protest transcended the Detroit city limits through the idea of Christian brotherhood and the theological perception of the "Body of Christ." In these Christian ideals lay the foundation for black collectivity and protest. The "Body of Christ" implied that all Christians were connected across space and time if they adhered to a belief in Jesus as God's only son. "Christian brotherhood" demanded that those who claimed to believe had to actively demonstrate their faith by meeting the needs of their fellow Christian brothers and sisters. For black ministers confronted with the atrocities of the Sweet case, providing a cup of water in the Lord's name or raising $500 for one of God's children in trouble were considered one and the same. And the NAACP, with some its local leadership held in the hands of charismatic black ministers across the nation, promoted these Christian principles in their communities. The sanctuaries of black churches across the nation created a "brotherhood of believers" that transcended spatial limitations. Black Christians joined their prayers and pooled their finances to back the Detroit defense team for the Sweets, as was seen in supporting letters from numerous black churches across the country, which flooded the offices of the local and national branches of the NAACP during 1925. Churches from New York, Philadelphia, Missouri, and even Chicago sent their support and held prayer meetings in support of the NAACP's efforts to back the defense of the Sweets. Abyssinian Baptist Church in New York City, for example, held a meeting on September 20, 1925, in support of Ossian Sweet and his family. The leadership of Abyssinian Baptist Church made sure to express their solidarity with the Detroit NAACP and the black community in Detroit in a telegram sent by the hand of Walter White.

> Authorizing me [Walter White] extend through you to the citizens of Detroit the congratulations of the citizens of New York on the magnificent fight you are making for Doctor O. H. Sweet . . . hearty sympathy and cooperation of the citizens of New York . . . it is felt here in New York that in making the fight you are making for Doctor Sweet you are fighting the Battle of everyone of the eleven million Negroes in the United States.[50]

Always savvy about his power, Reverend Bradby used his presidency of the NAACP during this period to lobby for a position as city councilman in Detroit. Again, taking advantage of the massive meetings organized for the Sweet defense, Bradby was not above tooting his own horn when it came to gaining more influence. The *Detroit Independent* caught this aspect of Bradby's personality when it recorded, "While the meeting was not of a political nature each speaker highly endorsed and pledged to support the candidacy of R. L. Bradby for councilman."[51] Though Bradby had accolades in his favor, such as of being president of the Detroit branch of the NAACP and the pastor of the city's largest black church, he was "soundly defeated in the primary election."[52] Speculation as to why Bradby was defeated ran the gamut from denominational prejudice in the mayor's committee to community displeasure of Bradby's personality.[53] Although 1925 would be Reverend Bradby's last foray into the political world as a candidate, the growing demands of Detroit's migrant population, his relationship with Ford Motor Company, and his position in the NAACP would cause the minister to grapple with other political overtones in the years to come.

Between lobbying for himself and maintaining his ministerial duties, Bradby, as president of the Detroit branch of the NAACP, continued his efforts to support the Sweets. During October 1925, his schedule was packed tight with Sunday morning sermons and fiery afternoon speeches at weekly meetings about the Sweet trial. By then, Walter White had taken to communicating directly with Bradby via telegram. The words wired on October 1, 1925, called upon Bradby to step beyond the platform of the black pulpit and move into the dark, dank cells of black incarceration—"communicate with all eleven defendants to settle definitely handling of case."[54] The meeting between Reverend Bradby, the eleven defendants, and their lawyers would eventually culminate in a dinner meeting at Bradby's house with Clarence Darrow, one of the most controversial lawyers in the early twentieth century. Recollections of a little girl wondering who the man was who came to dinner that night would be recounted over and over again to Bradby's granddaughters for over two decades. Gabrielle Bradby-Green, Bradby's granddaughter, fondly recalled how her Aunt Catherine, one of Bradby's daughters, remembered the austere attorney standing near their dining room table.[55]

While speculation arises around the nature of the interaction between Bradby and Darrow, it is clear that Clarence Darrow came to Detroit in October 1925 to defend the Sweets. Newspapers around the nation exploded with the news: "Clarence M. Darrow appeared in court yesterday as chief counsel for Dr. Ossian H. Sweet and 10 other prominent Detroit citizens. . . . Mr. Darrow was retained by the National Association for the Advancement of Colored People."[56] As the news continued to spread around the nation, Reverend Bradby worked with lawyers, other ministers, and national black leaders to secure financial support, now for the best defense team ever pulled together for the African American.[57]

Hiring Darrow and his defense team required the NAACP to raise the sum of $20,000. The national office of the organization called upon every local chapter in the nation to lend its support. A question that appeared in every black newspaper in America asked, "Will the colored people of the country furnish the ammunition for this fight upon which one of their most fundamental rights depends?" Requests for contributions from $100 to $1 were made of every black household in America. The national treasurer of the NAACP, J. E. Spingarn, received the donations made to his office. After eighty-four days in jail, the defendants were eligible for bail. The jury was at a stalemate. The hung jury put Sweet and his companions back at home, though for Sweet, home was still a dangerous place.

The NAACP celebrated the Sweet case as a victory, and Reverend Bradby proudly recognized the power of Second Baptist in the organization's triumph. The strategies Bradby and the NAACP used in the Sweet case would be used in the Scottsboro Boys case of 1933. While no longer the acting president of Detroit's NAACP, Reverend Bradby would again use the sacred space of the local black church for social and political action within the public sphere. In his endeavor, the minister would confront the shadows of communism in his fight for racial justice and equality.[58]

BRADBY, COMMUNISM, AND THE SCOTTSBORO BOYS TRIALS

Reverend Bradby's connection with the Ossian Sweet case demonstrates how the priestly and prophetic strains of black Christianity can invoke systems of resistance, create centers of economic capital, and even stimulate strategies for political power in oppressed communities. Second Baptist and its connection with the Scottsboro trials of the 1930s exposed a more nuanced perspective of the priestly and prophetic role of the black church. Here, Bradby's agenda for establishing the Kingdom of God was a fluid conceptualization of the priestly and prophetic that demanded the sacred institution of the black church to flow in and out of racially charged political events such as the Scottsboro trials.

By 1933 the infamous Scottsboro rape cases were already under way in the United States Supreme Court, and Reverend Bradby was no longer a working officer within Detroit's NAACP. Two years earlier, nine black youths had been accused of raping two white prostitutes on a freight train near Scottsboro, Alabama. Community sentiment among whites against the young boys (the eldest being twenty years old) made it necessary for National Guardsmen to protect the youths from mob violence. The NAACP immediately sent Chattanooga lawyer Stephen Roddy to the boys' defense. Working with Scottsboro lawyer Milo Moody, Roddy endeavored to secure the freedom of Clarence Norris, Ozie Powell, Haywood Patterson, Roy Wright, Charlie Weems, Eugene Williams, Andy Wright, Olen Montgomery, and Willie Roberson. Moody and Roddy's defense only served to get all nine of the boys convicted on April 9, 1931, leaving just one of them to escape death by the electric chair.[59] By 1932, the cases had been appealed to the United States Supreme Court in the landmark case *Powell v. Alabama* (287 U.S. 45). The US Supreme Court's 7–2 verdict in favor of the Scottsboro Nine argued that the young men had not been granted due process under the Fourteenth Amendment.[60]

However, one year before the appeal to the US Supreme Court, the International Labor Defense (ILD), a communist organization, came to the aid of the Scottsboro Boys by sending another Chattanooga lawyer and former attorney general for the state of Tennessee, George W. Chamlee. The ILD defended radicals and workers in the courts by providing legal counsel and through public gatherings, petitions, and letters. When the Scottsboro Nine had initially been arrested, the ILD distributed antilynching leaflets throughout Scottsboro. Once the ILD learned of the judgment rendered on April 9, they called for massive demonstrations and rallies in protest of the verdict. Meetings were held in various major cities throughout America under the theme, "free the Scottsboro Boys."[61]

The ILD was a communist group, yet blacks flooded the meetings and membership rolls of the organization. African Americans did not view communism like their white counterparts in 1931. Like A. Phillip Randolph, many African Americans believed that communism offered a medium of black advancement and racial reform in light of Jim Crow culture. The League of Struggle for Negro Rights (LSNR), for example, was a communist group that drew many black supporters, especially in 1931. Both the ILD and the LSNR held large meetings with speakers providing the details of the case. Many of the meetings were located in the sacred space of the black church.

The Communist Party, while firmly grounded in a Marxist approach, could not ignore the grassroots power of local black churches. Nor could it take lightly Marx's argument that "religious distress is at the same time the expression of real distress and the protest against real distress. Religion is the sigh of the oppressed creature, the heart of a heartless world, just as it is the spirit of an unspiritual situation. It is the opiate of the people."[62] Black religious communities were the expression of real distress, but as the Scottsboro trials progressed, the Communist Party realized that religion, as African Americans practiced it, was nothing close to being an opiate.[63] The appeal that the ILD and other communist front groups like LSNR held for African Americans across the country caused even the NAACP to applaud the strivings of the ILD in the Scottsboro affair. For example, William Pickens, field secretary of the NAACP, actually "praised the efforts of the ILD in the Scottsboro affair. 'This is one occasion for every Negro who has intelligence enough to read, to send aid to you [the Daily Worker] and to I.L.D.'"[64]

As the Communist Party gained strength among black supporters concerning the Scottsboro Nine, the NAACP found itself reeling from what appeared to be a political takeover from the ILD over the case as "both the NAACP and the ILD hoped to banish the other group from the cases as each organization coveted exclusive control of the defense." Each group vied for the expertise of white lawyers for the defense. Attorneys Clarence Darrow and Stephen Roddy were both first approached by the ILD, but each refused and lent their skills to the NAACP. Infighting between the NAACP and the ILD continued as the trials progressed and eventually caused attorneys Arthur Hays and Clarence Darrow to withdraw their participation from the NAACP's defense team, leaving the fate of the nine boys in the hands of the Communist Party and their Chattanooga lawyers.[65]

COMMUNISM IN DETROIT

As the Scottsboro trials progressed, the NAACP and the ILD sought the financial backing of the local black church and its surrounding communities for the defense team assigned to the case. In Detroit, black civic and religious organizations rallied to the call. With the hardships of the Great Depression making life decidedly more difficult for African Americans in the 1930s, the Communist Party held great appeal for black Detroiters.[66] In fact the Communist Party's popularity increased in Detroit and made the organization "stronger there than in most other U.S. Cities." The appeal of the Communist Party among African Americans came through its organizing efforts within local black communities. It had a reputation of fighting for the rights of evicted families and creating "a number of councils along neighborhood lines: one for the Hastings-Ferry Street area; one along Woodward Avenue north of Grand Circus Park; and a large one for the east side, where Italian, Jewish, and Eastern European families lived and the African American enclaves were located." The Scottsboro cases increased the black community's attention toward the Communist Party. Furthermore, the NAACP had initially endorsed the ILD in 1931, which also served to raise the credibility of the ILD in Detroit's black community. Writing to Rev. Bradby on May 19, 1933, the NAACP's national secretary, Walter White, wrote, "I thought you might be interested in seeing the enclosed statement . . . with regard to the part the N.A.A.C.P. is taking in raising money for the Scottsboro defense. Money raised by the N.A.A.C.P. will be used only for the payment of legal bills and will be paid directly to the persons to whom it is due."[67]

White's letter is written just six days after the pews of Second Baptist were filled with over five hundred Detroit citizens. The *Detroit Independent* got the word out that the Citizens' Steering Committee would be holding a meeting at the church on Sunday, April 30, in the afternoon. The *Detroit Tribune* cited Bradby's initiative to raise money for the defense team by writing, "The meeting was a marked manifestation of the keen interest shown by the people of the community in the nine ill-fated Scottsboro boys . . . the outgrowth of the meeting and upon the earnest plea of Rev. R. L. Bradby, pastor of Second Baptist, who was elected chairman, $340 was pledged by responsible citizens while $75 cash was raised through a collection which is to be used as part of the defense fund being used for the Scottsboro boys."[68] Listed among the members of the Citizens' Steering Committee were Reverend Bradby's longtime acquaintance Ossian Sweet and a host of ministers and black professionals. The event signaled the influence of churches like Second Baptist and its ability to draw its massive membership into the folds of black protest and activism.

Yet prior to Second Baptist's participation on behalf of the Scottsboro Nine, other ministers like Rev. William Peck, pastor of Bethel AME, had already risen to the call of the ILD and the NAACP in their efforts to raise funds for the Scottsboro defense team. Earlier that spring, Reverend Peck opened his church to host a meeting for the Scottsboro Boys sponsored by another committee designed to raise funds for the ILD—the Scottsboro Defense Fund Committee for Michigan. Under the direction of Ossian Sweet, the Scottsboro Defense Fund Committee sought to financially support the Scottsboro Nine under the same slogan as the ILD, "Free the Scottsboro Boys." As head of this committee, Sweet was outspoken in his protest against the Scottsboro trials and in his criticism of the apathy of the black community toward the cases. He wrote, "So far in the fight to free the nine Scottsboro Boys, Negroes as a group have done practically nothing and it is high time that we as a group get [solidly] behind these boys morally and financially to win their freedom." By the spring of 1933, Detroit was up in arms concerning the Scottsboro Boys. Local leaders had joined forces with area ministers to rally Detroit's black community in support of the ILD and their defense team. The Scottsboro Defense Fund Committee for Michigan was part of a larger branch of the national Scottsboro Defense Committee headed by Mr. William N. Jones, managing editor of the *Afro-American* of Baltimore. Under Sweet's direction, the Scottsboro Defense Fund Committee organized a "Scottsboro Boys Tag Day" on Saturday April 22 and a "Scottsboro Boys Day" on April 28. The latter event would be a collaboration of ministers of the city "speak[ing] in interest of the boys from the pulpits of the city." Here, the local black church worked with the black secular spheres of its community in order to confront the horrors of racism and protest against the injustice now levied against the Scottsboro Boys.[69]

The following day, April 23, 1933, numerous meetings all over Detroit were under way in continued support of the young boys and the communist-backed ILD. Under the title "The Scottsboro Defense Fund," the *Detroit Tribune* read, "Similar meetings are scheduled to occur at other public centers in the city on Sunday afternoon." The NAACP, for example, gathered a number of supporters at the Naval Armory in order to "stimulate the raising of contributions for the Scottsboro defense fund." Again, both the sacred institution of the black church and the secular organizations of the black community acted upon the opinions proclaimed in the *Detroit Tribune*—"This publication heartily endorses all of these meetings in behalf of the Scottsboro Boys, and we petition for them the loyal support of the general public. We cannot—we dare not forget that the lives of the nine innocent Negro boys are hanging in the balance. . . . They are our boys."[70]

As the trials progressed and conflict grew between the ILD and the NAACP, concerns over the correct appropriation of monies supplied by local organizations and branches of the NAACP became points of contention. By the summer of 1933, the NAACP had broken ties with the ILD. Walter White publicly declared the break from the ILD, stating, "The National Association for the Advancement of Colored People will not turn over 'unconditionally' all funds collected by it for the Scottsboro defense to the International Labor Defense." The NAACP accused the ILD of gross misappropriation of funds, declaring, "We are willing to help, but only in such fashion as will prevent the reputation of the N.A.A.C.P. for careful handling of funds from being damaged."[71]

Added to these pressures surrounding the funds raised for the ILD defense team was the NAACP's frustration with Detroit ministers and their tardiness in turning monies over to the local branch. Again, Reverend Bradby was depicted as a source of dissonance. Acting president of Detroit's NAACP then, Moses L. Walker, wrote, "Referring to the City Wide Committee of which Rev. Bradby is Chairman and of which I am a member of the Steering Committee, I beg to advise that I have been unable to do any good with this particular body in having these funds sent through us. . . . I am very much afraid that they prefer to handle their funds independently for reasons you know best."[72] Walker, a member of Second Baptist, knew well Bradby's inclination for control, especially over money. Despite these tensions, "the ILD was preparing for a new trial, the CP called for 'a solid front in the fight for the unconditional freedom of the Scottsboro Boys,' and by 1935 other organizations, including the NAACP, church groups, and civic associations had gotten involved." Like their more conservative counterparts, Rev. Charles Hill and Father Malcolm Dade of St. Cyprian's organized committees and meetings for raising defense funds in support of the Scottsboro Nine. As the court cases went on, "Reverend Hill and others like him began to appreciate the working classes, the Communist Party, and the need for militant (and interracial and interethnic) collective action as central to their struggle for justice."[73]

STRATEGIES OF BLACK RELIGIOUS ACTIVISM

Indeed, despite the varying views of Bradby and Hill with regard to the best forms of black activism, the two ministers converged in their strategies of racial protest and social service with regard to the Scottsboro Boys. Both ministers used their churches and their social networks to raise money for the defense teams of the Scottsboro Boys. And though both ministers realized the dangers of dealing with the Communist Party, neither man recoiled from interacting directly or indirectly with the party, because each minister believed that the welfare of the black race and the fight for justice outweighed the stain of alliances with such politically radical groups. Historian Angela Dillard notes that the pressures of the Great Depression "weaken[ed] traditional race improvement associations that depended on white philanthropy."

This may be part of the reason why Bradby was unusually open to financially supporting a communist-backed defense team on behalf of the Scottsboro Boys. From Dillard's view, "*service* was redefined—away from 'service to' to the working classes and toward a position of 'struggle with' them."[74]

This redefinition of "service" in the 1930s would coincide with Reverend Bradby's idea of the Kingdom of God. Social service programs that met the socioeconomic needs of the black community were also tied to sociopolitical strategies that protested race prejudice inside and outside the courtroom. Bradby's tenure as president of Detroit's NAACP chapter testified to the fact that he understood the Kingdom of God as a social as well as political reality that could be ushered in through the activism of lawyers connected with the NAACP. His support of the Ossian Sweet case in the mid-1920s and his ability to energize supporters and raise funds for the Sweet defense team also reflected his nuanced understanding of the Social Gospel and the concept of the Kingdom of God. The struggle with the black working classes for equality was part of making the Kingdom of God a reality for Reverend Bradby. The Communist Party and its connection with the ILD carved another pathway for Second Baptist's minister to usher in that Kingdom. Thus black religious activism, though often hidden by Reverend Bradby's accommodationist stance with labor unions, still maintained a space of prominence within Bradby's conceptualization of the Kingdom and created new spaces of influence in the making of Detroit's political spheres. Bradby's connection and activism in regard to the Sweet and Scottsboro cases also points to the "long arm" of the local black church in the social political arenas of the African American community. Local black churches often provided spiritual, emotional, financial, and political support for African Americans when faced with legal issues. And though fraught with tension at times, the relationship between the local black church and the NAACP during this period constituted one of the most powerful partnerships in the African American community, one that revealed the complex dialectic between the sacred paradigms of Christianity and the secular-sociopolitical realities of black life in the twentieth century.

CONCLUSION

The sage of the Negro People in Detroit . . . is interwoven with the life and inspiration of Dr. Bradby . . . the preacher—the priest—the leader.

Horace A. White, Plymouth Congregational Church

Rev. Robert L. Bradby was considered to be a man at the right place and the right time, and his rise to prominence in the Progressive Era allowed him to develop and clarify his sense of ministerial calling through the events of the Great Migration, Ford's five-dollar-a-day promise, and the interwar years, which demonstrated the minister's tenacity for employing a unique kind of Christian praxis. While some would argue that Bradby was driven by the need for power, control, and influence, one could never overlook the fact that he worked tirelessly for the advancement of African Americans. Christianity became the ideology and the local black church became the medium by which Bradby spread his gospel of black uplift. For him, Christianity was a faith that was always in touch with the social and political experiences of African Americans.

It is clear from Reverend Bradby's ministerial activities and his activism in Detroit on behalf of the migrant community that he read the Bible through the lens of black activism. His leadership of Second Baptist, Detroit's NAACP, and his relationship with automotive mogul Henry Ford reflected a continuum of black activist strategies. Operating within a black Christian ontology—the Kingdom of God—Reverend Bradby functioned in a black Christian praxis that was informed by the tenets of racial uplift. Here, the theology of the Kingdom of God operated as a cornerstone of rationale behind Bradby's strategy in courting liberal white elites like Henry Ford, as well as his programs of ministry toward impoverished southern migrants during the Great Migration. This Kingdom agenda even ordered Bradby's participation in Detroit's NAACP. Indeed, the priestly and the prophetic strains within African American Christianity, especially that created within black Baptist worship life, fashioned in Bradby a black theological ontology that wedded black uplift, racial advancement, and confrontational strategies to white supremacist power structures. Such a form of activism produced a particular type of black Christian praxis and constituted a type of *sacred resistance* on the part of those who followed the leadership and activism of Rev. Robert L. Bradby.

Aspects of Reverend Bradby's theology and this type of *sacred resistance* were seen in his 1923 address to the Wolverine-Ontario Baptists. Preaching in October, Bradby proclaimed, "The great Head of the Church, Christ, expected that the Church would meet all conditions of the world. . . . Shall we hear the call of this hour and turn every department of our church into a beehive of activity for Christ and his *Kingdom*?"[1] The answer to the rhetorical question, for Bradby, was an unequivocal "yes." Following the teachings of Christ and establishing God's Kingdom on earth became the driving force behind all the minister's activities. Bradby viewed society as an entity in need of reform and redemption from sin. The pulpit was the central conduit of the ideology of the Kingdom. Reverend Bradby's tenacity in the fight for black equality and his engagement in *sacred resistance* guided him to walk the Ford plants for twenty-six-years. His relationship with Charles Sorensen and Henry Ford was yet another aspect of his vision of establishing the Kingdom of God among those of his race. Building productive social networks for himself and his church had always been a part of Bradby's vision for the Kingdom. As early as 1907, Bradby maintained membership with such groups as the Amherstburg Regular Baptist Association and the Most Worshipful Grand Lodge of Ontario, North Star Lodge No. 7, Windsor. By 1923, the forty-six-year-old minister was an established public figure in Detroit. Along with his standing as the pastor of the largest church in Detroit, Reverend Bradby also served in a variety of national and local organizations. His participation in Detroit organizations afforded him a seat on the board of Detroit's Dunbar Hospital, made him president of the Wright Mutual Insurance Company, vice president of the Supreme Liberty Life Insurance Company, vice president of Detroit Memorial Park Cemetery, and first vice president of the Idlewild Summer Resort Development Company. The latter position spoke to Bradby's prominence among the black elite of Detroit's middle-class society. The minister also held memberships in lodges such as the Masons and Elks as well as an active standing in the Kappa Alpha Phi Fraternity.[2]

THE IDLEWILD CONNECTION

Idlewild was a famous African American resort located between the small towns of Baldwin and Reed City, Michigan, in the 1920s and 1930s. Four white land developers and their wives established the resort in the hamlet of Idlewild, Michigan, under the name Idlewild Resort Company.[3] Known among black communities in the United States as "the Black Eden of Michigan," the resort "had become one of the few places African Americans could find peace of mind, and could escape systematic practices of racism and discrimination."[4] Its reputation among black communities made it a national and international phenomenon of black bourgeois class and leisure. Between 1915 and 1927, blacks from Michigan, Ohio, Texas, Kentucky, Georgia, Canada, Massachusetts, Missouri, and Indiana made Idlewild the most noted northern vacation resort. Even people from Hawai'i and Liberia visited the place called Black Eden.[5]

Reverend Bradby often vacationed at Idlewild. Dr. Wilbur Lemon, one of the members of the Idlewild Resort Company, had personally solicited Bradby's presence at the resort and membership in the Idlewild Lot Owners Association in hopes of selling some of the land shares to the minister. Hoping to integrate the predominantly white committee, "Lemon thought it would be wise to have two blacks on the ISRDC board. Reverend R. L. Bradby, pastor of Second Baptist in Detroit . . . was viewed as an ideal candidate." Described as a "man of exemplary character, tempered with an indomitable will to do . . . right; a man of vision, diplomacy, and business efficiency which is the foundation of his present responsibility as pastor of a 5,000 membership church, president of the local branch of the NAACP, and president of the State Baptist Convention; a man whose personal property and other investments approximate $50,000," Reverend Bradby was a highly praised leader among black elites in Detroit. Once the Idlewild Resort Company was incorporated and chartered, Bradby became the organization's first vice president along with his purchase of 120 shares. Sharing Bradby's position as the only other black member of the group was attorney Charles A. Wilson of Chicago.[6]

BRADBY AND DETROIT POLITICS

Reverend Bradby used his position as a prominent black religious leader in Detroit to enter segments of Detroit's political world in order to build his

understanding of God's Kingdom. Solidly Republican in his political affiliations, he was not afraid to overstep the limits of the Republican Party in the
face of racism and inequality. Working on behalf of the Communist Party's
ILD in the Scottsboro case proved Bradby placed racial advancement over
political ties. Despite these subtle displays of radicalism, Bradby continued
to remain conservative in his strategies to advance his race. Writing in 1933
to state Republican headquarters, Bradby claimed, "We went up last night in
Saginaw with the governor, and we had one great meeting. The democrats
were in our meeting in full force. I think we won them all."[7]

His run for Detroit's City Council in 1925 was also part of Bradby's
agenda to establish the Kingdom of God. Reassessing how to pursue
Kingdom agendas after he failed to earn the seat, Bradby wrote, "I don't
believe that I could have been the help to the people as a city councilman
that I have been as a minister. And I am very sure the two could not associate
closely in one man."[8] For Reverend Bradby the pulpit and the sacred sphere
of the black church offered the best mediums for transformation and change
within the black community. Ultimately, Second Baptist's nineteenth pastor
loved and cherished his Christian faith and calling as a minister. As an *in-
between* figure in the social, economic, and sacred spheres of Detroit, his life
offers a glimpse into the making of Detroit during the interwar years.

FRIENDS AND ENEMIES

In retrospect, Reverend Bradby garnered both friends and enemies in his
pursuit of establishing the Kingdom of God. More radical activists like
Detroit's Garveyites, and ministers like Father Malcolm Dade, Cyprian Davis,
and Horace White, chided the minister for supporting servile relationships
with white power structures. NAACP members James Weldon Johnson and
Walter White, though frustrated with Bradby's power plays, could not ignore
the positive strides Bradby made in the fight for black equality. And even
through the tensions between himself and Second Baptist church members Moses L. Walker and William C. Osby, both who were part of Detroit's
NAACP, Bradby was still very much respected for his work within the black
community.

Bradby maintained congenial ties with a number of influential blacks
and white elites in Detroit. He held long-standing relationships with Rev.
William A. Peck of Bethel AME Church and labor union leader Rev. Charles
A. Hill. Reverend Bradby was also one of the earliest members of the Booker
T. Washington Trade Association in Detroit and often attended meetings of

the organization and supported Peck's leadership of the group.[9] Under Peck, this small group of black businessmen and professionals was organized in 1930 with the goal of confronting the hardships of the black community. Another friend of Bradby's was black female activist Nannie Helen Burroughs. Burroughs and Bradby had a mutually supportive friendship throughout Bradby's tenure at Second Baptist. In Detroit's white community, Reverend Bradby sustained connections with Henry Ford, Charles Sorensen, mayor of Detroit and US senator James Couzens, and Detroit Circuit Court judge Ira Jayne. The numerous letters between Bradby and these men reflected the minister's strategy of using high-powered connections to meet the needs of African Americans.

MOURNING

Reverend Bradby nurtured his family life with the same intensity of commitment he gave to his congregation. A loving husband and devoted father, Bradby's second wife, Marion Louise Taliaferro, often received letters with the phrase "Dear Wifie and Kiddies." One cannot help but see a softer, playful side to one of Second Baptist's most powerful ministers when reviewing a letter he wrote to his wife. The flirtatious words of the 1933 letter read, "I think perhaps the heat kind of effected [sic] my heart a little. Either the heat or your absence. Smile. I suppose that I will get my heat now and may be yours hereafter. With love and kindness, I am Your Hubby."[10]

Thirteen years later, Reverend Bradby would feel another kind of fluttering in his heart, one that was not sparked by the love of his wife. The beginnings of such palpitations were first signaled in June 1942, when Bradby vacationed with family and friends in Los Angeles, California. Visiting with close relatives by the name of Johnson, a recording of the time captures the minister's dry wit and humor as he recounts his last farewells with the family. One Johnson family member makes the remark that she hopes his time of rest "does . . . some good with your illness."[11] The illness referred to was a persistent heart condition, which the minister had been struggling with for several years.[12] By 1946, Bradby would suffer a heart attack and recover, only to have another on June 3, 1946. This last heart attack would end the minister's thirty-five-year tenure as pastor of Second Baptist Church. It was about 9:30 in the morning when Bradby, seated in his study at the church, "reached for a pen . . . [and] collapsed."[13] "Though the seventy-year old minister had been warned by his doctor not to exert himself, [Bradby] preached his regular sermon," which was to be his last, on Palm Sunday, June 2, 1946.

The day after Bradby's death, Second Baptist immediately instituted "Ninety Days of Mourning" on June 4, 1946. Within these ninety days, a number of memorial services and programs were organized to honor his life and ministry. The front of Reverend Bradby's funeral service program listed the title of his last sermon, "The Kind of Church I Would Like to Help Build."[14] Refusing to rest on the victories of the past, Second Baptist's nineteenth pastor was still about advancing the business of God's Kingdom.

And yet by 1945, Second Baptist had already become one of the most prominent beacons of Christian faith, black social reform, and racial uplift. In November of that year, Second Baptist celebrated its pastor's thirty-fifth anniversary through a series of special services and programs. Among those who honored Reverend Bradby for his service to the church and Detroit's black community were "the Rev. Benjamin E. Mays D.D., president of Morehouse College, Atlanta Ga., and first Negro elected a vice-president of the Federal Council of Churches; Dr. J. J. McClendon, president of the Detroit branch of the National Association for the Advancement of Colored People; and Miss Nannie Helen Burroughs, president of the National Trades and Professional School for Women and Girls, Washington."[15]

Burroughs and Carter G. Woodson, recognizing the minister's long-standing contributions to the black race, had been in attendance at Bradby's thirtieth anniversary, five years earlier.[16] Yet both Burroughs and Woodson would be conspicuously absent from Reverend Bradby's funeral in June 1946. And by November of that year, Burroughs, instead of attending Reverend Bradby's thirty-sixth anniversary of the pastorate, would find herself speaking at a special memorial service for Second Baptist's late pastor.[17]

THE FUNERAL

On Friday, June 7, 1946, Second Baptist and the larger Detroit community celebrated and mourned the dynamic life and contributions of Rev. Robert L. Bradby. As pastor of Detroit's largest church, Bradby had "served in [over] 1,716 Sunday services, preached [in excess of] 3,432 sermons, pastored [more than] 11,715 persons for Church membership, baptized [above] 2,244 Converts, and united [over] 1,617 Couples in Holy Wedlock."[18] These numbers do not include the thousands of individuals and families who received employment and housing through Bradby's recommendations not only to Ford but also to other agencies in Detroit.

Seven ministers presided at Bradby's funeral, some coming from as far away as California. Nine organists from various Detroit churches contributed throughout the funeral proceedings, and a host of deacons, trustees, ministers, and even businessmen were assigned pallbearers. Listed among those who made remarks at the service were representatives from the Detroit Council of Churches and the Federal Council of Churches of Christ in America. Irene Cole Croxton, one of the first converts and the first to be baptized under Reverend Bradby's ministry, sung "I've Done My Work" during the service. And Dr. Earl L. Harrison, pastor of Shiloh Baptist Church in Washington, DC, had the honor of giving Bradby's eulogy.[19]

Second Baptist's nineteenth pastor was buried at Detroit's Elmwood Cemetery. Established in 1846, Elmwood Cemetery memorialized a host of influential public figures in Detroit's history, both black and white. Notables among those laid to rest there include Lewis Cass, Michigan's territorial governor; Douglas Houghton, Michigan's first state geologist; and Fannie Richards, Detroit's first black schoolteacher.[20] Rev. Father Malcolm G. Davis, then rector of St. Cyprian Episcopal Church, remembered Bradby as a "great tower of strength and inspiration,"[21] whereas Horace A. White of Plymouth Congregational Church, a known critic of Bradby's leadership, could not deny that the minister's "life was one of great use to the people." White's words echoed those of Rev. Charles A. Hill, a prominent leader of black unionism in Detroit and pastor of Hartford Avenue Baptist Church. Both Hill and White were at odds with Bradby over the issue of black unions in the Ford Motor Company. Yet, like White, Hill could not ignore the strides Bradby made toward uplifting the social, economic, and political status of the race. Reflecting on Bradby's service to the black community in Detroit, Hill declared, "Rev. Bradby, former president of the NAACP, was always on the side of advancement of the Negro, economically, culturally, and religiously. As one of the earliest presidents of the NAACP, he worked diligently to bring about justice and democracy in Detroit."[22]

LEGACIES

Almost thirty-four years later, Second Baptist celebrated its most dynamic pastor again on March 29, 1981, during the church's 145th anniversary. This time, the occasion would not take place at Second Baptist, but on a connecting road in Detroit between Lafayette and Chene Streets. The connecting road was named Robert L. Bradby Drive and "some 500 members and friends of Second Baptist Church . . . gathered to honor the church's 19th pastor." It was an auspicious occasion that was long in coming, especially for members of Second Baptist's Worthwhile Missionary Club. Organized in

1931, this group of black churchwomen had petitioned Detroit's City Council at the time of his death for a street or a school to bear Reverend Bradby's name. In 1946 though, no school or church was available for such an action. A compromise was offered to the women of the Worthwhile Club. The City Council suggested the renaming of the Cardoni Recreation Center with the promise of further consideration of a naming a street in Bradby's honor at a later date. Located at 9721 Cardoni near Lynn Street, the Robert L. Bradby Recreation Center was opened to the public on March 21, 1957. It would take another twenty-two years before the Detroit City Council would make good on its promise to the Worthwhile Missionary Club. By 1980, Robert L. Bradby Drive was officially recognized in Detroit's City Council minutes and Bradby's name was made part of the city's landscape.[23]

Reverend Bradby's leadership of Detroit's Second Baptist Church during the interwar years reveals the multifaceted support networks that laced the black urban landscape. Further, the strategic partnerships the minister made with white elites like Henry Ford demonstrated the reciprocal, albeit at times even tumultuous, nature of race relations and racial progress in communities within urban Detroit. In all these things, Reverend Bradby's life and leadership stands as a window of insight into the formulations of black male ecclesiastic leadership within the black Baptist faith during the Progressive Era. His leadership of Second Baptist reveals the reciprocity between agendas of racial reform and black Christian theological schemas of *salvation* and the Kingdom of God. A man of his times, Bradby stands as Second Baptist's most celebrated minister and one of Detroit's most influential figures of the twentieth century. His life, leadership, and ministry were part and parcel of what he understood to be a divine mandate—to establish the Kingdom of God in the lives of Detroit's black urban community.

NOTES

INTRODUCTION

1. Albert J. Raboteau, *Slave Religion: The "Invisible Institution" in the Antebellum South* (New York: Oxford University Press, 1978).
2. Barbara Dianne Savage, *Your Spirits Walk beside Us: The Politics of Black Religion* (Cambridge, MA: Belknap Press of Harvard University Press, 2008), 9.
3. C. Eric Lincoln, foreword to Leonard E. Barrett's, *Soul-Force: African Heritage in Afro-American Religion* (Garden City, NY: Anchor Press, 1974), viii.
4. James H. Cone, *God of the Oppressed*, rev. ed. (Maryknoll, NY: Orbis, 1997).
5. Gayraud S. Wilmore, *Black Religion and Black Radicalism* (Maryknoll, NY: Orbis, 1996), xiii.
6. Wallace D. Best, *Passionately Human, No Less Divine: Religion and Culture in Black Chicago, 1915–1952* (Princeton, NJ: Princeton University Press, 2005), 2.
7. Beth Tompkins Bates, *The Making of Black Detroit in the Age of Henry Ford* (Chapel Hill: University of North Carolina Press, 2001), 5.
8. Kevin Boyle, *Arc of Justice: A Saga of Race, Civil Rights, and Murder in the Jazz Age* (New York: Henry Holt, 2004), 116.
9. Phyllis Vine, *One Man's Castle: Clarence Darrow in Defense of the American Dream* (New York: Harper Collins, 2004), 63.
10. Angela Dillard, *Faith in the City: Preaching Radical Social Change in Detroit* (Ann Arbor: University of Michigan Press, 2007), 41.
11. Victoria Wolcott, *Remaking Respectability: African American Women in Interwar Detroit* (Chapel Hill: University of North Carolina Press, 2001), 67–68.
12. Richard W. Thomas, *Life for Us Is What We Make It: Building Black Community in Detroit, 1915–1945* (Bloomington: Indiana University Press, 1992), 272.
13. Condensed narratives and theses on Rev. Robert L. Bradby can be found in Nathaniel Leach and Edith Gamble, *Eyewitness History, Second Baptist Church of Detroit, 1836–1976* (Detroit: Second Baptist Church of Detroit, 1976), Second Baptist Church Papers (Reel 3), Michigan Historical Collection, Bentley Historical Library, University of Michigan, Ann Arbor; Nathaniel Leach, *The Second Baptist Connection: Reaching Out to Freedom, History of Second Baptist Church of Detroit.* Revised Edition Eyewitness History Second Baptist Church (Detroit: Second Baptist Church, 1988); Cara L. Shelly, "Bradby's Baptist: Second Baptist Church of Detroit, 1910–1946," *Michigan Historical Review* 17, no. 1 (1991): 1–33.
14. Robin W. Winks, *The Blacks in Canada: A History*, 2nd ed. (Montreal: McGill-Queen's University Press, 1997), 338.

15. "Minutes of the Amherstburg Association, Pathfinders of Liberty and Truth, 1841–1940," pp. 1–2, Reel 2, Box 2, Second Baptist Church Papers, Michigan Historical Collection, Bentley Historical Library, University of Michigan.

16. Nathaniel Leach, *Second Baptist Connection Revised Edition Eyewitness History Second Baptist Church of Detroit* (Detroit: Second Baptist Church, 1988), 14.

17. "William C. Monroe," in Nathaniel Leach and Edith Gamble, *Eyewitness History Second Baptist Church of Detroit 1836–1976*, Reel 3, Second Baptist Church Papers, Michigan Historical Collection, Bentley Historical Library, University of Michigan.

18. Leach, *Second Baptist*, 14.

19. R. L. Bradby to C. E. Sorensen, General Manager of Ford Motor Company, September 24, 1931, Papers of Henry Ford, Accession 572, Box 28—Ford Motor Company Policies #12.7.3, Henry Ford Museum and Greenfield Village Research Center, Dearborn, Michigan.

20. Baz Dreisinger, *Near Black: White-to-Black in American Culture* (Amherst: University of Massachusetts Press, 2008), 3.

21. Kevin K. Gaines, *Uplifting the Race: Black Leadership, Politics, and Culture in the Twentieth Century* (Chapel Hill: University of North Carolina Press, 1996), xvii.

22. Ibid., xiv.

23. Ibid.

24. Reverend Robert L. Bradby, preface to *History of Second Baptist Church, 1836–1940* (Detroit: Second Baptist Church, 1940), 3.

25. Rauschenbusch's experiences in New York were written about in an article titled "Beneath the Glitter." Detailed documentation of the article can be found in Ronald C. White's *Liberty and Justice for All: Racial Reform and the Social Gospel (1877–1925)* (Louisville, KY: Westminster John Knox Press, 2002), v, n. 5. See also Dores Robinson Sharpe's *Walter Rauschenbusch* (New York: Macmillan, 1942), 80, n. 2.

26. Richard Hofstader, *The Progressive Movement, 1900–1915* (Englewood Cliffs, NJ: Prentice-Hall, 1963), 79.

27. Walter Rauschenbusch, *Christianity and Social Crisis* (New York: Macmillan, 1907), 367.

28. White, *Liberty and Justice for All*, xxv–xxvi.

29. Ibid., xix.

30. Ralph E. Luker, *The Social Gospel in Black and White: American Racial Reform, 1885–1912* (Chapel Hill: University of North Carolina Press, 1991), 174.

31. White, *Liberty and Justice for All*, xxiv.

32. Hofstader, *The Progressive Movement*, 80.

33. Ibid.

34. Frank Mason North, "The City and the Kingdom," in *Social Ministry: An Introduction to the Study and Practice of Social Service*, ed. Harry F. Ward (New York: Eaton and Mains, 1910), 293–318; Donald K. Gorrell, *The Age of Social Responsibility: The Social Gospel in the Progressive Era, 1900–1920* (Macon, GA: Mercer University Press, 1988), 124.

35. Gorrell, *The Age of Social Responsibility*, 124.

36. Ibid., 124–25.

37. Ibid., 125–26.

38. Savage, *Your Spirits Walk beside Us*, 9.

39. Gorrell, *The Age of Social Responsibility*, 124–26.

CHAPTER 1
1. R. L. Bradby to C. E. Sorensen, General Manager of Ford Motor Company, September 24, 1931, Papers of Henry Ford.
2. W.E.B. Du Bois, "The Forethought," in *Souls of Black Folk* (Cambridge: A. C. McClurg, 1903).
3. Christine B. Hickman, "The Devil and the One Drop Rule: Racial Categories, African Americans, and the U.S. Census," *Michigan Law Review* 95, no. 5 (1997): 1163.
4. Ibid., 1175.
5. Kevin R. Johnson, ed., *Mixed Race America and the Law: A Reader* (New York: New York University Press, 2002), 11.
6. Ibid., 15.
7. Ibid.
8. Hickman, "The Devil and the One Drop Rule."
9. Johnson, *Mixed Race America*, 15–16.
10. Joel Williamson, *New People: Miscegenation and Mulattoes in the United States* (Baton Rouge: Louisiana State University Press, 1995), 10, 13, and 65; Johnson, *Mixed Race America*, 15–16.
11. Johnson, *Mixed Race America*, 16; "Registration of Negroes and Mulattoes Free Papers," Charles City County Minute Book No. 3, 1838–1847, Court Order of August 20, 1840. Charles City County Historical Society, Charles City County, Virginia.
12. Melinda Micco, "'Blood and Money': The Case of Seminole Freedmen and Seminole Indians in Oklahoma," in *Crossing Waters, Crossing Worlds: The African Diaspora in Indian Country*, ed. Tiya Miles and Sharon Patricia Holland (Durham, NC: Duke University Press, 2006), 130.
13. Williamson, *New People*, 10, 13, and 65.
14. A. Leon Higginbotham, *In the Matter of Color: The Colonial Period* (New York: Oxford University Press, 1978), 58.
15. Edward Hastings Allard, "A Report of Some Descendants of Bolling Bradby of Charles City County, Virginia," December 2002, ii; Theodore Stern, "Chickahominy: The Changing Culture of a Virginia Indian Community," *Proceedings of the American Philosophical Society* 96, no. 2 (1952): 192.
16. Helen C. Rountree, *Pocahontas's People: The Powhatan Indians of Virginia through Four Centuries* (Norman: University of Oklahoma Press, 1990), 175; Stern, "Chickahominy: The Changing Culture of a Virginia Indian Community," 192.
17. "Registration of Negroes and Mulattoes Free Papers." Charles City County Minute Book No. 3, 1838-1847, Court Order of August 20, 1840. Charles City County Historical Society, Charles City County, Virginia.
18. Stern, "Chickahominy: The Changing Culture of a Virginia Indian Community."
19. Robert Keith Collins, "Katimih o Sa Chata Klyou (Why Am I Not Choctaw)? Race in the Lived Experiences of Two Black Choctaw Mixed-Bloods," in Miles and Holland, *Crossing Waters, Crossing Worlds*, 264.
20. Ibid.
21. Manifest Destiny was a theology and an economic philosophy that proclaimed the United States a nation divinely inspired by God to extend its borders from the east to the western shores of the North American continent.
22. W. O. Brown, "Racial Inequality: Fact or Myth," *Journal of Negro History* 16, no. 1 (1931): 48.

23. Thomas N. Ingersoll, *To Intermix with Our White Brothers* (Albuquerque: University of New Mexico Press, 2005), 203.

24. Fred Landon, "The Negro Migration to Canada after the Passing of the Fugitive Slave Act," *Journal of African American History* 5, no. 1 (1920): 22. http://links. jstor.org/sici?sici=0022-2992%28192001%295%3A1%3C22%3ATNMTCA%3 E2.0.CO%3B2-Z (accessed February 5, 2006, JSTOR database).

25. "Minutes of the Amherstburg Association, Pathfinders of Liberty and Truth, 1841–1940," Second Baptist Church Papers, 1–2 (Reel 2, Box 2), Michigan Historical Collection, Bentley Historical Library, University of Michigan, Ann Arbor; Dorothy Shadd Shreve and Alvin McGurdy, "The Africanadian Church: A Stabilizer of Blazing the Pathway in Ontario South" (1980), Archives of the Chatham Kent Historical Society, 11, WISH Center, Chatham, Ontario.

26. Breed, "Virginia Indians Fight to Reclaim Sovereignty," 4A.

27. Williamson, *New People*, 65; and Breed, "Virginia Indians Fight to Reclaim Sovereignty," 4A.

28. Sigrid Nicole Gallant, "Perspectives on the Motives for the Migration of African Americans to and from Ontario, Canada: From the Abolition of Slavery in Canada to the Abolition of Slavery in the United States," *Journal of African American History* 86, no. 3 (2001): 399. http://links.jstor.org/sici?sici=00222992%282001 22%2986%3A3%3C391%3APOTMFT%3E2.0.CO%3B2-D (accessed February 5, 2006, JSTOR database).

29. "Registration of Negroes and Mulattoes Free Papers," Charles City County Minute Book (No. 4, 1848–60, Court Order of August 17, 1856, and January 16, 1857), Center for Local History, Charles City County, Virginia.

30. Bolling Bradby's name is cited as "Belin Bradley" on James Eldridge Bradby's marriage certificate in 1870. The name Bradley has also been a common misspelling of the name Bradby; *Registrations of Marriages, 1869–1928*, MS932, Reel 2, Archives of Ontario, Toronto.

31. "Registration of Negroes and Mulattoes Free Papers," Charles City County Minute Book (No. 4, 1848–1860, Court Order of August 17, 1856, and January 16, 1857), 396, The Center for Local History, Charles City County, Virginia; Library and Archives Canada; Ottawa, Ontario; *Census Returns for 1861;* Roll c-1038-1039.

32. *Registrations of Marriages, 1869–1928*, MS932, Reel 2, Archives of Ontario, Toronto.

33. *Census of Canada, 1891. Oxford West, Oxford South, Ontario, Roll T-6361;* Family No. 31, Ottawa, Ontario; Library and Archives Canada; *Registrations of Deaths, 1869–1938.* MS935, Reel 112, Archives of Ontario, Toronto, Canada.

34. Stern, "The Changing Culture of a Virginia Indian Community," 206; Shreve and McGurdy, "The Africanadian Church," 10; Gabrielle Bradby-Green, "Bradby Descendants," March 8, 2003, interview by Julia Marie Robinson.

35. Bradby's mother died in Middlesex, Ontario, in 1884 (under the name Bradley). See "Subject of Sketch: Reverend Robert Lewis Bradby," Second Baptist Historical Collection, Second Baptist Church, Detroit, Michigan.

36. Betsy Bradby (Bradbury), the mother of James Eldridge Bradby, is not listed in the 1861 Census of Kent County, Chatham, Ontario. There is speculation as to her death sometime between 1857 and 1861, for she is registered upon the testimony of Allen Bradley that she is a "free person of color" in 1857. See "Registration of Negroes and Mulattoes Free Papers," Charles City County Minute Book

(No. 4, 1848–1860, Court Order of August 17, 1856, and January 16, 1857), 396, the Center for Local History, Charles City County, Virginia.

37. Williamson, *New People*, 18.
38. Winks, *The Blacks in Canada: A History*, 141.
39. Ibid.
40. "Subject of Sketch: Reverend Robert Lewis Bradby," Second Baptist Historical Collection, Second Baptist Church, Detroit, Michigan.
41. A cord of wood is equivalent to a sta·k of wood 4 feet x 4 feet x 8 feet (128 cubic feet).
42. "Subject of Sketch: Reverend Robert Lewis Bradby," Second Baptist Collection.
43. Gallant, "Perspectives on the Motives for the Migration," 402.
44. Baz Dreisinger, *Near Black: White to Black Passing in American Culture* (Amherst: University of Massachusetts Press, 2008), 3.
45. R. L. Bradby to C. E. Sorensen, General Manager of Ford Motor Company, September 24, 1931, Papers of Henry Ford.
46. Williamson, *New People*, 2.
47. Winks, *The Blacks in Canada: A History*, 289: Patricia Morton, "From Invisible Man to 'New People': The Recent Discovery of American Mulattoes," *Phylon* 46, no. 2 (1985): 120. http://links.jstor.org/sici?sici=0031–8906%28198532%2946%3A2%3C106%3AFIMT%22P%3E2.0.CO%3B2-F (accessed February 5, 2006, JSTOR database).
48. Morton, "From Invisible Man to 'New People.'"
49. Winks, *The Blacks in Canada: A History*, 338.
50. Many black settlers in Canada were known to "assemble themselves together to give praise to their God, who had delivered them from the bonds of slavery." See "Subject of Sketch: Reverend Robert Lewis Bradby," Second Baptist Historical Collection.
51. "Minutes of the Amherstburg Association, Pathfinders of Liberty and Truth, 1841–1940," Second Baptist Papers (Reel 2, 79).
52. "Chatham Church Celebrates Its Hundredth Anniversary," Archives of the Chatham Kent Historical Society, WISH Center, Chatham, Ontario.
53. "Subject of Sketch: Reverend Robert Lewis Bradby," Second Baptist Collection.
54. "Chatham Church Celebrates Its Hundredth Anniversary," Archives of the Chatham Kent Historical Society.
55. Mary Ann Shadd Shreve, compiler, *Pathfinders of Liberty and Truth: A Century with Amherstburg Regular Missionary Baptist Association* (Buxton, ON: 1940), 43–44; James Melvin Washington, *Frustrated Fellowship* (Macon, GA: Mercer University Press, 1991), 36.
56. Madison J. Lightfoot, Church Clerk "Minutes of the Amherstburg Association, Pathfinders of Liberty and Truth, 1841–1940," Second Baptist Papers.
57. "Minutes of the Amherstburg Association, Pathfinders of Liberty and Truth, 1841–1940," Second Baptist Papers; James Kennedy Lewis, "Religious Nature of the Early Negro Migration to Canada and the Amherstburg Baptist Association," *Ontario History* 57, no. 2 (1966): 121.
58. Shreve and McGurdy, "The Africanadian Church," 53 and 67.
59. "Minutes of the Sixty-Seventh Anniversary of Amherstburg Regular Baptist Association September 12th to 15th, 1907," Canadian Baptist Archives, 9, McMaster Divinity College, Hamilton, Ontario.

60. Winks, *The Blacks in Canada: A History*, 343; "Minutes of the Amherstburg Association, Pathfinders of Liberty and Truth, 1841–1940," Second Baptist Papers, 63.

61. "Minutes of the Amherstburg Regular Baptist Association and Sabbath School Convention held with the King Street Baptist Church, Chatham, ONT.; September 14 to 18, 1905"; "McMaster University, Arts and Science Calendars, 1901–1902 to 1911–1912"; "McMaster University Arts Theology Calendar 1906–1907"; Canadian Baptist Archives, McMaster Divinity College, Hamilton, Ontario.

62. "Deaths" in the *Ontario Death Records, 1869–1927*, Latter Day Saints Family History Center, film No. 1411568, Kalamazoo, Michigan; "Obituaries," *Amherstburg Echo*, January 12, 1906, 4, Marsh Collection, Amherstburg, Ontario.

63. "1901 Census—Kent County," Canada Census 1901, Ontario, Chatham, Chatham Library, Special Collections, microfilm, T06475, District: Ontario, Kent—Reel T6475, Chatham, Ontario.

64. "McMaster University Arts Theology Calendar 1906–1907"; Canadian Baptist Archives, McMaster Divinity College, Hamilton, Ontario.

65. Fifth Anniversary of the Pastorate of Robert Lewis Bradby . . . November 7–14, 1915 Commemorative Program, Second Baptist Collection.

66. Leach and Gamble, *Eyewitness History: Second Baptist Church of Detroit*, Second Baptist Church Papers (Reel 3, 17).

67. "Minutes of the Amherstburg Regular Baptist Association convened with the First Baptist Church of Windsor, September 9, 1909," 16, Canadian Baptist Archives, McMaster Divinity College, Hamilton, Ontario.

68. "Minutes of the Amherstburg Association, Pathfinders of Liberty and Truth, 1841–1940," Second Baptist Papers, 34.

69. Fifth Anniversary of the Pastorate of Robert Lewis Bradby . . . November 7–14, 1915, Second Baptist Collection; Winks, *The Blacks in Canada: A History*, 342; "Minutes of the Amherstburg Association, Pathfinders of Liberty and Truth, 1841–1940," Second Baptist Papers, 6 and 35–37.

CHAPTER 2

1. Joe William Trotter, *The Great Migration in Historical Perspective: New Dimensions of Race, Class, and Gender* (Bloomington: Indiana University Press, 1991), ix.

2. Nancy Tomes, "'Destroyer and Teacher': Managing the Masses during the 1918–1919 Influenza Pandemic," in *Public Health Reports* (1974–), vol. 125, supplement 3: The 1918–1919 Influenza Pandemic in the United States (April 2010), 50; Nell Irvin Painter, *Exodusters: Black Migration to Kansas after Reconstruction* (New York: Norton, 1992), viii; Trotter, *Great Migration*, ix; John R. Shillady, in *Thirty Years of Lynching in the United States, 1889–1913* (1919; National Association for the Advancement of Colored People; repr., New York: Negro Universities Press: A Division of Greenwood, 1969), 6; Langston Hughes, *Selected Poems of Langston Hughes: A Classic Collection of Poems by a Master of American Verse* (New York: Vintage, 1959), 173.

3. Thomas, *Life for Us Is What We Make It*, 27.

4. Ibid., 56.

5. "Brief Outline of Housing Conditions among the Negroes of Detroit, Michigan (May 2, 1917), Detroit Urban League Papers, Michigan Historical Collection,

Bentley Historical Library, University of Michigan (Box 1, Folders 1–5), Ann Arbor, Michigan.

6. "Approximate Number of Negroes in Detroit Industries" (November 21, 1925), Detroit Urban League Papers, Michigan Historical Collection, Bentley Historical Library, University of Michigan (Box 1, Folders 1–5), Ann Arbor, Michigan.

7. Martin, *Detroit and the Great Migration*, 4 and 16; Boyle, *Arc of Justice*, 7.

8. George Edmund Haynes, *Negro New-Comer in Detroit, Michigan: A Challenge to Christian Statesmanship, a Preliminary Survey* (New York: Home Mission Council, 1918), 8; Elaine Latzman Moon, *Untold Tales, Unsung Heroes: An Oral History of Detroit's African American Community, 1918–1967* (Detroit: Wayne State University Press, 1994), 24; Thomas, *Life for Us Is What We Make It*, 31.

9. Boyle, *Arc of Justice*, 5; David Lee Poremba, ed., *Detroit in Its World Setting: A Three Hundred Year Chronology, 1701–2001* (Detroit: Wayne State University Press, 2001), 237.

10. Wilhelmina Lewis Means, in Moon, *Untold Tales, Unsung Heroes*, 94.

11. Robert L. Bradby, "Second Baptist Church of Detroit Eyewitness History," in *The Second Baptist Advocate* (March 1976), 19, Second Baptist Historical Collection, Second Baptist Church, Detroit, Michigan. The *Second Baptist Advocate* was a quarterly organ of Second Baptist Church of Detroit, Michigan.

12. Brief Outline of Housing Conditions among the Negroes of Detroit, Michigan (May 2, 1917), Detroit Urban League Papers.

13. US Department of Commerce, Bureau of the Census, *Negroes in the United States, 1920–1926* (Washington, DC); Elizabeth Anne Martin, *Detroit and the Great Migration, 1916–1929* (Ann Arbor: Bentley Historical Library, University of Michigan, 1993), 3–4; Poremba, *Detroit in Its World Setting*, 237. Michele Mitchell, *Righteous Propagation: African Americans and the Politics of Racial Destiny after Reconstruction* (Chapel Hill: University of North Carolina Press, 2004), 162.

14. Boyle, *Arc of Justice*, 7.

15. Gaines, *Uplifting the Race*, xxi.

16. Ibid., 2.

17. Ibid., xiv.

18. Ibid., xv.

19. Ibid., 2.

20. Haynes, *Negro New-Comer in Detroit, Michigan*, 8.

21. Ibid.

22. Ibid.

23. "Baptist Christian Center," United Community Services—Central Files Collection, Archives of Labor and Urban Affairs, Box 6, Folder I, Wayne State University, Detroit, Michigan.

24. Haynes, *Negro New-Comer in Detroit, Michigan*, 10–11.

25. Ibid.; Mitchell, *Righteous Propagation*, 171.

26. Haynes, *Negro New-Comer in Detroit, Michigan*.

27. "A Brief History of St. Matthew's Church," Second Baptist Papers (Reel 2), Michigan Historical Collection, Bentley Historical Library, University of Michigan, Ann Arbor.

28. "A Brief History of St. Matthew's Church"; Dillard, *Faith in the City*, 66.

29. "A Brief History of St. Matthew's Church."

30. Thomas, *Life for Us Is What We Make It*, 53 and 59; Milton C. Sernett, *Bound for the Promised Land: African American Religion and the Great Migration* (Durham, NC: Duke University Press, 1997), 83.
31. Sernett, *Bound for the Promised Land*, 76.
32. Ibid., 81.
33. Preface, *History of Second Baptist Church 1836–1940*, Second Baptist Collection, Second Baptist Church, Detroit, Michigan.
34. Sernett, *Bound for the Promised Land*, 88; Julia Marie Robinson-Harmon, "Baptists," in *The Encyclopedia of the Great Black Migration*, ed. Steven A. Reich, Greenwood Milestones in African American History (Westport, CT: Greenwood Press, 2006), 1: 54–57.
35. Dr. Nathaniel Leach, interview, April 18, 2001.
36. Preface, *History of Second Baptist Church 1836–1940*, Second Baptist Collection; Dillard, *Faith in the City*, 32.
37. Other associate ministers acquired by Second under Bradby's tenure were Rev. Lee T. Clay, 1920–22; Rev. H. L. McNeil, 1922–26; Rev. Robert A. Moody, 1926–29; and Rev. Edward C. Simmons, 1935–; Preface, *History of Second Baptist Church 1836–1940*, Second Baptist Collection.
38. Dillard, *Faith in the City*, 39.
39. Ibid., 15.
40. Preface, *History of Second Baptist Church 1836–1940*, Second Baptist Collection.
41. Haynes, *Negro New-Comer in Detroit, Michigan*, 6–8.
42. Mitchell, *Righteous Propagation*, 147–49.
43. "Membership Manual," *Second Baptist Church of Detroit*, Second Baptist Church Papers, Michigan Historical Collection (Reel 2), Bentley Historical Library, University of Michigan, Ann Arbor.
44. Susan Lindley, "'Neglected Voices' and Praxis in the Social Gospel," *Journal of Religious Ethics* 18, no. 1 (1990): 75.
45. "Baptist Christian Center," United Community Services—Central Files Collection (Box 6, Folder I), Archives of Labor and Urban Affairs, Wayne State University, Detroit, Michigan.
46. Ibid.
47. Allen D. Grimshaw, ed., *Racial Violence in the United States* (Chicago: Aldine, 1969), 60–63, 73–75, and 87–88.
48. Mattie G. Anderson, "Baptist Christian Center," United Community Services Papers—Central Files Collection, Archives of Labor and Urban Affairs, Wayne State University, Detroit, Michigan; Sernett, *Bound for the Promised Land*, 245; Mattie G. Anderson, "Baptist Christian Center," United Community Services Papers—Central Files Collection.
49. Ellen Ross, "'Not the Sort That Would Sit on the Doorstep': Respectability in Pre–World War I London Neighborhoods," *International Labor and Working-Class History* 27 (Spring 1985): 39; see also Ellen Ross, *Love and Toil: Motherhood in Outcast London, 1870–1918* (New York: Oxford University Press, 1993).
50. Wolcott, *Remaking Respectability*, 4.
51. "Christian Center of Detroit Michigan—Baptist Christian Center," United Community Services—Central Files Collection, Archives of Labor and Urban Affairs, Wayne State University, Detroit, Michigan.
52. Haynes, *Negro New-Comer in Detroit, Michigan*, 10–11.

53. Ibid.; "Christian Center of Detroit Michigan—Baptist Christian Center," United Community Services—Central Files Collection, Archives of Labor and Urban Affairs, Wayne State University, Detroit, Michigan; and Mitchell, *Righteous Propagation*, 147.

54. Wolcott, *Remaking Respectability*, 64; Mitchell, *Righteous Propagation*, 155.

55. Ronald C. White Jr., "Social Christianity and the Negro in the Progressive Era, 1890–1920" (PhD diss., Princeton University, 1972), 2–3.

56. Ibid., 89.

57. Clarence Taylor, *Black Religious Intellectuals: The Fight for Equality from Jim Crow to the Twenty-First Century* (New York: Routledge, 2002), 93.

58. "Something Cooking at the Center," Women's American Baptist Home Mission Society flyer, 1946, Box 39, Folder 18; "Baptist Christian Center," United Community Services—Central Files Collection, Archives of Labor and Urban Affairs, Wayne State University, Detroit, Michigan; Wolcott, *Remaking Respectability*, 67.

59. "Christian Center of Detroit Michigan—Baptist Christian Center," United Community Services—Central Files Collection, 2, Archives of Labor and Urban Affairs, Wayne State University, Detroit, Michigan.

60. Mattie G. Anderson, "Baptist Christian Center," United Community Services—Central Files Collection, Archives of Labor and Urban Affairs, Wayne State University, Detroit, Michigan; "Christian Center of Detroit Michigan—Baptist Christian Center"; Mitchell, *Righteous Propagation*, 166.

61. Rosalie K. Butzel, "The Baptist Christian Center," United Community Services—Central Files Collection, Archives of Labor and Urban Affairs, Wayne State University, Detroit, Michigan.

62. "Rededication Baptist Christian Center," United Community Services—Central Files Collection (Box 6, Folder I), Archives of Labor and Urban Affairs, Wayne State University, Detroit, Michigan.

63. "Baptist Christian Center," United Community Services—Central Files Collection (November 1939, 1), Archives of Labor and Urban Affairs, Wayne State University, Detroit, Michigan.

64. Susan Curtis, *A Consuming Faith: The Social Gospel and Modern Culture* (Baltimore: Johns Hopkins University Press, 1991), 82–83.

65. Taylor, *Black Religious Intellectuals*, 14.

66. Curtis, *A Consuming Faith*, 83.

67. Ibid., 84.

68. Taylor, *Black Religious Intellectuals*, 14.

69. Curtis, *A Consuming Faith*, 4, 57 and 187; Norman Kenneth Miles, "Home at Last: Urbanization of Black Migrants in Detroit, 1916–1929" (PhD diss., University of Michigan, 1978), 170.

70. Dress Well Club, Dress Well Club Card, 1917, Detroit Urban League Papers, Michigan Historical Collection, Bentley Historical Library, University of Michigan (Box 1, Folders 1–5), Ann Arbor.

71. Martin Summers, *Manliness and Its Discontents: The Black Middle Class and the Transformation of Masculinity, 1900–1930* (Chapel Hill: University of North Carolina Press, 2004), 1 and 4.

72. *Second Baptist Herald*, September 5, 1926, October 3, 1926, June 17, 1928, Second Baptist Collection, Second Baptist Church, Detroit, Michigan.

73. Wolcott, *Remaking Respectability*, 64–66; Shelly, "Bradby's Baptist: Second Baptist Church of Detroit, 1910–1946," 29; Miles, "Home at Last," 169–70.

74. Wolcott, *Remaking Respectability*, 66; Henry Pratt, *Churches and Urban Government in Detroit and New York, 1895–1994* (Detroit: Wayne State University Press, 2004), 22.

75. Justine Rebecca Hamilton, "Second Baptist," interview, March 3, 1997.

76. Dillard, *Faith in the City*, 40.

77. Ibid., 46.

78. Ibid.

79. Ramla M. Bandele, *Black Star: African American Activism in the International Political Economy* (Urbana: University of Illinois Press, 2008), 89 and 95.

80. Judith Stein, *The World of Marcus Garvey: Race and Class in Modern Society* (Baton Rouge: Louisiana State University Press, 1986), 275–76; Thomas, *Life for Us Is What We Make It*, 196.

81. Thomas, *Life for Us Is What We Make It*.

82. Marcus Garvey, "An Exposé of the Caste System among Negroes," August 31, 1923, quoted in Garvey, *The Philosophy and Opinions of Marcus Garvey; or, Africa for Africans*, the New Marcus Garvey Library, no. 9 (Dover, MA: Majority Press, 1986), 58.

83. Rev. Robert Bagnall, "The Madness of Marcus Garvey," *Messenger* (March 1923): 638–48; "2,000 Negroes Hear Garvey Denounced," *New York Times*, August 21, 1922, reprinted in Robert A. Hill, *The Marcus Garvey and Universal Negro Improvement Association Papers, Vol. IV: Sept. 1921–Sept. 1922* (Berkeley: University of California Press, 1986), 932–33.

84. Thomas, *Life for Us Is What We Make It*, 195–96; Stein, *The World of Marcus Garvey*, 228–34.

85. David Allen Levine, *Internal Combustion: The Races in Detroit, 1915–1926* (Westport, CT: Greenwood Press, 1976), 101.

86. For more detailed analysis on Garveyism, see Colin Grant, *Negro with a Hat: The Rise and Fall of Marcus Garvey* (New York: Oxford University Press, 2008); Stein, *The World of Marcus Garvey*; Edmund David Cronon, *Black Moses: The Story of Marcus Garvey and the Universal Negro Improvement Association* (Madison: University of Wisconsin Press, 1955), 19; Levine, *Internal Combustion*, 101.

87. C. Eric Lincoln, foreword to Leonard E. Barrett's *Soul Force: African Heritage in Afro-American Religion* (New York: Anchor Press, 1974), viii.

88. Ibid.

89. Wolcott, *Remaking Respectability*, 129.

90. Preface, *History of Second Baptist Church 1836–1940*, Second Baptist Collection.

91. Nannie H. Burroughs to Robert L. Bradby, November 7, 1925, "Souvenir Program 15th Anniversary of Second Baptist Church, 1910–1925 (Reel 3, Box 2, 43), Second Baptist Church Papers, Michigan Historical Collection, Bentley Historical Library, University of Michigan, Ann Arbor; Evelyn Brooks Higginbotham, "Religion, Politics, and Gender: The Leadership of Nannie Burroughs," in *This Far by Faith: Readings in African-American Women's Religious Biography*, ed. Judith Weisenfeld and Richard Newman (New York: Routledge, 1996), 154.

92. Ched Myers, *Who Will Roll Away the Stone?: Discipleship Queries for First World Christians* (Maryknoll, NY: Orbis, 1994), xxvii and 163.

93. Neil R. McMillen, *Dark Journey: Black Mississippians in the Age of Jim Crow* (Urbana: University of Illinois Press, 1990), 285.
94. R. L. Bradby, "Detroit's Confusion and God's Remedy," April 8, 1933 to June 24, 1933, Rev. Robert L. Bradby Papers, Burton Collection, Detroit Public Library, Detroit, Michigan; *History of Second Baptist Church 1836–1949*, Second Baptist Collection, 6–7, Second Baptist Church, Detroit, Michigan.

CHAPTER 3

1. Burroughs to Bradby, November 7, 1925, in "Souvenir Program—15th Anniversary 1910–1925."
2. Evelyn Brooks Higginbotham, *Righteous Discontent: The Women's Movement in the Black Baptist Church, 1880–1920* (Cambridge, MA: Harvard University Press, 1993), 175.
3. Ibid., 176.
4. Bettye Collier-Thomas, *Jesus, Jobs, and Justice: African American Women and Religion* (New York: Knopf, 2010), 160–61.
5. "Dr. Bradby Begins 35th Year Sunday," Rev. Robert L. Bradby Papers, Burton Collection, Detroit Public Library, Detroit, Michigan.
6. Collier-Thomas, *Jesus, Jobs, and Justice*, 59.
7. W.E.B. Du Bois, *Darkwater: Voices from within the Veil* (1920; New York: Dover, 1999), 104.
8. Collier-Thomas, *Jesus, Jobs, and Justice*, 58.
9. Nannie Helen Burroughs, "Black Women and Reform," *Crisis* 10, no. 4 (1915): 187.
10. "The Negro in Detroit," Report Prepared for the Mayor's Inter-Racial Committee by Special Survey Staff under the General Direction of the Detroit Bureau of Government Research, Section III (Detroit, Michigan, 1926), 3; Burroughs, "Black Women and Reform," 187; for more information on other black denominations in Detroit in 1926, see "The Negro in Detroit," Report Prepared for the Mayor's Inter-Racial Committee by Special Survey staff under the General Direction of the Detroit Bureau of Government Research; "The Negro in Detroit," Report Prepared for the Mayor's Inter-Racial Committee by Special Survey Staff under the General Direction of the Detroit Bureau of Government Research, Section III (Detroit, Michigan, 1926), 32–33.
11. "Minutes of the Seventh Annual Session of the Women's Division of the Metropolitan Baptist Association held with the Second Baptist Church Ypsilanti, Michigan," Second Baptist Church Papers, 27, Michigan Historical Collection, Bentley Historical Library, University of Michigan, Ann Arbor.
12. Anne Meis Knupfer, *Toward a Tenderer Humanity and a Nobler Womanhood: African American Women's Clubs in Turn-of-the-Century Chicago* (New York: New York University Press, 1996), 15; C. Eric Lincoln and Lawrence H. Mamiya, *The Black Church in the African American Experience* (Durham, NC: Duke University Press, 1990), 12–13; see also White, *Liberty and Justice for All*, xxv.
13. Second Baptist Collection, 11, Second Baptist Church, Detroit, Michigan.
14. Knupfer, *Toward a Tenderer Humanity and a Nobler Womanhood*; Wolcott, *Remaking Respectability*, 162.
15. Wolcott, *Remaking Respectability*, 149.
16. Ibid., 5; Ross, "Not the Sort That Would Sit on the Doorstep," 39; Higginbotham, *Righteous Discontent*, 100.

17. Curtis, *A Consuming Faith*, 5.
18. Wolcott, *Remaking Respectability*, 4.
19. By 1927 the churchwomen had paid off the debt of the Francis Harper Home and burned the mortgage. "Church History," *History of Second Baptist Church, 1836–1940*, 5, Second Baptist Collection, Second Baptist Church, Detroit, Michigan.
20. "The Earnest Worker's Club," *History of Second Baptist Church, 1836–1940*, 75, Second Baptist Collection, Second Baptist Church, Detroit, Michigan; "Scrap Book, History of the Earnest Worker's Club of Second Baptist Church, 1908–1946," Second Baptist Collection, Second Baptist Church, Detroit, Michigan.
21. Wolcott, *Remaking Respectability*, 65.
22. Leach, *The Second Baptist Connection*, 39.
23. "Second Baptist Church of Detroit Members Manual," 29, Second Baptist Church Papers, Michigan Historical Collection, Bentley Historical Library, University of Michigan, Ann Arbor; Leach and Gamble, *Eyewitness History: Second Baptist Church of Detroit*, 22; "Robert L. Bradby Drive Dedication: Work of the Worthwhile Missionary Club," Rev. Robert L. Bradby Papers, Burton Collection, Detroit Public Library, Detroit, Michigan; Leach, *The Second Baptist Connection*, 61; "Second Baptist Church of Detroit Members Manual," 45, Second Baptist Church Papers, Michigan Historical Collection, Bentley Historical Library, University of Michigan, Ann Arbor.
24. "Cavalcade of Second Baptist Church," March 29, 1937 (Reel 2, 14), Second Baptist Church Papers, Michigan Historical Collection, Bentley Historical Library, University of Michigan, Ann Arbor.
25. "Church History," *History of Second Baptist Church, 1836–1940*, 5, Second Baptist Collection, Second Baptist Church, Detroit, Michigan.
26. "Cavalcade of Second Baptist Church," 14, Second Baptist Church Papers, Michigan Historical Collection, Bentley Historical Library, University of Michigan, Ann Arbor.
27. "Cavalcade of Second Baptist," 14–13.
28. Wolcott, *Remaking Respectability*, 242.
29. "History of Second Baptist," Second Baptist Historical Collection, Second Baptist Church, Detroit, Michigan; "Missionary Social Worker (Reid), 1925–1926," Second Baptist Church Papers, Michigan Historical Collection, Bentley Historical Library, University of Michigan, Ann Arbor; "Baptist Christian Center," United Community Services—Central Files Collection (Box 6, Folder I), Archives of Labor and Urban Affairs, Wayne State University, Detroit, Michigan.
30. Robert L. Bradby, "Report for Quarter, Oct 28–Dec 31, 1921 of Baptist Christian Center," United Community Services—Central Files Collection (Box 75, Folder 21), Archives of Labor and Urban Affairs, Wayne State University, Detroit, Michigan; Itemized Report of the Archives of the Christian Center, 28 October–31 December 1921, United Community Services—Central Files Collection (Box 75, Folder 21), Archives of Labor and Urban Affairs, Wayne State University, Detroit, Michigan; Wolcott, *Remaking Respectability*, 67–68; "Baptist Christian Center," November 1939, 1, United Community Services—Central Files Collection (Box 6, Folder I), Archives of Labor and Urban Affairs, Wayne State University, Detroit, Michigan.
31. Wolcott, *Remaking Respectability*, 67 and 161; see also "Christian Center of Detroit Michigan," n.d., 3; Joseph Campau, "Baptist Christian Center," November 1939,

1; and "Baptist Christian Center," n.d., 1, United Community Services—Central Files Collection (Box 7, Folder I), Archives of Labor and Urban Affairs, Wayne State University, Detroit, Michigan.

32. Few of Bradby's sermons have survived. Although the aforementioned sermon titles are cited, the actual content of each sermon was not found among archive materials at Second Baptist Church or the Bentley Historical Library; "Pastor To Initiate A Series of Vital Addresses," May 5, 1929, Second Baptist Papers (Box 5, Reel 10), Michigan Historical Collection, Bentley Historical Library, University of Michigan, Ann Arbor.

33. Wolcott, *Remaking Respectability*, 67–68.

34. "When the Going Is Hard," *Second Baptist Herald*, September 20, 1931, Accession 572, Ford Motor Company Policies 12.7.3, Ford Papers (Box 28), Henry Ford Museum and Greenfield Village Research Center, Dearborn, Michigan.

35. Lillian E. Johnson, "Reminiscences," typescript, March 2, 1928, Detroit Study Club Collection (Box 2), Burton Historical Collection, Detroit Public Library, Detroit, Michigan.

36. Detroit Study Club Thirtieth Anniversary 1898–1928," Detroit Study Club Collection (Box 2), Burton Historical Collection, Detroit Public Library, Detroit, Michigan.

37. "Detroit Study Club Thirtieth Anniversary 1898–1928," Detroit Study Club Collection; Wolcott, *Remaking Respectability*, 151.

38. Frances Welker, "The History of the Detroit Study Club," February 21, 1928, Detroit Study Club Collection (Box 2), Burton Historical Collection, Detroit Public Library, Detroit, Michigan. See also Wolcott, *Remaking Respectability*, 44–45.

39. Lillian E. Johnson, "The Founding," typescript, March 19, 1938, Detroit Study Club Collection (Box 2), Burton Historical Library, Detroit Public Library, Detroit, Michigan; Lillian Johnson, Fortieth Anniversary Speech, March 18, 1938, 2, Detroit Study Club Collection (Box 2), Burton Historical Collection, Detroit Public Library, Detroit, Michigan.

40. Wolcott, *Remaking Respectability*, 151.

41. "Scrap Book, History of Earnest Worker's Club of Second Baptist Church, 1908–1946, Second Baptist Collection, Second Baptist Church, Detroit, Michigan; Mary E. Glenn, "Mary E. Glenn," Glenn Papers (Box 10), Burton Historical Collection, Detroit Public Library, Detroit, Michigan.

42. Mary E. Glenn, "Mary E. Glenn," Glenn Papers (Box 10), Burton Historical Collection, Detroit Public Library, Detroit, Michigan.

43. The Association for the Study of Negro Life and History, founded in 1915, changed its name to Association for the Study of Afro-American Life and History in 1972. Today the organization is known as the Association for the Study of African American Life and History.

44. "Sign Up Sheet for Attending the Association for the Study of Negro Life and History at Second Baptist Church," February 8–15, 1948, Glenn Papers (Box 16), Burton Historical Collection, Detroit Public Library, Detroit, Michigan; "Memorandum—Lorenzo J. Greene," Glenn Papers (Box 17), Burton Historical Collection, Detroit Public Library, Detroit, Michigan.

45. Carter G. Woodson to Mary Etta Glenn, February 1, 1938, Glenn Papers (Box 16), Burton Historical Collection, Detroit Public Library, Detroit, Michigan.

46. Mary Etta Glenn to Robert L. Bradby, October 15, 1943, Glenn Papers (Box 16), Burton Historical Collection, Detroit Public Library, Detroit, Michigan.
47. Higginbotham, *Righteous Discontent,* 100 and 145.
48. "Minutes of the Seventh Annual Session of the Women's Division of the Metropolitan Baptist Association held with the Second Baptist Church Ypsilanti, Michigan," July 7–10, 1926, 17, Second Baptist Church Papers, Michigan Historical Collection, Bentley Historical Library, University of Michigan, Ann Arbor.
49. Minutes of the Seventh Annual Session of the Women's Division of the Metropolitan Baptist Association held with the Second Baptist Church Ypsilanti, Michigan," July 7–10, 1926, 25, Second Baptist Church Papers, Michigan Historical Collection, Bentley Historical Library, University of Michigan, Ann Arbor.
50. Higginbotham, "Religion, Politics, and Gender," 146.
51. Minutes of the Seventh Annual Session of the Women's Division of the Metropolitan Baptist Association held with the Second Baptist Church Ypsilanti, Michigan," July 7–10, 1926, 27, Second Baptist Church Papers, Michigan Historical Collection, Bentley Historical Library, University of Michigan, Ann Arbor.
52. "Minutes of the Seventh Annual Session of the Women's Division of the Metropolitan Baptist Association held with the Second Baptist Church Ypsilanti, Michigan," 28.
53. "Minutes of the Seventh Annual Session of the Women's Division of the Metropolitan Baptist Association held with the Second Baptist Church Ypsilanti, Michigan."
54. Pierre Bourdieu, *Masculine Domination,* trans. Richard Nice (Stanford, CA: Stanford University Press, 2001), 1.
55. Ibid., 1–2.
56. Robert L. Bradby, "Editorial," *Second Baptist Herald,* August 4, 1929, Second Baptist Church Papers (Box 4, Reel 10), Michigan Historical Collection, Bentley Historical Library, University of Michigan, Ann Arbor.
57. Leach, *The Second Baptist Connection,* 68; Darlene Clark Hine, *When the Truth Is Told: A History of Black Women's Culture and Community in Indiana, 1875–1950,* Nation Council of Negro Women, Indiana Section, 1981, 21; Collier-Thomas, *Jesus, Jobs, and Justice,* xxx.

CHAPTER 4

1. Robert L. Bradby to C. E. Sorensen, August 4, 1930, Benson Ford Research Center (Accession 572, Box 28), Dearborn, Michigan.
2. Robert L. Bradby to C. E. Sorensen, April 22, 1929, Benson Ford Research Center (Accession 572, Box 28), Dearborn, Michigan.
3. Georgios Paris Loizides, "'Making Men' at Ford: Ethnicity, Race, and Americanization during the Progressive Period," *Michigan Sociological Review* 21 (Fall 2007): 110.
4. Ibid.
5. Douglas Brinkley, *Wheels for the World: Henry Ford, His Company, and a Century of Progress, 1903–2003* (New York: Penguin, 2004), 276.
6. Ibid.
7. Ibid.
8. Loizides, "Making Men," 113.
9. Ibid.

10. Robert E. Park and Ernest W. Burgess, *Introduction to the Science of Sociology* (1921; Chicago: University of Chicago Press, 1969), 139; Paul Reinsch, "The Negro Race and European Civilization," *American Journal of Sociology* 11, no. 2 (1905): 149, 151, and 156; Loizides, "Making Men," 113.

11. Robert Lacey, *Ford: The Men and the Machine* (Boston: Little, Brown, 1986), 222; Labor-Policies-Promotion of Jews, Benson Ford Research Center (Accession 940, Box 16), Dearborn, Michigan.

12. David L. Lewis, *The Public Image of Henry Ford: An American Folk Hero and His Company* (Detroit: Wayne State University Press, 1987), 11.

13. Ford's parents were extremely liberal in their views and therefore had no influence on Ford's known anti-Semitic views. Ford's racist views were formed, in part, by "anti-Semitic passages that appeared with great frequency in the *McGuffey Eclectic Readers* he was weaned on." Brinkley, *Wheels for the World*, 9–10, 137.

14. Robert R. Morton to Charles E. Sorensen, March 20, 1935, Benson Ford Research Center (Accession 572, Box 28), Dearborn, Michigan; William Jay Schieffelin to Charles E. Sorensen, September 5, 1935, Benson Ford Research Center (Accession 572, Box 28), Dearborn, Michigan; "Ford saw to it that African-Americans and whites worked side by side and that all were paid the same wages for the same job," Benson Ford Research Center (Accession 935, File: African American Workers), Dearborn, Michigan.

15. Lewis, *The Public Image of Henry Ford*, 135 and 137.

16. Victoria Saker Woeste, "Insecure Equality: Louis Marshall, Henry Ford, and the Problem of Defamatory Antisemitism, 1920–1929," *Journal of American History* 91, no. 3 (2004): 883.

17. Ibid.

18. Lewis, *The Public Image of Henry Ford*, 138.

19. Robert S. Wistrich, *Routledge Who's Who in Nazi Germany*, rev. ed. of *Who's Who in Nazi Germany* (New York: Routledge, 1995), 222.

20. The *Dearborn Independent* drew six hundred thousand readers at the height of its circulation in the mid-1920s. Woeste, "Insecure Equality," 883.

21. Ibid.

22. Ibid.

23. By 1916, Ford Motor Company employed people of sixty-two nationalities, more than nine hundred disabled persons, six hundred ex-convicts, and a "number of former prostitutes." "Ford saw to it that African-Americans and whites worked side by side and that all were paid the same wages for the same job," Benson Ford Research Center (Accession 935, File: African American Workers), Dearborn, Michigan.

24. Personal Notes of Henry Ford, Benson Ford Research Center (Accession 23, Box 14), Dearborn, Michigan.

25. In 1939, Henry Ford built the George Washington Carver School for black children in Richmond Hill, Georgia. "A Chronology of Information Illustrating Nondiscriminatory Policies and Practices at Ford Motor Company," Benson Ford Research Center (Accession 935, File: African American Workers), Dearborn, Michigan; "Ford saw to it that African-Americans and whites worked side by side and that all were paid the same wages for the same job," Benson Ford Research Center (Accession 935, File: African American Workers), Dearborn, Michigan; Lewis, *The Public Image of Henry Ford*, 253.

26. Beth Tompkins Bates, *Pullman Porters and the Rise of Protest Politics in Black America, 1925–1945* (Chapel Hill: University of North Carolina Press, 2001), 4.

27. Ibid.

28. Historian Angela Dillard builds on Randolph's perspective and argues that Second Baptist engaged in a "system of white patronage that was divisive within the black community and generally troublesome for the labor-civil rights community as a whole." Dillard, *Faith in the City*, 64.

29. Thomas, *Life for Us Is What We Make It*, 272.

30. David Lewis, "During the 1920s and 30s the percentage of African-Americans employed at Ford exceeded the ratio of Detroit's black population," 29, V. F. African American Workers, Benson Ford Research Center, Dearborn, Michigan.

31. Thomas, *Life for Us Is What We Make It*, 272; Lewis, "During the 1920s and 30s."

32. Bates, *Pullman Porters and the Rise of Protest Politics in Black America*, 32.

33. In 1914, Ford's Five Dollar a Day Plan privileged married workers, workers with dependents, older workers, and those who could maintain sobriety. Although most blacks were hired after the termination of the Five Dollar a Day Plan in 1922, black workers continued to seek employment at Ford, many being employed at a steady pace. By 1937, 9,825 out of 84,096 workers in Detroit were employed by Ford. By 1940, the Ford Motor Company employed 11.5 percent of black workers out of its total working population, indicating that nearly half of Detroit's black male working class was on the Ford payroll. "A Chronology of Information Illustrating Nondiscriminatory Policies and Practices at Ford Motor Company," Benson Ford Research Center (Accession 935, File: African American Workers), Dearborn, Michigan.

34. Thomas N. Maloney and Warren C. Whatley, "Making the Effort: The Contours of Racial Discrimination in Detroit's Labor Markets, 1920–1940," *Journal of Economic History* 55, no. 3 (1995): 478; see also Stephen Meyer, *The Five Dollar Day: Labor Management and Social Control in the Ford Motor Company, 1908–1921* (Albany: State University of New York Press, 1981), 6; "A Chronology of Information Illustrating Nondiscriminatory Policies and Practices at Ford Motor Company," Benson Ford Research Center (Accession 935, File: African American Workers), Dearborn, Michigan.

35. Lloyd H. Bailer, "Negro Labor in the Automobile Industry" (PhD diss., University of Michigan, 1943), 29.

36. Ibid., 31–32.

37. John L. Dancy served as director of the Detroit Urban League from 1918 to 1960; see Boyle, *Arc of Justice*, 365; and "John L. Dancy Papers," Michigan Historical Collection, Bentley Historical Library, University of Michigan, Ann Arbor.

38. "Detroit Urban League on Urban Conditions among Negroes—1918 Leaflet from EAD Files," Benson Ford Research Center (Accession 572, Box 28), Dearborn, Michigan.

39. "Detroit Urban League on Urban Conditions Among Negroes—1918 Leaflet from EAD Files."

40. David L. Lewis, "History of Negro Employment in Detroit Area Plants of Ford Motor Company, 1914–1941" (PhD diss., University of Michigan, 1954), 16, found in Benson Ford Research Center (Accession 423, File: African American Workers), Dearborn, Michigan; "A Chronology of Information Illustrating Nondiscriminatory Policies and Practices at Ford Motor Company," Benson Ford

Research Center (Accession 935, File: African American Workers), Dearborn, Michigan.

41. August Meier and Elliot Rudwick, *Black Detroit and the Rise of the UAW* (New York: Oxford University Press, 1979), 9–10. See also Allan Nevins and Frank E. Hill, *Ford: Expansion and Challenge, 1915–1933* (New York: Charles Scribner's Sons, 1957), 15.

42. Martin, *Detroit and the Great Migration*, 17; Glenn E. Carlson, "The Negro in the Industries of Detroit" (PhD diss., University of Michigan, 1929), 142–43; and Bailer, "Negro Labor in the Automobile Industry," 78.

43. Meier and Rudwick, *Black Detroit and the Rise of the UAW*, 9–10; "Remarks by R. L. Bradby," September 28, 1931, Second Baptist Church Papers (Reel 3), Michigan Historical Collection, Bentley Historical Library, University of Michigan, Ann Arbor.

44. Leach, *The Second Baptist Connection*, 69; Leach and Gamble, *Second Baptist Church Eyewitness History*, 46, Second Baptist Church Papers (Reel 3); "Ford saw to it that African-Americans and whites worked side by side and that all were paid the same wages for the same job," Benson Ford Research Center (Accession 935, File: African American Workers), Dearborn, Michigan; Lewis, "History of Negro Employment in Detroit Area Plants of Ford Motor Company, 1914–1941," 18.

45. Thomas, *Life for Us Is What We Make It*, 273.

46. Lewis, "History of Negro Employment in Detroit Area Plants of Ford Motor Company, 1914–1941," 18.

47. Nathaniel Leach, interview by Julia Marie Robinson, Detroit, Michigan, April 18, 2001.

48. Historian Elizabeth Anne Martin writes that Bradby's recommendation was "considered tantamount to securing a Ford Job." Martin, *Detroit and the Great Migration*, 21.

49. Lewis, "History of Negro Employment in Detroit Area Plants of Ford Motor Company, 1914–1941," 12–14.

50. William Perry, hired prior to Price, was sponsored by Ford himself and remained on the Ford payroll until his death. Ibid.

51. "Horace L. Sheffield," *Detroit News*, July 2, 1964, papers of Henry Ford, V. R. African American Workers, Henry Ford Museum and Greenfield Village Research Center, Dearborn, Michigan.

52. *Second Baptist Herald* 12, no. 1 (1929), Second Baptist Historical Collection, Second Baptist Church, Detroit, Michigan.

53. "Horace L. Sheffield," *Detroit News*, July 2, 1964, Papers of Henry Ford, V. R. African American Workers, Henry Ford Museum & Greenfield Village Research Center, Dearborn, Michigan.

54. Robert L. Bradby to C. E. Sorensen, General Manager of Ford Motor Company, December 8, 1931, Papers of Henry Ford (Accession 285, Box 1274–12BRAA–BRADF), Henry Ford Museum and Greenfield Village Research Center, Dearborn, Michigan.

55. Bailer, "Negro Labor in the Automobile Industry," 155.

56. Lewis, "History of Negro Employment in Detroit Area Plants of Ford Motor Company, 1914–1941," 21 and 35.

57. Bailer, "Negro Labor in the Automobile Industry," 113; Levine, *Internal Combustion*, 98; Robert L. Bradby to Donald Marshall, Special Investigator in Personnel Department, November 20, 1931, Second Baptist Collection, Second Baptist Church, Detroit, Michigan; and Shelly, "Bradby's Baptist: Second Baptist Church of Detroit, 1910–1946," 17.

58. Robert L. Bradby to Charles E. Sorensen, June 7, 1929; Robert L. Bradby to Charles E. Sorensen, October 14, 1937; Charles E. Sorensen to Robert L. Bradby, October 5, 1937, Benson Ford Research Center (Accession 38, Box 125), Dearborn, Michigan.

59. Robert L. Bradby to Charles E. Sorensen, April 25, 1934, Benson Ford Research Center (Accession 572, Box 28), Dearborn, Michigan.

60. Charles. E. Sorensen to Robert L. Bradby, April 27, 1934, Benson Ford Research Center (Accession 572, Box 28), Dearborn, Michigan.; Robert L. Bradby to Donald Marshall, November 20, 1931, Second Baptist Papers (Reel 3), Michigan Historical Collection, Bentley Historical Library, University of Michigan, Ann Arbor.

61. Thomas H. Jairison to Robert L. Bradby, May 1, 1932, Second Baptist Church Papers (Box 2, Reel 3), Michigan Historical Collection, Bentley Historical Library, University of Michigan, Ann Arbor.

62. Thomas further notes that "among all the contributions Ford made to the social and economic well being of the black community, nothing excelled his assistance to blacks in Inkster during the Great Depression." Thomas, *Life for Us Is What We Make It*, 274.

63. Robert L. Bradby to Donald Marshall, May 3, 1932, Second Baptist Church Papers (Box 2, Reel 3), Michigan Historical Collection, Bentley Historical Library, University of Michigan, Ann Arbor.

64. "A Chronology of Information Illustrating Nondiscriminatory Policies and Practices at Ford Motor Company," Benson Ford Research Center (Accession 935, File: African American Workers), Dearborn, Michigan; Robert L. Bradby to Charles E. Sorensen, 1931, Benson Ford Research Center (Accession 572, Box 28), Dearborn, Michigan; Robert L. Bradby to C. J. Winniegar, May 26, 1931, Second Baptist Collection, Second Baptist Church, Detroit, Michigan.

65. Robert L. Bradby to C. J. Winniegar, May 26, 1931; Sernett, *Bound for the Promised Land*, 148.

66. Robert L. Bradby to Charles E. Sorensen, September 15, 1930, Benson Ford Research Center (Accession 572, Box 28), Dearborn, Michigan.

67. Charles E. Sorensen to Henry Ford, 1931, Benson Ford Research Center (Accession 572, Box 28), Dearborn, Michigan.

68. "Departmental Communication," December 31, 1930 and October 7, 1930, Papers of Henry Ford, Benson Ford Research Center Accession 572, Box 28-FMC Policies # 12.7.3, Dearborn, Michigan.

69. On some occasions, Ford did charge Bradby for coal deliveries to Second Baptist, but at a cheaper price. Robert L. Bradby to Charles E. Sorensen, October 8, 1930, Benson Ford Research Center (Accession 572, Box 28), Dearborn, Michigan; Charles E. Sorensen, October 20, 1931, Benson Ford Research Center (Accession 38, Box 118), Dearborn, Michigan.

70. Robert L. Bradby to Charles E. Sorensen, April 25, 1934, Benson Ford Research Center (Accession 572, Box 28), Dearborn, Michigan.

71. Charles E. Sorensen to Robert L. Bradby, November 2, 1925, in "15th Anniversary Souvenir Program," 38, Second Baptist Church Papers (Box 2, Reel 3), Michigan Historical Collection, Bentley Historical Library, University of Michigan, Ann Arbor.

72. Nevins and Hill, *Ford: Expansion and Challenge*, 540.

73. Brinkley, *Wheels for the World*, 427–28; "Henry Ford and the Negro," *Michigan Chronicle*, November 9, 1963, V. F. African American Workers, Benson Ford Research Center, Dearborn, Michigan; Dillard, *Faith in the City*, 67.

74. "Henry Ford and the Negro," *Michigan Chronicle*, November 9, 1963, V. F. African American Workers, Benson Ford Research Center, Dearborn, Michigan.

75. Leach, *The Second Baptist Connection*, 37.

76. Miles, "Home at Last," 81.

77. Detroit historian Steve Babson notes, "Ford Sr. subsidized several black churches, including St. Matthew's (for whom he built a parish house)." Steve Babson, *Working Detroit: The Making of a Union Town* (Detroit: Wayne State University Press, 1986), 42.

78. Charles Denby [Matthew Ward], *Indignant Heart: A Black Worker's Journal* (Detroit: Wayne State University Press, 1989), 35–36.

79. "The Negro in Detroit," Report Prepared for the Mayor's Inter-Racial Committee by Special Survey Staff under the General Direction of the Detroit Bureau of Government Research, Section III (Detroit, Michigan, 1926).

80. "Employers also used stereotypes as an excuse to place blacks in the hottest jobs." Martin, *Detroit and the Great Migration*, 16.

81. Herman Feldman, *Racial Factors in American Industry*, based on a Bruno Lasker study (New York: Harper, 1931), 43.

82. Ibid., 62 and 68. For the report given by Louis I. Dublin and Robert J. Vane Jr., see Louis I. Dublin and Robert J. Vane Jr., *Causes of Death by Occupation*, US Bureau of Labor Statistics, R. 507 (1930), 49–50; Bailer, "Negro Labor in the Automobile Industry," 62 and 68.

83. Thomas, *Life for Us Is What We Make It*, 274.

84. Dock Hornbuckle to Robert L. Bradby, April 1, 1930, Second Baptist Church Papers (Box 2, Reel 3), Michigan Historical Collection, Bentley Historical Library, University of Michigan, Ann Arbor.

85. Maloney and Whatley, "Making the Effort," 489.

86. Ibid.; Nevins and Hill, *Ford: Expansion and Challenge*, 561–63.

87. "Top Negro Machinist Developed By Ford Co.," *Michigan Chronicle*, December 7, 1963, Benson Ford Research Center (Accession 935, File: African American Workers), Dearborn, Michigan; "A Chronology of Information Illustrating Non-discriminatory Policies and Practices at Ford Motor Company," Benson Ford Research Center (Accession 935, file: African American Workers), Dearborn, Michigan. For other information concerning the Ford Trade School see S. Gaft, "The History of the Henry Ford Trade School, 1916–1953" (PhD diss., University of Michigan, 1998).

88. "A Chronology of Information Illustrating Nondiscriminatory Policies and Practices at Ford Motor Company," accession 935, file: African American Workers.

89. Charles Voorhess, "The Reminiscences of Mr. Charles Voorhess, Vol. II (November 1952), Ford Motor Company Archives Oral History Section (Accession 65), Ford Benson Research Center, Dearborn, Michigan.

90. Tom Phillips, "The Reminiscences of Mr. Charles Voorhess," Vol. II (November 1951), Ford Motor Company Archives Oral History Section (Accession 65), Ford Benson Research Center, Dearborn, Michigan.

91. "A Chronology of Information Illustrating Nondiscriminatory Policies and Practices at Ford Motor Company," Benson Ford Research Center (Accession 935, file: African American Workers), Dearborn, Michigan; Maloney and Whatley, "Making the Effort," 466.

92. Babson, *Working Detroit*, 44–45.

93. Christopher C. Alston, *Henry Ford and the Negro People*, Issued by the National Negro Congress and the Michigan Negro Congress, 6, V. F. African American Workers, Benson Ford Research Center , Dearborn, Michigan.

94. Bates, *The Making of Black Detroit in the Age of Henry Ford*, 8.

95. "Remarks by R. L. Bradby," September 28, 1931, Second Baptist Church Papers (Box 2, Reel 3), Michigan Historical Collection, Bentley Historical Library, University of Michigan, Ann Arbor.

96. A. Friend to Robert L. Bradby, 1931, Benson Ford Research Center (Accession 572, Box 28), Dearborn, Michigan; Robert L. Bradby to Charles E. Sorensen, 17 November 1931, Benson Ford Research Center (Accession 572, Box 28), Dearborn, Michigan; Robert L. Bradby to Mayor Frank Murphy, 17 November 1931, Second Baptist Church Papers (Box 2, Reel 3), Michigan Historical Collection, Bentley Historical Library, University of Michigan, Ann Arbor.

97. Robert L. Bradby to Donald Marshall, November 20, 1931, Second Baptist Church Papers (Box 2, Reel 3), Michigan Historical Collection, Bentley Historical Library, University of Michigan, Ann Arbor.

98. Robert L. Bradby to Donald Marshall, November 20, 1931.

99. Dillard, *Faith in the City*, 67.

100. "Remarks by R. L. Bradby," September 28, 1931, Second Baptist Church Papers (Reel 3), Michigan Historical Collection, Bentley Historical Library, University of Michigan, Ann Arbor; Shelly, "Bradby's Baptist: Second Baptist Church of Detroit, 1910–1946," 1–33.

101. Dillard, *Faith in the City*, 70; Horace A. White, "Who Owns the Negro Churches?" *Christian Century* 55, no. 6 (1938): 177.

102. Dillard, *Faith in the City*, 51, 68, and 69.

103. "The city government employed 2,745 African Americans in 1926, including 486 in the Post Office and 2,200 in the Department of Public Works, most of whom worked as street-cleaners or did minor repair work."

104. White, "Who Owns the Negro Churches?," 176–77.

105. Thomas, *Life for Us Is What We Make It*, 279 and 276.

106. Leach, *The Second Baptist Connection*, 40.

107. Moon, *Untold Tales, Unsung Heroes*, 97.

108. White, "Who Owns the Negro Churches?," 177.

109. Leach, *The Second Baptist Connection*, 40.

110. Christopher C. Alston, *Henry Ford and the Negro People*, Issued by the National Negro Congress and the Michigan Negro Congress, 14, V. F. African American Workers, Benson Ford Research Center, Dearborn, Michigan.

111. Dillard, *Faith in the City*, 68.

112. Ibid.

113. The Battle of the Overpass took place in May of 1937 when UAW organizers Robert Kantor, Walter Reuther, Richard Frankensteen, and J. J. Kennedy were severely beaten at the Ford Service Department. The Chrysler Motor Company strike in 1939 occurred on October 6 of that year when the company fired several stewards from the Dodge Main body plant, leading to a "lock-out" and strike. During this strike, African American leaders Reverend Horace White, Senator Charles Diggs Sr., Reverend Charles Hill, and Louis Martin were principle figures connected with this action. Leach, *The Second Baptist Connection*, 40; Thomas, *Life for Us Is What We Make It*, 293; and Babson, *Working Detroit*, 92–101.

114. "Banquet Brochure" 1941, Second Baptist Historical Collection, Second Baptist Church, Detroit, Michigan.

115. Thomas, *Life for Us Is What We Make It*, 293.

116. Ibid.; Meier and Rudwick, *Black Detroit and the Rise of the UAW*, 85.

117. African Americans who were hired during strikes were typically "discharged as soon as white workers were available for work"; Lewis, "History of Negro Employment in Detroit Area Plants of Ford Motor Company, 1914–1941," 3.

118. Meier and Rudwick, *Black Detroit and the Rise of the UAW*, 94 and 102.

119. Ibid., 138.

120. Ibid., 147.

121. Ibid., 119.

CHAPTER 5

1. Susan Curtis, *A Consuming Faith: The Social Gospel and Modern Culture* (Baltimore: Johns Hopkins University Press, 1991), 130.

2. Ibid.

3. Ibid.

4. Father Robert W. Bagnall was pastor of St. Matthew's Episcopal Church in Detroit. In January 1921, he began working with the NAACP in New York.

5. Walter White to R. L. Bradby, March 4, 1925, Papers of the NAACP, 1913–1939 (Reel 12, Part 12), text-film.

6. "Detroit N.A.A.C.P. Reorganized Rev. Robert L. Bradby, New President—Immediate Release," March 6, 1925, Papers of the NAACP, 1913–1939 (Reel 12, Part 12), text-film.

7. Robert W. Bagnall to Rev. R. L. Bradby, July 27, 1926, Papers of the NAACP, 1913–1939 (Reel 12, Part II), text-film.

8. For more on this case, see Boyle, *Arc of Justice*, 120; W. Hayes McKinney to Walter White, April 20, 1921, Papers of the NAACP, 1913–1939 (Reel 11, Part 12), text-film.

9. W. Hayes McKinney to Walter White, April 20, 1921, Papers of the NAACP, 1913–1939 (Reel 11, Part 12), text-film.

10. Walter White to Rev. Robert L. Bradby, April 22, 1921, Papers of the NAACP, 1913–1939 (Reel 11, Part 12), text-film.

11. Walter White to W. Hayes McKinney, May 6, 1921, Papers of the NAACP, 1913–1939 (Reel 11, Part 12), text-film.

12. Lillian E. Johnson, "Report of Detroit, Michigan Branch To Branch Bulletin," June 8, 1921, Papers of the NAACP, 1913–1939 (Reel 11, Part 12), text-film.

13. Lillian E. Johnson to Secretary—N.A.A.C.P, September 23, 1921, Papers of the NAACP, 1913–1939 (Reel 11, Part 12), text-film.
14. Robert W. Bagnall to Rev. R. L. Bradby, July 12, 1922, Papers of the NAACP, 1913–1939 (Reel 11, Part 12), text-film.
15. Gary Marx, "Religion: Opiate or Inspiration of Civil Rights Militancy?" in *The Black Church in America*, ed. Hart Nelson, Raytha Yokley, and Anne Nelsen (New York: Basic Books, 1971), 150–60.
16. Robert L. Bradby to Mr. R. M. Bagnall, March 26, 1925, Papers of the NAACP 1913–1939 (Reel 12, Part 12), text-film.
17. Arthur G. C. Randall, Colonel, to Mr. Robert W. Bagnall, April 26, 1925, Papers of the NAACP 1913–1939 (Reel 12, Part 12), text-film.
18. "Baby Contest," *Detroit Independent*, April 10, 1925, Papers of the NAACP 1913–1939 (Reel 12, Part 12), text-film.
19. "Report of Baby Contest for NAACP," May 4, 1925, Papers of the NAACP 1913–1939 (Reel 12, Part 12), text-film.
20. "N.A.A.C.P. Takes Up Swimming Pool Discrimination," *Detroit Independent*, April 3, 1925, Papers of the NAACP 1913–1939 (Reel 12, Part 12), text-film.
21. "Our Recent Legal Achievements," *Detroit Independent*, May 30, 1925, Papers of the NAACP 1913–1939 (Reel 12, Part 12), text-film.
22. James Weldon Johnson to Hon. Ira W. Jayne, July 22, 1925; James Weldon Johnson to Rev. R. L. Bradby, July 30, 1925; Robert L. Bradby to James Weldon Johnson, July 28 1925, Papers of the NAACP 1913–1939 (Reel 12, Part 12), text-film.
23. "Report of Baby Contest for N.A.A.C.P.," April 29, 1925, Papers of the NAACP 1913–1939 (Reel 12, Part 12), text-film.
24. James Weldon Johnson to Hon. Ira W. Jayne, June 10, 1925, Papers of the NAACP 1913–1939 (Reel 12, Part 12), text-film.
25. Ira W. Jayne to James Weldon Johnson, June 15, 1925, Papers of the NAACP 1913–1939 (Reel 12, Part 12), text-film.
26. Boyle, *Arc of Justice*, 105.
27. James Weldon Johnson to Rev. R. L. Bradby, July 22, 1925, Papers of the NAACP 1913–1939 (Reel 12, Part 12), text-film.
28. R. L. Bradby to James Weldon Johnson, July 27, 1925, Papers of the NAACP 1913–1939 (Reel 12, Part 12), text-film.
29. R. L. Bradby to James Weldon Johnson, July 27, 1925, Papers of the NAACP 1913–1939 (Reel 12, Part 12), text-film; Boyle, *Arc of Justice*, 145.
30. Boyle, *Arc of Justice*, 115.
31. Walter White to James Weldon Johnson, September 16, 1925, Papers of the NAACP 1913–1939 (Reel 2, Part 5), text-film.
32. R. L. Bradby to William Pickens, July 31, 1925, Papers of the NAACP 1913–1939 (Reel 12, Part 5), text-film.
33. "Cosmopolitan League," Papers of the NAACP 1913–1939 (Reel 2, Part 5), text-film.
34. Vine, *One Man's Castle*, 115–19.
35. "Detroit Race Riot Kills One," *Evening Post*, New York City (September 10, 1925), Papers of the NAACP 1913–1939 (Reel 2, Part 5), text-film.
36. John Weldon Johnson to Rev. R. L. Bradby, "Western Union Telegram," September 11, 1925, Papers of the NAACP 1913–1939 (Reel 2, Part 5), text-film.

37. W. Hayes McKinney to James Weldon Johnson, September 12 1925, Papers of the NAACP 1913–1939 (Reel 2, Part 5), text-film.

38. W. Hayes McKinney to James Weldon Johnson.

39. "Mass meeting 3 p.m. tomorrow . . . Suggestions appreciated"; W. Hayes McKinney to James Weldon Johnson, "Western Union Telegram," September 12 1925, Papers of the NAACP 1913–1939 (Reel 2, Part 5), text-film.

40. "On the Test Up in Detroit Clash Trial: Ten Negroes Must Face Murder Trial for Shooting Whites in Fight to Protect Home," *St. Louis Argus*, Saint Louis, Missouri, September 18, 1925, Papers of the NAACP 1913–1939 (Reel 2, Part 5), text-film.

41. "On the Test Up in Detroit Clash Trial: Ten Negroes Must Face Murder Trial for Shooting Whites in Fight to Protect Home," *St. Louis Argus*, Saint Louis, Missouri, September 18, 1925, Papers of the NAACP 1913–1939 (Reel 2, Part 5), text-film; Walter White to James Weldon Johnson, September 16, 1925, Papers of the NAACP 1913–1939 (Reel 12, Part 5), text-film.

42. M. L. Walker to Walter White, September 18, 1925, Papers of the NAACP 1913–1939 (Reel 12, Part 5), text-film.

43. Moses L. Walker was also the secretary for the National Association United States Customs Inspectors of the Detroit, Michigan, Branch. M. L. Walker to Walter White, September 22, 1925, Papers of the NAACP 1913–1939 (Reel 12, Part 5), text-film.

44. Walter White to James Weldon Johnson, September 16, 1925, Papers of the NAACP 1913–1939 (Reel 12, Part 5), text-film. For more information on the lawyers connected with the Sweet case, see Vine, *One Man's Castle*; and Boyle, *Arc of Justice*.

45. "Mass Meeting at St. John C.M.E. Church, Interest of Sweet Fund: Large and Enthusiastic Crowd at Second Baptist Church Last Sunday," *Detroit Independent*, Detroit, Michigan, September 25, 1925, Papers of the NAACP 1913–1939 (Reel 12, Part 5), text-film.

46. "Mass Meeting at St. John C.M.E. Church, Interest of Sweet Fund: Large and Enthusiastic Crowd at Second Baptist Church Last Sunday," *Detroit Independent*, Detroit, Michigan, September 25, 1925; "City Wide Committee for Sweet Fund Is Organized," *Detroit Independent*, Detroit, Michigan, October 2 1925, Papers of the NAACP 1913–1939 (Reel 2, Part 5), text-film.

47. Walter White to Robert L. Bradby, "Western Union Telegram," September 19, 1925, Papers of the NAACP 1913–1939 (Reel 2, Part 5), text-film.

48. "City Wide Committee for Sweet Fund Is Organized," *Detroit Independent*, Detroit, Michigan, October 2, 1925, Papers of the NAACP 1913–1939 (Reel 2, Part 5), text-film.

49. "A.M.E. Ministers Pledge to Support Sweet Case," *Detroit Independent*, Detroit, Michigan, October 2, 1925, Papers of the NAACP 1913–1939 (Reel 2, Part 5), text-film.

50. Walter White to Rev. Robert L. Bradby, "Western Union Telegram," September 21, 1925, Papers of the NAACP 1913–1939 (Reel 2, Part 5), text-film.

51. "N.A.A.C.P. Holds Another Successful Meeting for Sweet Fund at St. John's C.M.E. Church," *Detroit Independent*, October 2, 1925, Papers of the NAACP 1913–1939 (Reel 2, Part 5), text-film.

52. Miles, "Home at Last," 167; see also Record of Detroit Election Commission, 1920–1975, Old City County Building, Detroit, Michigan.

53. Miles, "Home at Last."

54. Walter White to Judge Ira W. Jayne, "Western Union Telegram," October 1, 1925, Papers of the NAACP 1913–1939 (Reel 2, Part 5), text-film.

55. Gabrielle Bradby-Green, "One Drop Rule," interview, March 8, 2003, by Julia Marie Robinson.

56. "Famous Criminal Lawyer to Be Associated with Arthur Garfield and Other Noted Lawyers in Effort to Clear Detroit Physician and 10 Others of Homicide Charge," *Washington Daily American*, Washington, DC, October 19, 1925, Papers of the NAACP 1913–1939 (Reel 2, Part 5), text-film.

57. Other newspapers that marked this historic move by the NAACP were the *St. Louis Argus*, Saint Louis, Missouri, October 30, 1925; the *Detroit Independent*, Detroit, Michigan, October 23, 1925; and *The World*, New York City, October 30, 1925, Papers of the NAACP 1913–1939 (Reel 2, Part 5), text-film.

58. Vine, *One Man's Castle*, 238.

59. "Case to the Supreme Court: New Picture of Scottsboro Boys," *Detroit Tribune*, April 14, 1933; *Detroit Tribune*, April 14, 1933–December 25, 1933, microfilm 605, Burton Collection, Detroit Public Library, Detroit, Michigan.

60. Dan T. Carter, *Scottsboro: A Tragedy of the American South* (Baton Rouge: Louisiana State University Press, 2007), 162–63.

61. Hugh T. Murray Jr., "The NAACP versus the Communist Party: The Scottsboro Rape Cases, 1931–1932," *Phylon* 28, no. 3 (1967): 277–78.

62. Karl Marx, "Toward the Critique of Hegel's Philosophy of Right," in *Basic Writings on Politics and Philosophy*, by Karl Marx and Friedrich Engels, ed. Louis S. Feuer (London: Fontana, 1969), 304.

63. Ibid.

64. Murray, "The NAACP versus the Communist Party," 278.

65. Ibid.

66. Dillard, *Faith in the City*.

67. Walter White to Dr. Bradby, May 19, 1933, Series C, Papers of the NAACP 1913–1939 (Reel 13, Part 12), text-film.

68. Dillard, *Faith in the City*, 57; "Reverend Bradby Heads Defense Committee," *Detroit Tribune*, May 13, 1933, *Detroit Tribune*, April 14, 1933–December 25, 1933, Burton Collection (Microfilm 605, Part 12), Detroit Public Library, Detroit, Michigan, text-film.

69. "Local Physician Heads Defense Fund," *Detroit Tribune*, April 14, 1933, *Detroit Tribune*, April 14, 1933–December 25, 1933, Burton Collection (Microfilm 605, Part 12), Detroit Public Library, Detroit, Michigan, text-film.

70. "The Scottsboro Defense Fund," *Detroit Tribune*, April 22, 1933, *Detroit Tribune* April 14, 1933–December 25, 1933 (Microfilm 605, Part 12), Burton Collection, Detroit Public Library, Detroit, Michigan, text-film.

71. "Refuse to Turn Over Scottsboro Funds to I.L.D.," *Detroit Tribune*, June 24, 1933, *Detroit Tribune*, April 14, 1933–December 25, 1933, Burton Collection (microfilm 605, Part 12), Detroit Public Library, Detroit, Michigan, text-film.

72. M. L. Walker to Walter White, May 23, 1933, Series C, Papers of the NAACP 1913–1939 (Reel 13, Part 12), text-film.

73. Dillard, *Faith in the City*, 60–61.

74. Ibid., 61–62.

CONCLUSION

1. Reverend Robert L. Bradby in Dorothy Shadd Shreve and Alvin McGurdy, "The African Canadian Church: A Stabilizer or Blazing the Pathway in Ontario South" (unpublished diss.), 167, Chatham Historical Society—WISH Center, Chatham, Ontario.

2. Dorothy Shadd Shreve and Alvin McGurdy, "The African Canadian Church: A Stabilizer or Blazing the Pathway in Ontario South" (unpublished diss.), 99 and 167, Chatham Historical Society—WISH Center, Chatham, Ontario; "Proceedings of Grand Lodge and Jurisdiction 1891–1909, Masonic Papers, Chatham Historical Society—WISH Center, Chatham, Ontario; "Obituary of Robert L. Bradby, Sr." Rev. Robert L. Bradby Papers, Burton Collection, Detroit Public Library, Detroit, Michigan.

3. Ronald Jemal Stephens, *Idlewild: The Black Eden of Michigan* (Chicago: Arcadia, 2001), 10.

4. Ibid., 11.

5. Lewis Walker and Benjamin C. Wilson, *Black Eden: The Idlewild Community* (East Lansing: Michigan State University Press, 2002), 30 and 34.

6. Bradby bought stock in the ILOA for $25 per share; Walker and Wilson, *Black Eden*, 30.

7. Robert L. Bradby to Mr. C. D. Burbank, November 8, 1932, Second Baptist Church Papers (Reel 3, Box 2), Michigan Historical Collection, Bentley Historical Library, University of Michigan, Ann Arbor.

8. Robert L. Bradby to Rev. J. Reese Saunders, June 5, 1931, Second Baptist Church Papers (Reel 3, Box 2), Michigan Historical Collection, Bentley Historical Library, University of Michigan, Ann Arbor.

9. "Last Rites for Bradby on Friday," *Michigan Chronicle*, June 8, 1946, Rev. Robert L. Bradby Papers, Burton Collection, Detroit Public Library, Detroit, Michigan.

10. "Robert L. Bradby to Wifie, June 30, 1933," Second Baptist Church Papers (Reel 3, Box 2), Michigan Historical Collection, Bentley Historical Library, University of Michigan, Ann Arbor.

11. Robert L. Bradby, "Sounding Recording of Time with Johnson Family in Los Angeles California," Sound Recording, June 1942, Compact Disc. Angela Bradby and Gabrielle Bradby-Greene Family Historical Collection, Detroit, Michigan.

12. "Bradby Built Church by Social Service during the First World War," *Michigan Chronicle*, June 8, 1946, Rev. Robert L. Bradby Papers, Burton Collection, Detroit Public Library, Detroit, Michigan.

13. "Rev. Robt. Bradby Dies; Funeral Set for Friday," *Michigan Chronicle*, June 8, 1946, Rev. Robert L. Bradby Papers, Burton Collection, Detroit Public Library, Detroit, Michigan; "Obituary of Robert L. Bradby, Sr." Rev. Robert L. Bradby Papers, Burton Collection, Detroit Public Library, Detroit, Michigan.

14. "Obituary of Robert L. Bradby, Sr." Rev. Robert L. Bradby Papers, Burton Collection, Detroit Public Library, Detroit, Michigan.

15. "Dr. Bradby Honored by Second Baptists," *Detroit News*, November 10, 1945, Rev. Robert L. Bradby Papers, Burton Collection, Detroit Public Library, Detroit, Michigan.

16. "30th Anniversary," *Detroit News*, November 2, 1940, Rev. Robert L. Bradby Papers, Burton Collection, Detroit Public Library, Detroit, Michigan.

17. "Month's Services Honor Dr. Bradby," *Detroit News*, November 2, 1946, Rev. Robert L. Bradby Papers, Burton Collection, Detroit Public Library, Detroit, Michigan.

18. "Program of the Thirty-Third Anniversary of Dr. Robert L. Bradby, D.D. LL.D.," Second Baptist Church Papers (Reel 3, Box 2), Michigan Historical Collection, Bentley Historical Library, University of Michigan, Ann Arbor.

19. "Obituary of Robert L. Bradby, Sr.," Rev. Robert L. Bradby Papers, Burton Collection, Detroit Public Library, Detroit, Michigan.

20. "History of Elmwood Historic Cemetery," www.elmwoodhistoriccemetery.org (accessed July 30, 2012). Website detailing the historical significance of Elmwood cemetery in Detroit, Michigan.

21. "Bradby Mourned by Citizens of Motor City," *Michigan Chronicle*, June 8, 1946, Rev. Robert L. Bradby Papers, Burton Collection, Detroit Public Library, Detroit, Michigan.

22. "Bradby Mourned by Citizens of Motor City," *Michigan Chronicle*, June 8, 1946, Rev. Robert L. Bradby Papers, Burton Collection, Detroit Public Library, Detroit, Michigan; "Bradby Built Church by Social Service during First World War," *Michigan Chronicle*, June 8, 1946, Rev. Robert L. Bradby Papers, Burton Collection, Detroit Public Library, Detroit, Michigan.

23. "Robert L. Bradby Drive Dedication: Work of the Worthwhile Missionary Club," Rev. Robert L. Bradby Papers, Burton Collection, Detroit Public Library, Detroit, Michigan; Detroit's Common Council was organized in 1824 and retained its name until July 1, 1974, when it was renamed Detroit City Council; "Robert L. Bradby Drive Dedication: Work of the Worthwhile Missionary Club," Rev. Robert L. Bradby Papers, Burton Collection, Detroit Public Library, Detroit, Michigan.

BIBLIOGRAPHY

PUBLISHED SOURCES

Babson, Steve. *Working Detroit: The Making of a Union Town*. Detroit: Wayne State University Press, 1986.

Barrett, Leonard E. *Soul-Force: African Heritage in Afro-American Religion*. Garden City, NY: Anchor Press, 1974.

Bates, Beth Tompkins. *The Making of Black Detroit in the Age of Henry Ford*. Chapel Hill: University of North Carolina Press, 2012.

———. *Pullman Porters and the Rise of Protest Politics in Black America, 1925–1945*. Chapel Hill: University of North Carolina Press, 2001.

Best, Wallace D. *Passionately Human, No Less Divine: Religion and Culture in Black Chicago, 1915–1952*. Princeton, NJ: Princeton University Press, 2005.

Boesak, Allan. *Black and Reformed: Apartheid, Liberation, and the Calvinist Tradition*. Edited by Leonard Sweetman. New York: Orbis, 1986.

Bourdieu, Pierre. *Masculine Domination*. Translated by Richard Nice. Stanford, CA: Stanford University Press, 2001.

Boyle, Kevin. *Arc of Justice: A Saga of Race, Civil Rights, and Murder in the Jazz Age*. New York: Henry Holt, 2004.

Breed, Allen G. "Virginia Indians Fight to Reclaim Sovereignty." *Detroit News*, December 25, 2005, 4A.

Brinkley, Douglas. *Wheels for the World: Henry Ford, His Company, and a Century of Progress, 1903–2003*. New York: Penguin, 2004.

Brown, W. O. "Racial Inequality: Fact or Myth." *Journal of Negro History* 16, no. 1 (1931): 43–60.

Carter, Dan T. *Scottsboro: A Tragedy of the American South*. Rev. ed. Baton Rouge: Louisiana State University Press, 2007.

Collier-Thomas, Bettye. *Jesus, Jobs, and Justice: African American Women and Religion*. New York: Knopf, 2010.

Collins, Robert Keith. "Katimih o Sa Chata Klyou (Why Am I Not Choctaw)? Race in the Lived Experiences of Two Black Choctaw Mixed-Bloods." In *Crossing Waters, Crossing Worlds: The African Diaspora in Indian Country*, edited by Tiya Miles and Sharon Holland. Durham, NC: Duke University Press, 2006.

Cone, James H. *God of the Oppressed*. Rev. ed. Maryknoll, NY: Orbis, 1997.

Cronon, Edmund David. *Black Moses: The Story of Marcus Garvey and the Universal Negro Improvement Association*. Madison: University of Wisconsin Press, 1955.

Curtis, Susan. *A Consuming Faith: The Social Gospel and Modern American Culture*. Baltimore: Johns Hopkins University Press, 1991.

Denby, Charles [Matthew Ward]. *Indignant Heart: A Black Worker's Journal.* Detroit: Wayne State University Press, 1989.

Dillard, Angela. *Faith in the City: Preaching Radical Social Change in Detroit.* Ann Arbor: University of Michigan Press, 2007.

Dreisinger, Baz. *Near Black: White to Black Passing in American Culture.* Amherst: University of Massachusetts Press, 2008.

Dublin, Louis I., and Robert J. Vane Jr. *Causes of Death by Occupation.* US Bureau of Labor Statistics, R. 507 (1930).

Du Bois, W.E.B. *Darkwater: Voices from within the Veil.* 1920; New York: Dover, 1999.

———. *The Souls of Black Folk: Essays and Sketches.* London: Archibald Constable, 1905.

Feldman, Herman. *Racial Factors in American Industry.* Based on a Bruno Lasker study. New York: Harper, 1931.

Franklin, John Hope, and August Meier, eds. *Black Leaders of the Twentieth Century.* Urbana: University of Illinois Press, 1982.

Frazier, E. Franklin. *The Negro Church in America.* New York: Schocken, 1963.

Frazier, Nancy. "Rethinking the Public Sphere: A Contribution to the Critique of Actually Existing Democracy." *Social Text* 25/26 (1990): 56–80.

Gaines, Kevin. *Uplifting the Race: Black Leadership, Politics, and Culture in the Twentieth Century.* Chapel Hill: University of North Carolina Press, 1996.

Gallant, Sigrid Nicole. "Perspectives on the Motives for the Migration of African Americans to and from Ontario, Canada: From Abolition of Slavery in Canada to the Abolition of Slavery in the United States." *Journal of African American History* 86, no. 3 (2001): 391–408.

Garvey, Marcus. *The Philosophy and Opinions of Marcus Garvey; or, Africa for Africans.* The New Marcus Garvey Library, no. 9. Dover, MA: Majority Press, 1986.

Genovese, Eugene. *Roll Jordan Roll: The World the Slaves Made.* New York: Pantheon, 1974.

Gladden, Washington. *The Church and the Kingdom.* New York: Fleming H. Revell, 1894. In *Social Gospel in America, 1870–1920: Gladden, Ely Rauschenbusch,* edited by Robert T. Handy, 102–18. New York: Oxford University Press, 1966.

Gorrell, Donald K. *The Age of Social Responsibility: The Social Gospel in the Progressive Era, 1900–1920.* Macon, GA: Mercer University Press, 1988.

Grant, Colin. *Negro with a Hat: The Rise and Fall of Marcus Garvey.* New York: Oxford University Press, 2008.

Grimshaw, Allen D., ed. *Racial Violence in the United States.* Chicago: Aldine, 1969.

Harding, Vincent. *There Is a River: The Black Struggle for Freedom in America.* New York: Harcourt Brace Jovanovich, 1981.

Harris, Fredrick C. *Something Within: Religion in African-American Political Activism.* New York: Oxford University Press, 1999.

Hartgrove, W. B. "The Story of Maria Louise Moore and Fannie M. Richards." *Journal of African American History* 1, no. 1 (1916): 22–33.

Haynes, George Edmund. *Negro New-Comer in Detroit, Michigan: A Challenge to Christian Statesmanship, a Preliminary Survey.* New York: Home Mission Council, 1918.

Hickman, Christine B. "The Devil and the One Drop Rule: Racial Categories, African Americans, and the U.S. Census." *Michigan Law Review* 95, no. 5 (1997): 1161–265.

Higginbotham, Evelyn Brooks. "Religion, Politics, and Gender: The Leadership of Nannie Helen Burroughs." In *This Far by Faith: Readings in African American Women's Religious Biography*, edited by Judith Wisenfeld and Richard Newman, 140–57. New York: Routledge, 1996.

———. *Righteous Discontent: The Women's Movement in the Black Baptist Church, 1880–1920*. Cambridge, MA: Harvard University Press, 1993.

Higginbotham, Leon A. *In the Matter of Color: The Colonial Period*. New York: Oxford University Press, 1978.

Hill, Robert A. *The Marcus Garvey and Universal Negro Improvement Association Papers*. Vol. IV: *Sept. 1921–Sept. 1922*. Berkeley: University of California Press, 1986.

Hine, Darlene Clark. *Hine Sight: Black Women and the Re-Construction of American History*. Bloomington: Indiana University Press, 1994.

———. *When the Truth Is Told: A History of Black Women's Culture and Community in Indiana, 1875–1950*. National Council of Negro Women, Indiana Section, 1981.

Hofstader, Richard. *The Age of Reform*. New York: Vintage, 1955.

———. *The Progressive Movement, 1900–1915*. Englewood Cliffs, NJ: Prentice-Hall, 1963.

Holli, Melvin G., ed. *Detroit*. New York: New Viewpoints, 1976.

Hughes, Langston. *Selected Poems of Langston Hughes: A Classic Collection of Poems by a Master of American Verse*. New York: Vintage, 1959.

Ingersoll, Thomas N. *To Intermix with Our White Brothers*. Albuquerque: University of New Mexico Press, 2005.

Johnson, Kevin R., ed., *Mixed Race America and the Law: A Reader*. New York: New York University Press, 2002.

Knupfer, Anne Meis. *Toward a Tenderer Humanity and a Nobler Womanhood: African American Women's Clubs in Turn-of-the-Century Chicago*. New York: New York University Press, 1996.

Lacey, Robert. *Ford: The Men and the Machine*. Boston: Little, Brown, 1986.

Landon, Fred. "Negro Migration to Canada after the Passing of the Fugitive Slave Act." *Journal of African American History* 5, no. 1 (1920): 22–36.

Leach, Nathaniel. *The Second Baptist Connection: Reaching Out to Freedom, History of Second Baptist Church of Detroit*. Rev. ed. Eyewitness History. Detroit: Second Baptist Church, 1988.

Leach, Nathaniel, and Edith Gamble. *Eyewitness History: Second Baptist Church of Detroit, 1836–1976*. Detroit: Second Baptist Church, 1976.

Levine, David Allan. *Internal Combustion: The Races in Detroit, 1915–1926*. Westport, CT: Greenwood Press, 1976.

Lewis, David L. *The Public Image of Henry Ford: An American Folk Hero and His Company*. Detroit: Wayne State University Press, 1987.

Lewis, James Kennedy. "Religious Nature of the Early Negro Migration to Canada and the Amherstburg Baptist Association." *Ontario History* 57, no. 2 (1966): 121.

Lincoln, C. Eric, and Lawrence H. Mamiya. *The Black Church in the African American Experience*. Durham, NC: Duke University Press, 1990.

Lindley, Susan. "Neglected Voices and Praxis in the Social Gospel." *Journal of Religious Ethics* 18, no. 1 (1990): 75–102.

Loizides, Georgios Paris. "'Making Men' at Ford: Ethnicity, Race, and Americanization during the Progressive Period." *Michigan Sociological Review* 21 (Fall 2007): 109–48.

Luker, Ralph E. *The Social Gospel in Black and White: American Racial Reform, 1885–1912*. Chapel Hill: University of North Carolina Press, 1991.

Martin, Elizabeth Anne. *Detroit and the Great Migration, 1916–1929.* Ann Arbor: Bentley Historical Library, University of Michigan, 1993.

Marx, Gary. "Religion: Opiate or Inspiration of Civil Rights Militancy?" In *The Black Church in America,* edited by Hart Nelson, Raytha Yokley, and Anne Nelsen, 150–60. New York: Basic Books, 1971.

Marx, Karl. "Toward the Critique of Hegel's Philosophy of Right." In *Basic Writings on Politics and Philosophy,* by Karl Marx and Friedrich Engels, edited by Louis S. Feuer, 262–66. London: Fontana, 1969.

Matthews, Shailer. "Social Gospel." In *A Dictionary of Religion and Ethics,* edited by Shailer Matthews and Gerald Birney Smith, 416. New York: Macmillan, 1921.

Mays, Benjamin E., and Joseph W. Nicholson. "The Genius of the Negro Church." In *African American Religious History: Documentary Witness,* 2nd ed., edited by Milton C. Sernett, 423–34. Durham, NC: Duke University Press, 1999.

Mbiti, John. *African Religions and Philosophy.* 2nd ed. Oxford: Heinemann, 1990.

McMillen, Neil R. *Dark Journey: Black Mississippians in the Age of Jim Crow.* Urbana: University of Illinois Press, 1990.

Meier, August, and Elliot Rudwick. *Black Detroit and the Rise of the UAW.* New York: Oxford University Press, 1979.

Meyer, Stephen. *The Five Dollar Day: Labor Management and Social Control in the Ford Motor Company, 1908–1921.* Albany: State University of New York Press, 1981.

Micco, Melinda. "'Blood and Money': The Case of Seminole Freedmen and Seminole Indians in Oklahoma." In *Crossing Waters, Crossing Worlds: The African Diaspora in Indian Country,* edited by Tiya Miles and Sharon Patricia Holland. Durham, NC: Duke University Press, 2006.

Mitchell, Michele. *Righteous Propagation: African Americans and the Politics of Racial Destiny after Reconstruction.* Chapel Hill: University of North Carolina Press, 2004.

Moon, Elaine Latzman. *Untold Tales, Unsung Heroes: An Oral History of Detroit's African American Community, 1918–1967.* Detroit: Wayne State University Press, 1994.

Morton, Patricia. "From Invisible Man to 'New People': The Recent Discovery of American Mulattoes." *Phylon* 46, no. 2 (1985): 106–22.

Murray, Hugh T., Jr. "The NAACP versus the Communist Party: The Scottsboro Rape Cases, 1931–1932." *Phylon* 28, no. 3 (1967): 276–87.

Myers, Ched. *Binding the Strong Man: A Political Reading of Mark's Story of Jesus.* Maryknoll, NY: Orbis, 2008.

———. *Who Will Roll Away the Stone?: Discipleship Queries for First World Christians.* Maryknoll, NY: Orbis, 1994.

Nevins, Allan, and Frank Hill. *Ford: Expansion and Challenge, 1915–1933.* New York: Charles Scribner's Sons, 1957.

North, Frank Mason. "The City and the Kingdom." In *Social Ministry: An Introduction to the Study and Practice of Social Service,* edited by Harry F. Ward, 293–319. New York: Eaton and Mains, 1910.

Norton, Mary Beth, and David M Katzman, eds. *A People and a Nation: A History of The United States.* Boston: Houghton Mifflin, 1982.

Painter, Nell Irvin. *Exodusters: Black Migration to Kansas after Reconstruction.* New York: Norton, 1992.

Park, Robert E., and Ernest W. Burgess. *Introduction to the Science of Sociology.* Chicago: University of Chicago Press, 1921.

Poremba, David Lee, ed. *Detroit in Its World Setting: A Three Hundred Year Chronology, 1701–2001*. Detroit: Wayne State University Press, 2001.

Pratt, Henry. *Churches and Urban Government in Detroit and New York, 1895–1994*. Detroit: Wayne State University Press, 2004.

Raboteau, Albert J. *Slave Religion: The "Invisible Institution" in the Antebellum South*. New York: Oxford University Press, 1978.

Rauschenbusch, Walter. "Belated Races and the Social Problems." *Methodist Quarterly* (South) 62 (1914): 252–59.

———. *Christianity and Social Crisis*. New York: Macmillan, 1907.

Robinson-Harmon, Julia Marie. "Baptists." In *The Encyclopedia of the Great Black Migration*, edited by Steven A. Reich, 1: 54–57. Greenwood Milestones in African American History. Westport, CT: Greenwood Press, 2006.

Ross, Ellen. *Love and Toil: Motherhood in Outcast London, 1870–1918*. New York: Oxford University Press, 1993.

———. "Not the Sort That Would Sit on the Doorstep: Respectability in Pre–World War I London Neighborhoods." *International Labor and Working-Class History* 27 (1985): 39–59.

Rountree, Helen C. *Pocahontas's People: The Powhatan Indians of Virginia through Four Centuries*. Norman: University of Oklahoma Press, 1990.

Rowland, Christopher, and Mark Corner. *Liberating Exegesis: The Challenge of Liberation Theology to Biblical Studies*. Louisville, KY: John Knox Press, 1989.

Salvatore, Nick. *Singing in a Strange Land: C. L. Franklin, the Black Church, and the Transformation of America*. New York: Little, Brown, 2005.

Satter, Beryl. "Marcus Garvey, Father Divine, and Gender Politics of Race Difference and Race Neutrality." *American Quarterly* 48, no. 1 (1996): 43–76.

Savage, Barbara Dianne. *Your Spirits Walk beside Us: The Politics of Black Religion*. Cambridge, MA: Belknap Press of Harvard University Press, 2008.

Schechter, Patricia A. *Ida B. Wells-Barnett and American Reform, 1880–1930*. Chapel Hill: University of North Carolina Press, 2001.

Sernett, Milton C. *Bound for the Promised Land: African American Religion and the Great Migration*. Durham, NC: Duke University Press, 1997.

Sharpe, Dores Robinson. *Walter Rauschenbusch*. New York: Macmillan, 1942.

Shelly, Cara. "Bradby's Baptist: Second Baptist Church of Detroit, 1910–1946." *Michigan Historical Review* 17, no. 1 (1991): 1–33.

Stein, Judith. *The World of Marcus Garvey: Race and Class in Modern Society*. Baton Rouge: Louisiana State University Press, 1986.

Stephens, Ronald Jemal. *Idlewild: The Black Eden of Michigan*. Chicago: Arcadia, 2001.

Stern, Theodore. "Chickahominy: The Changing Culture of a Virginia Indian Community." *Proceedings of the American Philosophical Society* 96, no. 2 (1952): 157–225.

Summers, Martin. *Manliness and Its Discontents: The Black Middle Class and the Transformation of Masculinity, 1900–1930*. Chapel Hill: University of North Carolina Press, 2004.

Taylor, Clarence. *The Black Churches of Brooklyn*. New York: Columbia University Press, 1994.

———. *Black Religious Intellectuals: The Fight for Equality from Jim Crow to the Twenty-First Century*. New York: Routledge, 2002.

Thomas, Richard W. *Life for Us Is What We Make It: Building Black Community in Detroit, 1915–1945*. Bloomington: Indiana University Press, 1992.

———. *State of Black Detroit: Building from Strength, The Black Self-Help Tradition in Detroit*. Detroit: Detroit Urban League, 1987.

Tomes, Nancy. "'Destroyer and Teacher': Managing the Masses during the 1918–1919 Influenza Pandemic." In *Public Health Reports* (1974–), vol. 125, supplement 3: The 1918–1919 Influenza Pandemic in the United States (April 2010), 48–62.

Trotter, Joe William, Jr. *Black Milwaukee: The Making of an Industrial Proletariat, 1915–45*. Urbana: University of Illinois Press, 1985.

———, ed. *The Great Migration in Historical Perspective: New Dimensions of Race, Class, and Gender*. Bloomington: Indiana University Press, 1991.

Turman, Kevin. "A Word from Our Pastor . . . Rev. Kevin M. Turman." In *Second Baptist 159th Anniversary Celebration Souvenir Book*, 5. Detroit: Second Baptist Church, 1995.

Vine, Phyllis. *One Man's Castle: Clarence Darrow in Defense of the American Dream*. New York: Harper Collins, 2004.

Walker, Lewis, and Benjamin C. Wilson. *Black Eden: The Idlewild Community*. East Lansing: Michigan State University Press, 2002.

Washington, James Melvin. *Frustrated Fellowship*. Macon, GA: Mercer University Press, 1991.

Weems, Renita. "Reading Her Way through the Bible: African American Women and the Bible." In *Stony the Road We Trod: African American Biblical Interpretation*, edited by Cain Hope Felder, 57–79. Minneapolis: Fortress Press, 1991.

Weisenfeld, Judith, and Richard Newman. *This Far by Faith: Readings in African-American Women's Religious Biography*. New York: Routledge, 1996.

Wench, Julie. "James Forten, Conservative Radical." In *Black Conservatism: Essays in Intellectual and Political History*, edited by Peter Eisenstadt, 3–24. New York: Garland, 1999.

White, Horace A. "Who Owns the Negro Churches?" *Christian Century* 55, no. 6 (1938): 176–77.

White, Ronald C., Jr. *Liberty and Justice for All: Racial Reform and the Social Gospel (1877–1925)*. San Francisco: Harper and Row, 1990.

Wiebe, Robert H. *The Search for Order, 1877–1920*. New York: Hill and Wang, 1967.

Williamson, Joel. *New People: Miscegenation and Mulattoes in the United States*. Baton Rouge: Louisiana State University Press, 1995.

Wilmore, Gayraud S. *Black Religion and Black Radicalism*. Maryknoll, NY: Orbis, 1996.

Winks, Robin W. *The Blacks in Canada: A History*. 2nd ed. Montreal: McGill-Queen's University Press, 1997.

Wistrich, Robert S. *Routledge Who's Who in Nazi Germany*. Revised edition of *Who's Who in Nazi Germany*. New York: Routledge, 1995.

Woeste, Victoria Saker. "Insecure Equality: Louis Marshall, Henry Ford, and the Problem of Defamatory Antisemitism, 1920–1929." *Journal of American History* 91, no. 3 (2004): 877–905.

Wolcott, Victoria. *Remaking Respectability: African American Women in Interwar Detroit*. Chapel Hill: University of North Carolina Press, 2001.

Zunz, Olivier. *The Changing Face of Inequality: Urbanization, Industrial Development Immigrants in Detroit, 1880–1920*. Chicago: University of Chicago Press, 1982.

UNPUBLISHED SOURCES

Allard, Edward Hastings. "A Report of Some Descendants of Bolling Bradby of Charles City County, Virginia." December 2002.

Bailer, Lloyd H. "Negro Labor in the Automobile Industry." PhD diss., University of Michigan, 1943.

Bradby-Green, Gabrielle. "Bradby Descendants." Interview by Julia Robinson-Harmon, March 8, 2003.

Carlson, Glenn E. "The Negro in the Industries of Detroit." PhD diss., University of Michigan, 1943.

Hamilton, Justine Rebecca. "Second Baptist." Interview with author, March 3, 1997.

Miles, Norman Kenneth. "Home at Last: Urbanization of Black Migrants in Detroit, 1916–1929." PhD diss., University of Michigan, 1978.

Shelly, Cara. "Bradby's Baptist: Second Baptist Church of Detroit, 1910–1946." PhD diss., University of Michigan, 1990.

White, Ronald C., Jr. "Social Christianity and the Negro in the Progressive Era, 1890–1920." PhD diss., Princeton University, 1972.

MANUSCRIPT COLLECTIONS

Bradby, Rev. Robert L., and family members photos, sound recordings, letters, vital records. Angela Bradby and Gabrielle Bradby-Greene Family Historical Collection, Detroit, Michigan.

Bradby, Rev. Robert L., and prominent members of Second Baptist Church, anniversary pamphlets, letters, and memoirs. Second Baptist Collection, Second Baptist Church, Detroit, Michigan.

Bradby, Rev. Robert L., and Second Baptist Church of Detroit, correspondence, church minutes, anniversary booklets, and miscellaneous papers. Second Baptist Church Papers, Michigan Historical Collection, Bentley Historical Library, University of Michigan, Ann Arbor.

Dancy, John L., papers. Michigan Historical Collection, Bentley Historical Library, University of Michigan, Ann Arbor. Includes detailed information on John L. Dancy's leadership of the Detroit Urban League.

Detroit Urban League Papers, Michigan Historical Collection, Bentley Historical Library, University of Michigan, Ann Arbor. Includes detailed information on Detroit's African American community during the turn of the century.

Ford, Henry, and Ford Motor Company, correspondence. Benson Ford Research Center, Dearborn, Michigan.

Ford, Henry, papers. Henry Ford Museum and Greenfield Village Research Center, Dearborn, Michigan.

Glenn, Mary Etta, Second Baptist member, correspondence and miscellaneous materials. Glenn Papers, Burton Historical Collection, Detroit Public Library, Detroit, Michigan.

Johnson, Lillian E., Second Baptist member, correspondence and miscellaneous materials. Detroit Study Club Collection, Burton Historical Collection, Detroit Public Library, Detroit, Michigan.

NAACP, papers, 1913–39. Text-film.

ARCHIVE MATERIALS

"1850 Federal Census of Charles City County, Virginia." Center for Local History, Charles City County, Virginia.

"Approximate Number of Negroes in Detroit Industries" (November 21, 1925), Detroit Urban League Papers, Michigan Historical Collection, Bentley Historical Library, University of Michigan (Box 1, Folders 1–5), Ann Arbor, Michigan.

"Brief Outline of Housing Conditions among the Negroes of Detroit, Michigan (May 2, 1917), Detroit Urban League Papers, Michigan Historical Collection, Bentley Historical Library, University of Michigan (Box 1, Folders 1–5), Ann Arbor.

Census of Canada, 1891. Oxford West, Oxford South, Ontario, Roll: T-6361; Family No: 31, Ottawa, Ontario, Canada: Library and Archives of Canada.

"Deaths," *Ontario Death Records, 1869–1927,* film No. 1411568. Latter Day Saints Family History Center, Kalamazoo, Michigan.

"McMaster University Arts Theology Calendar, 1906–1907." Canadian Baptist Archives, McMaster Divinity College, Hamilton, Ontario.

"Minutes of the Sixty-Seventh Anniversary of Amherstburg Regular Baptist Association September 12th to 15th, 1907." Canadian Baptist Archives, McMaster Divinity College, Hamilton, Ontario.

National Association for the Advancement of Colored People. *Thirty Years of Lynching in the United States, 1889–1913* (1919; repr.: New York: Negro Universities Press; A Division of Greenwood, 1969).

The Negro in Detroit: Report of the Mayor's Committee on Race Relations. Detroit: Detroit Bureau of Government Research, 1926.

———. Report Prepared for the Mayor's Inter-Racial Committee by Special Survey under the General Direction of the Detroit Bureau of Government Research. Detroit: 1926.

"Negroes in the United States, 1920–1926." US Department of Commerce, Bureau of the Census.

"Obituaries." *Amherstburg Echo.* January 12, 1906, 4. Marsh Collection, Amherstburg, Ontario.

"Papers on the Baptist Christian Center." United Community Services—Central Files Collection. Archives of Labor and Urban Affairs, Wayne State University, Detroit, Michigan.

Records of the Detroit Election Commission, 1920–1925. Old County Building, Detroit Michigan.

Registration of Deaths, 1869–1939. MS935, Reel 112, Archives of Ontario, Toronto, Ontario, Canada.

Registration of Marriages, 1869–1928. MS932, Reel 2, Archives of Ontario, Toronto, Canada.

"Registration of Negroes and Mulattoes Free Papers." Charles City County Minute Book No. 3, 1838-1847, Court Order of August 20m 1840. Charles City County Historical Society, Charles City County, Virginia.

"Registration of Negroes and Mulattoes Free Papers." Charles City County Minute Book No. 4, 1848–1860, Court Order of August 17, 1856, and January 16, 1857. The Center of Local History, Charles City County, Virginia.

Shadd Shreve, Mary Ann, compiler. *Pathfinders of Liberty and Truth: A Century with Amherstburg Regular Missionary Baptist Association* (Buxton, ON: 1940.) Archives of the Chatham Kent Historical Society, WISH Center, Chatham, Ontario.

Shreve, Dorothy Shadd, and Alvin McGurdy. "The Africanadian Church: A Stabilizer of Blazing the Pathway in Ontario South" (1980). Archives of the Chatham Kent Historical Society, WISH Center, Chatham, Ontario.

INDEX